Voices in Revolution

Voices in

Revolution

oetry and the Auditory Imagination
1 Modern China

John A. Crespi

 University of Hawai'i Press
Honolulu

14 13 12 11 10 09   6 5 4 3 2 1

Library of Congress Cataloging-in-Publication Data

Crespi, John A.
    Voices in revolution : poetry and the auditory imagination
in modern China / John A. Crespi.
      p.   cm.
    ISBN 978-0-8248-3365-7 (alk. paper)
    1. Revolutionary poetry, Chinese.   2. Oral interpretation
of poetry.   3. Chinese poetry—20th century—History and
criticism.   4. Social movements in literature.   I. Title.
    PL2309.R48C74 2009
    895.1'150935851—dc22
                                          2009010039

University of Hawai'i Press books are printed on acid-free
paper and meet the guidelines for permanence and
durability of the Council on Library Resources.

Designed by the University of Hawai'i Press production staff

Printed by The Maple-Vail Book Manufacturing Group

To my father and mother

Contents

Acknowledgments

It is easy during the long, often secluded hours of writing and research to forget the uncountable instances of intellectual, material, financial, and spiritual aid that have made a project like this one possible. The small ritual of writing acknowledgments reminds us that, whatever we do, we are never alone.

My interest in the rather improbable topic of poetry recitation came about while I was doing graduate research based at Beijing University in 1995–1996 funded by the Committee for Scholarly Communications with China. During that time abroad, Professor Qian Liqun of the Peking University Department of Chinese generously gave of his time and energy, all the while serving as a model of serious commitment to the modern Chinese intellectual legacy he has inherited. I also thank my friends on the staff of the National Library of China, formerly known as the National Beijing Library, and comrades Zhou and Wu in particular, for making the time-consuming task of gathering and copying my materials both congenial and expeditious.

For intellectual support on a project that has changed shape and shed its skin more times than I can remember, a debt of gratitude extends to Prasenjit Duara for helping me keep an eye on the bigger picture, to Paul Friedrich for reminding me that poetry is less something we read than something we already are, to Gregory B. Lee for guidance from near and afar in the construction of this humble hacienda, and to William Sibley for stepping up to the plate when it really counted. A word of thanks also goes to Margot Browning and the folks at the University of Chicago Franke Institute of the Humanities for providing me with a very quiet place to think and write during the 1999–2000 academic year, and to Jason McGrath and Xiaobing Tang for making me a part of the productively cacophonous "China's Long Twentieth-Century Workshop."

A Fulbright Program China Studies Research Award in 2005–2006 made possible my own immersion in the world of poetry and poetry recitation in and beyond Beijing. Alongside that support was, of course, the generous assistance of colleagues at Colgate University, including not just the careful counseling of the Grants Office, but also the continuing advice and mentorship of Gloria Bien, who made my position at Colgate possible through a start-up grant from the Henry R. Luce

Fund for Asian Studies. I also thank the Colgate Research Council for a publication subsidy.

Among the many friends and associates who have contributed to this project are Maghiel van Crevel, Graham Hodges, Yu Jian, Zang Di, Sun Wenbo, Wang Jiaxin, Jiang Tao, Bei Ta, Xie Mian, Wang Benchao, Cao Can, Zhu Lin, Yin Zhiguang, George O'Connell, Hei Dachun, Sun Jigang, Yu Zhenzhi, and the members of the Capital Friends of Recitation club, especially Xu Lianyong, Wang Aiping, and Ji Guosheng. Special thanks go as well to Matthew Forney and Paola Zuin for making my every return to Beijing a welcome one.

Chapter 6 was published in an earlier version but with the same title in *Modern Chinese Literature and Culture* 13, no. 2 (2001). Chapter 7 appeared previously in a Chinese-language version in *New Poetry Review* (*Xinshi pinglun*) with the title "Cong 'yundong' dao 'huodong': Shi langsong zai dangqian Zhongguo de jiazhi" (From *yundong* to *huodong*: The value of poetry recitation in today's China), trans. Wu Hongyi, no. 6 (November 2007). I thank both publications for permission to reprint these materials.

Most of all, I thank my parents for their unflagging, loving encouragement; Henry and Emma for creating a positive imbalance between work time and play time; and Botao for holding up half my sky, and then some.

Introduction

Let us consider: who are the peoples these days that lack a voice?
Can we hear the voice of the Egyptians? Can we hear the voice of the
Vietnamese or Koreans? Aside from Tagore, is there any other voice
from India?
    —Lu Xun, "Silent China"

Hearing Voices

Orated to an audience of young people in a Hong Kong YMCA in 1927, these
words of Lu Xun rest upon a commonplace and far-reaching assumption: that to
find one's voice is to locate and express an identity true, inalienable, and at times
almost mystical in its sources. Such a premise leads easily to the association of the
human voice with what has been called an "ancient magic" connected with "the
center of human existence," the idea that the spoken word "reaches deep into a re-
gion of lived experience where it escapes conceptual formulas and where prescience
alone operates" (Ong 1990, x; Zumthor 1990, 6). Voice thus imagined becomes a
trope that cuts deeply across discussions of political, historical, and literary rep-
resentation to become perhaps *the* master metaphor for discussing identity and
agency. Notwithstanding the deconstructionist demolition of voice as metaphysical
presence, the closely linked fields of literature and cultural studies have generated
an intellectual industry built upon the express or implied intent of giving "voice"
or "speech" to previously silenced subjectivities. As a consequence, we continue
to see innumerable literary anthologies and book series invoking the trope of
voice to index categories of gender, class, race, ethnicity, and national or regional
belonging.

Similarly, practitioners of most major types of cultural studies almost intui-
tively cast problems of representation and power in terms of voice: oppositional
voices, listening for voices, letting the subaltern "speak," and other variations on
the theme of placing faith in such vocally imagined "possibilities for expression,

articulation, agency" (R. Chow 1998, 2-3). Even among poststructuralists wise to the metaphysics of presence and determined to pronounce the author dead, the evocative power of the human voice can remain a seductive ideal. How else to explain Roland Barthes on one hand declaring writing "the destruction of every voice," and on the other turning his creed of semiotic surface play inside out to find therein an authentic animal pleasure in the voice's elusive "grain"? (1977, 142–148, 179–189). Even in the Lacanian scheme of the subject, voice assumes central significance as the flip side of presence, as the "object voice" introducing a "rupture at the core of self-presence" with its ineradicable otherness, *jouissance*, and feminine essence (Dolar 1996, 25).

Encountered today in academic and literary discourse, use of the voice trope is organized overwhelmingly by an ideology of multiculturalism. But, as scholars have noted, when applied to literary studies, the multicultural ethos typically relies upon the problematic representational models of reflectionism and authenticity, wherein "ethnicity" functions "as a kind of repressed truth that awaits liberation" (Bernheimer 1995, 8–9; R. Chow 1998, 101). In a world saturated with and at times bitterly divided by competing and clashing claims to the voicing of identity in and through literature, it should not be forgotten that such representational politics comes to us as younger cousin to an older but still powerful ideology: nationalism. Though by no means its only possible rhetorical application, the metaphor of voice has done long service as a means of asserting the presence of the nation as a living, evolving, self-aware cultural entity in its own right. When and how the trope of voice became coopted by any particular nation-building project might be impossible to determine with absolute precision, but the epistemic shift that made possible the identification of voice with expression, articulation, and agency can be roughly located in nineteenth-century Romantic-nationalist thought. This was the period, argues Michel Foucault, in which the understanding of language became humanized, when a faith in linguistic nominalism, in language's transparency with things, gave way to "a tendency to attribute to language profound powers of expression" originating in the will of the human subject. Thus, "Language is 'rooted' not in the things perceived, but in the active subject," where it "is no longer linked to the knowing of things, but to men's full freedom." This new imagination of language, Foucault continues, was a discovery that "[t]hroughout the 19th Century . . . was to have profound political reverberations" (1970, 290–291).

These reverberations, Foucault might have added, have echoed throughout the nineteenth and twentieth centuries' obsession with the making of nations. Given the corollary that the people constitute the nation (Hobsbawm 1990, 18–19), it is a short step from imagining language as expressing the collective will of human subjects to identifying the living language of the people with the unique and sovereign voice of the nation itself. Out of this simple equation have come innumerable movements to recover and revitalize an imagined authentic voice of national identity located in combinations and recombinations of indigenous traditions of spoken vernaculars and the updated and renovated art-languages of "new" national literatures.

Returning to Lu Xun, himself one of the preeminent figures in the establishment of China's new vernacular national literature, we see how he, too, promotes the idea that delivering China into modern nationhood meant restoring the sound of the nation's voice through a renewal of language, literature, and, as his mention of Tagore suggests, poetry. In his 1927 speech, Lu Xun told his youthful auditors that to save their homeland from the fate of its colonized counterparts—Egypt, Vietnam, Korea, and India—China had to speak and be heard, had to escape the silence imposed by an outmoded classical language to "speak its own, modern words," for "only a true voice can move the emotions of Chinese people and people of the world" (1981, 15). Lu Xun's advice to youth was informed, of course, by China's vernacular reform movement begun some ten years before. But turning back even twenty or more years before 1927 we find that many of the canonical moments in Lu Xun's mission to revive China—its people, language, and literature—are at a fundamental level informed by this same metaphor of the sounding voice.

In the famous "Preface" to his 1923 collection of short stories, *Outcry* (*Nahan*), Lu Xun portrays his turn from medicine to literature, from curing China's bodies to reviving its spirit, as a moment that might have been sparked by vision but was at the same time immersed in a nationally inflected opposition of voice and silence. At the Sendai Medical School, in a classroom of clapping and *banzai*-shouting Japanese medical students, Lu Xun describes himself sitting and watching as the instructor projects the lantern slide of an accused Chinese spy, surrounded by silent, passively onlooking countrymen, awaiting execution during the 1904-1905 Russo-Japanese War then being waged in southern Manchuria and Korea. Quite understandably, scholars have emphasized the visual, observational perspective in this well-known episode in modern Chinese literary history (R. Chow 1995; Anderson 1990, 77-79). But to my mind the crucially overlooked dimension of this seminal anecdote lies in its stark contrast between the seen and the heard. For at the same moment in which Lu Xun visually encounters a reflection of his own silent self in the enlarged, dumb, static tableau of benighted "Chinamen," his ears ring with the riotous voices of another Asian nation, one that had not only defeated China in the Sino-Japanese War ten years previously, but was at that moment achieving an unprecedented military victory over a major Western power, Russia. To be vanquished is to be voiceless, to be seen and not heard—perhaps this was the message that prompted Lu Xun to leave medical school and, so the story goes, make his first attempt at a national revival through literature.

After several abortive projects at publishing progressive literature, followed by the grand disillusionment of China's 1911 Revolution, it was a decade before Lu Xun was again convinced to turn his hand to the mission of national revival through literature. Here once more he casts the dilemma of national awakening in the figures of voice and silence. Approached by linguist Qian Xuantong in 1917 for contributions to the progressive journal *New Youth* (*Xin Qingnian*), an older and more skeptical Lu Xun replies with the famous conundrum of the "iron house": "Imagine an iron house without windows, absolutely indestructible, with many people fast asleep inside who will soon die of suffocation. But you know since they will die in their sleep, they will not feel the pain of death. Now if you cry aloud to wake a few of the lighter sleepers, making those unfortunate few suffer the agony of irrevocable death, do you think you are doing them a good turn?" (Lu Xun 1977, 5). The trope of voice is present still, but qualified by a deep ambivalence. By this time, however, the movement to regenerate a voice for China through the medium of modern vernacular literature was gaining ground fast, and there were few who troubled themselves with such agonized self-doubt. Among Lu Xun's cohort of new and enlightened literati, what carried the day was enthusiasm for the vernacular language, a new, modernized literature, and the liberating potential of the new ideas this modern language and modern writing promised to deliver. Observes one historian of modern China, once the voice of hope rang out, "there was no turning back for the awakened nationalist" (Fitzgerald 1996, 102).

* * *

How modern China's imagination of sound and voice emerged, and how it echoed across a century, is the subject of this book. To understand this history of the heard, I listen in on a specific aspect of the Chinese literary experience: poetry recitation (*shige langsong*). As an excursion into the culture of aurality in China's new poetry, the project might be regarded as an attempt—almost literally—to recover voices lost to history by resurrecting this poetry as it sounded in its day. My motivation, however, is not to reconstruct or restore to rights an obscured or oppressed subjectivity. Instead, I attend to a nationally inflected ideology of voice that consistently informed the auditory dimensions of the modern Chinese poem. The result is a history of the sounded poem in modern Chinese literary practice over a period of about a century: from Lu Xun's 1908 essay "On the Power of Mara Poetry" (Moluo shi li shuo), to the practice of poetry recitation in China as it happens now, at the outset of the twenty-first century. Throughout these ten decades, the attempts to give voice to new poetry through recitation do, to be sure, entwine with the ideology of a national voice. But even though the problematic of nation functioned as one of the dominant factors directly and indirectly shaping the imagination and realization of reciting poetry, the practice of giving voice to modern Chinese poems cannot be reduced to matters of national awareness and awakening. As detailed in subsequent chapters, modern China's performed poetry has done many things: resolved problems of aesthetics, mourned the dead, established bonds of literary solidarity, excited mass sentiment, tapped the sources of revolutionary passion, and most recently, engaged in ambivalent symbiosis with the market economy. Moreover, these multifarious functions of the recited poem have been far from mutually exclusive; any single poetic event could and did combine several overlapping effects.

So even as an approach to modern Chinese poetry's sound and voice might remind one of the insistent imperative of nation, the contingencies of poetry in living action move in many directions, revealing multilayered, real-world dimensions of poetic creation and reception. One reason approaching poetry as event rather than as printed text can achieve this complexity of perspective is that listening, as opposed to the more familiar academic practice of reading, forces the critic to abandon, or at least supplement, traditional approaches to interpreting the poetic text. Through its orientation toward the aural, I hope to open our ears to new critical approaches to poetry and its place in modern Chinese history. To do so requires engagement with a comparative theoretical perspective, one that joins the study of poetry recitation in modern China to an increasing scholarly interest in critical approaches, not only to the sound and performance of modern and contemporary poetry, but to the importance of auditory culture in literary and historical experience.

Sounding Out an Approach

"While the performance of poetry is as old as poetry itself," writes poet and critic Charles Bernstein, "critical attention to modern and contemporary poetry performance has been negligible, despite the crucial importance of performance to the practice of the poetry of this century" (Bernstein 1998, 3). Bernstein's statement holds as true for the twentieth-century English-language poetry he refers to as for the Chinese poetry produced during that same period. A review of recent work on auditory culture points to several general and important factors that can help explain this state of general neglect. First, and perhaps most fundamentally, though sound can be "the most forceful stimulus that human beings experience," its fugitive and fleeting nature makes it a difficult object of study (Smith 2003, 128). Unlike most visually perceived media—written texts, paintings, photographs, and so on—which may be viewed at leisure, and usually without any special equipment, sound is at best an ephemeral object of study, even with the aid of mechanical or digital recording devices. Due in part to the impossibility of capturing sound *as* sound and holding it motionless in state, critical vocabulary for talking about the poem as live, active voice remains relatively undeveloped. Thus even though the voicing of an orally produced text may constitute a "thing" whose "material qualities" of "tone, timbre, volume, register" each possesses symbolic value, at the same time voice "cannot be objectified and thus remains enigmatic, nonspecular" (Zumthor 1990, 5, 9). Put in more traditionally poetic terms, the "audiotext" of a poem "is a semantically denser field of linguistic activity than can be charted by means of meter, assonance, alliteration, rhyme, and the like" (Bernstein 1998, 13). In short, because of the nature of sound itself, the acoustically realized poem evades close "reading" even as its aural fullness and complexity exceed the diagnostic abilities of traditional prosodic analysis.

Another, more subtly pervasive issue relegating the study of sound to secondary status is the dominance of vision over hearing, of the eye over the ear, or the idea that, as Douglas Kahn observes in his pioneering exploration of sound and modernism, "Visuality overwhelms aurality in the cultural balance of the senses" (1999, 158). Scholars account for this sensory bias by pointing either singly or in combination to a range of philosophical, historical, and economic factors, including but not limited to Aristotelian philosophy, Renaissance perspectivism, the print revolution, and the spectacularized society of postindustrial capitalism (Debord 1994; Ihde 1976; Jay 1993; Levin 1993; McLuhan 1962). The resulting "visualist paradigm," as Steven Connor (1997) calls it, has not only dominated Western modes of thinking and perceiving, but deeply informs the interpretive models used by various academic disciplines (B. R. Smith 2003). Such embedded perceptual and conceptual bias is at its most pernicious when applied to the study of sound; for, as Kahn asks, "How . . . can listening be explained when the subject in recent theory has been situated, no matter how askew, in the web of the gaze, mirroring, reflection, the spectacle, and other ocular tropes?" (1992, 4).

A growing body of scholarly work that recognizes and seeks to remedy this ingrained visual bias has begun to emerge during the past decade or so. The disciplines that have begun to attune themselves to sound range widely—from anthropology to history, media studies, religious studies, literature, and cultural studies (Feld 1996; Schmidt 2000; M. M. Smith 2001; Kahn 1999; Morris 1997b). Such research has opened up experimentation in critical methodologies of sound, proving that sound does indeed occupy an important, though by no means autonomous, dimension of human experience in terms of subject formation, class conflict, literary history and imagination, senses of space and place, and religious belief.

Although such research has made significant headway toward creative and meaningful engagement with sounds historical, literary, sacred, and technologized, few have applied their theoretical insights outside the Western Hemisphere. With the exception of Steven Feld's groundbreaking anthropological work, the human experiences considered so far have belonged to the cultures and histories of Europe and North America, and in particular the impact of modernity on consciousness of voice and sound. Given the shared premise among all these studies of the heard—

that sound and voice, like any perceptual phenomenon, are culturally and historically constructed—to neglect non-Euro-American cultures and histories can easily create the illusion that Western ways of hearing the modern are the only ways. Following Lu Xun, we might now observe that awareness of the "voice" of China—not its presumed national voice, but its historically distinct narratives and imaginations of the aural experience of modernity—remains in a state of neglect and obscurity.

Thus while aurality may no longer be called "the unthought in accounts of modernity" (Lastra 2000), to speak of sound and modernity in the Chinese experience remains, so to speak, unheard of. It is my contention, then, that listening in to the aural dimensions of Chinese poetry over the past century or so presents an opportunity to expand understanding of the heard world of modernity beyond primarily Western constructs. This is so because, as Kahn asserts, the study of sound presents "a means through which to investigate issues of cultural history and theory . . . existing behind the peripheral vision and selective audition of established fields of study" (1999, 2). The sounds of modern Chinese poetry, I argue, offer precisely this sort of alternative apprehension of Chinese modernity.

But how is it possible to apprehend modernity through a sensory regime itself so resistant to sustained, stable apprehension? Or, in more concrete terms, how does one go about studying the sounds of voices whose echoes have long since died away? Especially given the rarity of recording equipment in China until the past several decades, how can one constitute an object of inquiry at all? As suggested already in the discussion of Lu Xun, the discourse of sound in its modern manifestations is not limited to direct experience of specific acoustic events, but rather expands into those representations of sound that constitute and shape the social, cultural, intellectual, and historical experience of how and what one hears. The definition of "sound" extends beyond commonsense reckoning and into a broader realm that includes "*sounds, voices, aurality*—all that might fall within or touch on auditive phenomena, whether this involves actual sonic or auditive events or ideas about sound or listening; sounds actually heard or heard in myth, idea, or implication; sounds heard by everyone or imagined by one person alone; or sounds as they fuse with the sensorium as a whole" (Kahn 1999, 3). Sound, and for me this includes the sound of poetry, thus refers both to physical acoustics *and* to entire realms of imagining that make sound a historically and culturally distinct human construct. Sound may be a fleeting medium in its phenomenal substance, yet ideas and imaginations of sound are inscribed with greater permanence, not just in sound reproduction media, but also in the material domain of the written, pictorial, and even architectural record.

In the absence of preserved recorded media for recited poetry, especially during the first half of the twentieth century, it is the written record of poetry and writing on poetry that this study primarily relies upon. These records include not just ear-witness accounts of recitations, but also writings that contributed more broadly to a "constructed aural order" (M. M. Smith 2000) by figuring the imagined sound of the poetic voice through deployment of aurally inspired metaphor. In rereading the history of modern Chinese poetry with an ear attuned to the aural imagination, I gesture toward a literary-critical agenda that revises the way in which we encounter the poetic text by opening it up to the world. The recited poem, because it is a sounded, performed text, cannot be disengaged from its spatial, temporal, and social moment. Encounters with these performed poetic words thus naturally work against the tendency to isolate poetry from its social and historical context, and thereby counter the conventional inclination "[t]o constitute a literary text as a static, truth-telling object, abstruse, hieratic, and linear," and thus place it "in a private, timeless, hermetic isolation" (Morris 1997a, 5). Attention to the orally produced text goes beyond the ahistorical reading because its words are *embodied* words, words whose extension into the medium of the heard orients them toward "a specific body, point of view, and history" (Middleton 1998, 268). Or, in Paul Zumthor's coinage, the performed poem is "sociocorporeal" in that it "resists . . . any perception that might sever it from its social function, from its place within a real community, from an acknowledged tradition, and from the circumstances in which it is heard" (1994, 221). It is precisely within these functions, communities, traditions, and circumstances that I hope to find a new, auditory medium of Chinese modernity.

Rethinking Recitation

As mentioned, reasons for the relative neglect of the performed modern and contemporary poem include the ephemeral nature of sound, the inadequacy of current critical vocabulary to conceptualize sound-based phenomena, and a conceptual as well as theoretical bias toward visuality. While such general concerns explain much, the lack of critical attention to the genre of the performed modern and contemporary Chinese poem also must be understood within the historically specific context of the discipline of modern and contemporary Chinese literature as pursued by scholars both outside and inside mainland China.

Among scholars based outside of China, it is certain that most, if not all, have attended, organized, or even taken part in Chinese-language poetry recitations, as they are typically held now in mostly academic and literary settings. Few, however, have considered the history of Chinese poetry recitation as it has evolved since the 1920s. As for the fewer still who have written about recitation, none have done more than either mention the subject in passing or offer condensed surveys based almost exclusively on secondary sources. Regarding the former, one brief account of wartime recitation is worth noting primarily for ambiguous citation and reproduction of factual error.[1] Such inaccuracies can in part be attributed to the relative

lack of secondary sources on recitation, but it may also reflect a negligence result-
ing from the discipline's failure to conceive of modern poetry as having literary
or historical significance beyond its presence in print artifacts. As for the survey
approach, Russian sinologist L. E. Cherkasskii provides the most substantial treat-
ment of the subject in his discussion of poetry recitation during the War of Resis-
tance (1980, 225-234). But due to an apparent lack of access to primary sources,
and perhaps as well to the ideological demands of his time and place in Soviet-era
Russia, Cherkasskii's account does little more than reproduce the ideas of Chinese
literary historians writing in the 1950s through the 1970s, who for their own part
simply approached poetry recitation as one among many modern literary "move-
ments" (yundong).

As for recent research by scholars based in mainland China, existing studies
of modern poetry recitation do offer more empirical detail than the English- and
Russian-language work already mentioned, but for quite specific historical reasons
have not explored the topic with the interest and energy applied to other aspects
of Chinese modern poetry. In the broadest terms, scholars have avoided the study
of recitation due to a persistent dialectic tension that dates from the invention of
modern Chinese literature early in the twentieth century. This tension plays out
between the poles of an autonomous "art for art's sake" and a socially engaged "art
for life's sake." The positions and counterpositions in this dialectic have assumed
multiple forms and vocabularies in Chinese literary discourse over the past cen-
tury or so: "commoner" versus "aristocratic," "proletarian" versus "Europeanized,"
"official" versus "independent," "popular" versus "intellectual," and so on. At its
core, however, the issue hinges on the problematic mission posed first and most
forcefully during the May Fourth period (1919-1925)—namely, to invent a national
literature that is cosmopolitan and modern but can also reach a nonelite audience
thought to require ideological betterment. The War of Resistance against Japan
(1937-1945) period, in particular, stands as a historical watershed marking a shift
away from elite modes of writing and toward a politically motivated popularization
of cultural production, including new poetry. With some notable exceptions, the
felt need on the part of many wartime poets to reinvent themselves and their verse
to serve, or at least not offend, the cause of national salvation retarded the 1930s
development of poetic modernism. Moreover, and as discussed in Chapter 2, during
this same period advocates of poetry recitation attacked Chinese poetic modernism
with special vehemence, inveighing against it as an effete literary practice fatally de-
tached from the people and the national situation. This ideological shift away from
elite forms of new literature received its greatest impetus from Mao Zedong's plat-
form for an indigenous revolutionary literature, the 1942 *Talks at the Yan'an Forum
on Literature and Art*. Subsequently enshrined by the Chinese communist state after
1949 as the last word in literary policy, Mao's *Talks* identifies the fundamental task

of literature and art as serving China's worker, peasant, and soldier masses. Poetry recitation, because it is a literary practice strongly associated not just with wartime movements for literary massification and national defense but also with Mao-era literary orthodoxy, has been closely identified with this patriotic and populist strand of new Chinese literature.

Poetry recitation's historical affiliation with mainstream Mao-era culture is the main factor shaping its reception as an object of serious research during the post-Mao era. This reception results in large part from two general tendencies in China's literary criticism during the past twenty to twenty-five years. On one hand, China's political and intellectual liberalization since the 1980s has encouraged a strong reaction *against* the stifling constraints of politically mainstream national-popular "art for life's sake." At the same time, a continuing, nationalist impulse to depict all patriotic literary activities during the War of Resistance in a sympathetic if not heroic light still influences a significant—if declining—number of researchers. Although Chinese literary critics' relation to the national past has changed immensely as the immediacy of the war has faded and the ideological restrictions of the Mao era have relaxed, recent scholarship on poetry recitation—or more accurately, the lack of such studies—bears the imprint of the life/art, populist/elitist dichotomies. In actual critical practice, this legacy of the national literary past means that the history of poetry recitation is either ignored or its original claims are taken at their word.

It is ignored by researchers who have made the most of the loosening of ideological restrictions on scholarship since the 1980s. Freed from the Mao era's intellectually crippling injunctions for politically correct methodology and subject matter, scholars of China's modern poetry began intensive investigations of pre-Liberation-era poets and poetic schools—labeled as Formalism, Symbolism, and, most notably, Modernism—that had for decades been decreed off-limits due to their "elitist," "bourgeois," or "decadent" tendencies. Driving such research, observes Jiang Tao in a recent study of early new poetry, was a desire on one hand to refute the narrowly political literary history and criticism of the Mao era and, on the other, to modernize Chinese literature by drawing from its own past (2005, 5). As for the impulse to modernize, most scholars of Chinese modern poetry, if they are not poets themselves, associate closely with working poets. Thus when looking back at their poetic predecessors, they often do so with an eye to recovering the more aesthetically sophisticated poetic insights of the pre-Liberation period. From such a position, the tradition of patriotic recitation that began during the War of Resistance and was coopted by the Chinese communist literary-cultural apparatus in the 1950s and 1960s seems artistically retrograde. Although such official-style recitation remains an active cultural practice to this day, practicing poet-scholars tend to discount it as a form of repugnantly politicized literary atavism. My own first encounter with this critical stance took place at Peking University in the 1990s, when I first came up with the idea of working on this project. I clearly recall the disbelieving, and vaguely suspicious, expression that came across one young literary scholar's face when I mentioned my interest in researching recitation poetry. It was a look that asked, with an undertone of mild distaste, "What would you want to do *that* for?"

On the other side of the critical fence, where Mao-era attitudes continue to hold sway, two of the more substantial pieces on poetry recitation illustrate well the tendency toward heroic oversimplification and uncritical reproduction of wartime discourse. For example, one survey history of Chinese new poetry flatly states that "the Poetry Recitation Movement continued undiminished from the early stage of the War of Resistance up to the eve of national liberation. It forcefully expedited the War of Resistance Salvation Movement as well as the later Democracy Movement of the Guomindang-controlled areas, and greatly advanced the development of new poetry itself" (Yang 1992, 186). As we shall see in the chapters to follow, close examination of poetry recitation activity during that period shows it to be far from this sort of internally coherent, self-confident, historically continuous, politically and aesthetically constructive "movement." A more accurate characterization would describe poetry recitation from 1937 to 1949 as a series of exploratory fits and starts intended at first to awaken the masses to national consciousness, but later recognizing its own shortcomings and consolidating itself as a cultural form by and for the literary elite.

Another way of attributing literary-historical coherence to poetry recitation has been to label it a literary "school" (*pai*); specifically, a "recitation poetry school" (*langsongshi pai*) covering more or less the same period from 1937 to 1949 (Chen Anhu 1997, 558–570). While this approach offers a more finely grained account of poetry recitation, defining a "school" requires coming up with a list of aesthetic features shared by a group of practitioners. The problem here is that the list of features draws uncritically from ideas of direct communication, formal liberation, emotion, and voice that were current during the 1930s and 1940s. One reads, for example, that: "recitation poetry . . . directs the realistic content of battle and the emotion of the nation directly into and among the popular masses"; "Recitation poetry is another instance of the liberation of poetic form"; and "The poetry of the recitation school is poetry of the impassioned battle cry. The soul of the poetry is fervent emotion, and recitation poetry is the voice of high emotion" (Chen Anhu 1997, 568–569). Such assumptions do represent important and persistent elements in the ideology of the sounding voice in modern Chinese poetry; but as ideology they should not be taken at face value. My own approach is to reconsider statements like these in a manner that not only locates them in their historically specific circumstances of utterance, but also makes sense of them as a part of a complex, sometimes contradictory hundred-year process of articulating the sounding voice of poetry to multiform elements of a modern Chinese experience.

Poetic Voices from *Dao* to Now

This book follows a roughly chronological, though by no means historically comprehensive, path through the history of modern Chinese poetry and poetry recitation. The book's seven chapters proceed from a period of invention and experimentation in poetic voicing roughly congruent with new, vernacular poetry's establishment in the first several decades of the twentieth century, to consolidation of poetry recitation between 1937 and 1948 (the War of Resistance and Civil War period), on to the development of poetry recitation as a performance genre during the socialist and postsocialist eras in the People's Republic of China. Chapter 1, "Poetic Interiorities: From Civilization to Nation" lays the groundwork for understanding the Chinese modern imagination of the poetic voice. It does so by examining how a shift in the myth of linguistic authority, engineered by modernizing literati, marked the transition from empire to nation in the early twentieth century. Where the imperial system drew authority from written language's presumed manifestation of a universal Way or *dao*, proponents of a new nationalist ideology searched for the sources of authority in a "living" spoken language generated from an individual or collective national genius. By giving value to the spoken, this shift implied an emphasis on the heard over the seen; and because poetry had for millennia been regarded as the premier genre for manifesting the *dao*, it was a reinvented poetry that reformers imagined as the bearer of a popular voice. From a discussion of traditional ideologies of writing and poetry, the chapter moves on to analyze ideologies of nation and voice in the work of figures active in the vernacular reform and new literature movements, including Lu Xun, Qian Xuantong, Hu Shi, Zhou Zuoren, and Yu Pingbo.

Building on Chapter 1's argument that an imagination of the sounding voice animated modern Chinese poetry from its inception, the subsequent chapter, "Poetry Off the Page: Sound Aesthetics in Print," asks how poets experimenting with this new literary genre "voiced" their poems on paper, in performance, or through a combination of print and performance. Here we find that through the 1920s and 1930s, well before poetry recitation of political agitation became an established practice in China, poets of a populist bent deployed paralinguistic, typographic, and formal devices to construct a "recitational aesthetic" of inscribed voice meant to transcend the visible, written text while projecting an imaginary volume and emotive presence. At the same time, academic poets who made a regular practice of reciting poetry in Beiping's cosmopolitan salons created a visually oriented aesthetics of textual self-reference designed to establish poetry as a discourse independent from natural, spoken language.[2] Although this latter, linguistically self-oriented, poetry frequently incorporated an important sound component in its prosodic structure, it nonetheless came under attack from the populist poets, who condemned it as a static, opaque, printed poetry of the "eye" unable to project a *sound* of poetry that might achieve wide emotive resonance among a national populace. The conflicted intersections of the seen and the heard in these two poetic currents are significant, first, for how, during their chosen genre's formative years, poets engaged in an often vituperative battle over what makes poetry *poetry*, and second, for the latter camp of poets' determination to establish a metanarrative of national modernity grounded in the register of the sounding voice.

The war years of the 1930s and 1940s, and in particular the eight years of the War of Resistance, represent the most important period in the developing practice of modern Chinese poetry recitation. It was during this time of geographical dislocation, national trauma, and literary massification that poetry recitation, as well as its literary realization in print as "recitation poetry" (*langsong shi*), took hold as a meaningful category of literary performance. Chapters 3 through 5 approach wartime poetry recitation from several complementary angles. Chapter 3 examines the assumptions underlying the production of "recitation poetry" as an object of literary discourse, as well as the breakdown of these assumptions in later war-period poems. On the one hand, early wartime recitation poems and wartime writing on poetry recitation amplified the notions of vocal aesthetics and national interiority invented in the preceding decades, and in the case of works labeled "recitation poems" even vocalized a poetic soundscape of wartime geography. Midway through the war, however, one finds poems by leading practitioners of poetry recitation, such as Guang Weiran (Zhang Guangnian) and Gao Lan (Guo Dehao), which complicate and even undermine the imagined powers of poetic voice and sound.

There was, of course, much more going on at the time than writing and discussing recitation poems. This was, after all, poetry for performance. Chapter 4 narrates the historical drama of wartime recitation by reconstructing the sights, sounds, personalities, and institutions of poetry performance during the War of Resistance period. Drawing upon diaries, memoirs, news dispatches, performance reviews, and of course the poems themselves, this chapter narrates the heroic ideal of recitation as it encountered the quotidian realities of live performance under conditions often both physically and politically unforgiving. The story begins with the poetry recitation activities of Pu Feng and the poets of the Guangzhou-based China Poetry Forum Society (Zhongguo shitan she) in 1937–1938, moves on to the early wartime rallies in and around the city of Hankou, and from there to efforts at poetry recitation by the War Song Society (Zhan'ge she) in Yan'an, Shanghai's Rank and File Society (Hanglie she), and various recitation events sponsored by the Chongqing, Chengdu, and Guilin branches of the All-China Resistance Association of Writers and Artists (Zhonghua quanguo wenyijie kangdi xiehui).

Available accounts of these events make it quite clear that, despite the grand theoretical claims for heard poetry as an avenue into mass consciousness, and despite the brave ambition written into so many of the recitation poems themselves, practitioners of new poetry recitation could do little more than feel their way through an often painful process of trial and error. But despite poetry recitation's undeniably spotty record of success, recitation advocates did not abandon the efforts to bring poetry to the public ear. Instead, by the end of the war literary circles had adopted modern poetry recitation as a cultural form flexible enough to accommodate the desire for both entertainment and political education—a dual legacy revived years later for the socialist mass culture of the early 1960s.

Chapter 5 moves several years beyond the War of Resistance to the eve of the 1949 revolution, when the restive college campuses of Beiping generated a dynamic new model of poetry recitation. Writing within the ferment of student protest and civil war, the erstwhile poet and newly radicalized Tsinghua University professor Zhu Ziqing reconceived recitation. His formulation, which I call "situational practice," warrants attention, because whereas former theorists of the recited poem had located this poetry's potential for intervention in a reified regime of voice-mediated emotion, Zhu reimagined the voiced poetic text as coextensive with the social text of collective action, as an integral element of the entire situation created by the shifting and unstable space-time of live performance. By linking Zhu's theory to student recitation poetry and an actual historical situation, this chapter revises notions of what constitutes a poetic text while adding to our understanding of a neglected period of Chinese literary history.

The final two chapters compare what has become an established culture of poetry recitation in the Mao and post-Mao eras. Chapter 6 revisits the popular peak of official-style poetry recitation during the early 1960s, a time when poetry took over the stages of China's theaters and culture palaces as a mass-performance art displaying and engaging national aspirations for a New China. Performed by professional actors in urban centers and popularized through recitals, radio broadcasts, amateur training courses, and symposia, poetry recitation became the hallmark genre of a lyricized socialist enthusiasm. And yet, when given voice on the public stage, poetic expression encountered a subtle but unavoidable contradiction: did the voice of poetry spontaneously capture and project the era's ideal of a deep, authentic "revolutionary passion" (*geming de jiqing*), or was it simply a consciously cultivated, and thus ideologically suspect, art of dramatic performance? Through analysis of actors' own discourse on the art of recitation as well as poetry recitation primers of the time, this chapter makes sense of the tension between poetic passion and dramatic art, while also complicating the idea of Mao-era art as a seamlessly monolithic system of cultural production and reception.

The seventh and final chapter brings this study of performed poetry up to the present. Here I offer an explanation of why, even as the current postsocialist market economy has swept contemporary poetry to the cultural fringes, poetry recitation events flourish as never before in China's urban centers. Professional language artists, amateur recitation enthusiasts, and, of course, poets themselves, recite in venues ranging from private homes to the Great Hall of the People, from trade exhibitions to avant-garde "happenings," and from high-brow academic conferences to mass-culture tourism festivals. This minor explosion of poetry recitation, sometimes referred to as a "recitation renaissance," suggests that, instead of falling prey to the culturally leveling influences of the market economy, the practice of poetry recitation has adapted to the new economic and cultural configurations of postsocialist China. Why does recitation live on? Here I argue that whereas socialist-era poetry recitation was a creature of that period's political institution of the coercive "mass campaign" or *yundong*, postsocialist recitation thrives in the more autonomous, decentralized, and fluid institution of the cultural "event" or *huodong*. The point here is that, despite many significant differences, both *yundong* and *huodong* represent means for mobilizing the population to meet state development goals: the former designed to advance the Mao-era socialist economy, and the latter a key component of the currently booming sector of the "culture-economy." More important, however, is how the category of the *huodong* encompasses multiple varieties of poetry recitation: from events bearing the unmistakable stamp of official ideology to those carrying the earmarks of "independent" artistic practice.

These chapters can hardly claim to be a complete critical history of sound and voice in Chinese modernity. For one thing, exclusive attention to a single form of literary and cultural practice—in this case, poetry recitation—can account only partially for the vast dynamic range of auditory culture in modern China. Also, even within this strictly delimited generic zone, my narration has left gaps to be filled by researchers interested in extending, modifying, or contravening my arguments. There is much more to be said, for example, on recitation during the early years of the People's Republic, when performed poetry was initially institutionalized to support campaigns such as those accompanying the war in Korea. The April 1976 Tiananmen demonstrations in memory of Zhou Enlai, in which poetry functioned prominently as an expression of protest and grief, represent another high-water mark in the history of recitation. Significant, too, was the role of recitation in the small cults of poetic celebrity enlivening university campuses, and Peking University in particular, during the culture-hungry 1980s.[3]

What this book can do is amplify some of the most salient intellectual, historical, and literary features that constitute how the past century or so has been heard. It can also remind readers that similar and possibly even richer representations of sound and voice not only cut across all modern Chinese literary genres but find important expression as well in film, drama, art, and, of course, music. Turning one's

ear even further afield, attention to the auditory imagination of modern China
has potentially even broader significance when pursued through other disciplines,
such as history, architecture, urban studies, anthropology, and sociology. In short,
I harbor no ambition to be the last word on the heard world of modern China. If
my book can renew understanding of the modern Chinese poem, that would be
good. If it can at the same time begin to restructure our current sense of Chinese
modernity, even better. Best of all, however, would be simply to remind its readers
that the closer you listen, the more you might hear.

* * *

Finally, a few words on the translation of key terms. Different languages, as Yurii
Lotman suggestively describes, are by nature semiotically asymmetrical (Lotman
1990, 127). This means that the translator who seeks precise semantic correspon-
dences across languages seeks in vain. While writing a book in English about a
performance form that developed in a Chinese linguistic context, I have inevitably
encountered such asymmetries when negotiating between two sets of English and
Chinese words, each referring, with a good degree of slippage, to past, present, and
emerging modes of orally performing poetry in the Anglophone and Chinese tradi-
tions. In current English usage, the most commonly used terms for these modes are
reading, recitation, speaking, and declamation. The first of these, reading, is the
one most often used today in the United States, due to the contemporary conven-
tion of poets and other authors who literally read their work aloud in the setting of
a university or college, literature workshop, or book-release event. "Reading" natu-
rally implies that the performer relies on a printed script, such as a book or manu-
script, although that is not always the case. In contrast, the less commonly used
"recitation" implies that the performance text has been committed to memory,
with the further suggestion that such speaking from memory relates to some sort of
pedagogical task, as when a student recites his or her lessons. Closely related, and
more or less interchangeable with recitation, are "poetry speaking" or "verse speak-
ing," terms that emerged from the United Kingdom's "verse-speaking movement"—
an efflorescence of competitions and festivals, peaking between 1920 and 1950
but continuing to this day mostly in schools—that promoted poetry recitation as a
means of education in the arts (Sivier 1983b). Poetry "declamation," while generally
interchangeable with the term "recitation," suggests a dramatic or impassioned style
of oral delivery.

A set of more or less direct Chinese cognates for these terms would not be
hard to find. *Songdu* or *langdu*, which share the character *du*, meaning "read" or
"read aloud," would seem to correspond to "reading," with *songdu* suggesting more
of a chanting style of delivery, and *langdu* more of a clear, ringing spoken enuncia-
tion. *Beisong*, where *bei* refers to memorization, would seem to correlate well with

the English "recitation" and its implied reliance on committing texts to memory. *Langsong* might then be aligned with the relatively high-volume, relatively stylized delivery that declamation connotes. As in English, however, the borders among these several terms are not clearly delineated. *Langdu, songdu, langsong, du,* and even the term *yinsong,* which normally refers to a chanting or even melodic sing-song style of recitation used for classical poems, were all used with varying frequencies up until the War of Resistance to refer to the oral performance of modern poetry. It was not until the announcement of a "recitation movement" (*langsong yundong*) during the early war years that *langsong* became a more or less conventionalized term referring to the recitation of poetry or other literary works, whether based on memory or a written script.[4] In mainland China, the region on which my study focuses, *langsong* has remained the dominant term up to the present. For want of precise correlates between the English and Chinese languages, and to avoid confusion, I use "recitation" as shorthand for all the varieties of the oral performance of modern Chinese poetry, and have provided pinyin Romanization of Chinese terms wherever clarification is desirable.

CHAPTER 1

Poetic Interiorities

From Civilization to Nation

THIS CHAPTER EXPLORES the construction of poetic voice across one of the most profound ideological divides in modern Chinese history: the early twentieth-century transition from empire to nation. To do so I investigate the mediations between politics and poetics, that is, how the shift from an imperial to a national ideal revised the imagination of language, how the new linguistic imagination inspired a reimagined poetry, and how a reimagined poetry brought with it the reinvention of poetic voice. In other words, the modern Chinese poetic voice emerged from the dynamic integration of old and new elements in the overlapping domains of political, linguistic, and poetic discourse. It was an integration facilitated by analogous imaginations of poetic voice—one local and tied to the political ideology of Chinese empire, the other imported and linked to the political ideology of nation. Only by turning an ear to linguistic and poetic resonances between the local and global, the imperial and the national or, to use more common but notoriously imprecise terms, the traditional and the modern, can one begin to understand the logics and tensions animating discourse on the sounding voice of poetry during the ensuing one hundred years.

I begin by discussing the imperial myth of the Chinese written language as manifestation of the *dao* or Way but then explore the allied civilizational myth of poetry, with special attention to poetry's oral imagination and the political ramifications attached to the expressive, suasive poetic voice canonized through the "Great Preface" (Daxu) to the *Book of Songs* (*Shijing*, a.k.a. the *Odes*). To introduce modern, post-Imperial thought, I then turn to sound and voice imagery in Lu Xun's 1908 essay "The Power of Mara Poetry," discerning there the formation of an expressive "national interiority" associated with the sounding poetic voice. The construct of a linguistic national interiority, I then demonstrate, reemerges about a decade later in New Culture intellectuals' interpretation of China's dual-language or diglossic situation in terms of a Romantic-nationalist model of language that situates the source of language in a national interiority coterminous with a popular voice.

Finally, I examine how the template of this expressive linguistic national interiority, when aligned with the expressive logic of the "Great Preface," creates the imagination of a modern poetic national interiority, one located ambiguously between a popular collective and elite individual voice. Here I turn to Hu Shi's 1919 theoretical piece "On New Poetry," Zhou Zuoren's writing on folk song, and Yu Pingbo's 1922 essay "Return to Origins in the Evolution of Poetry." While these several texts cannot represent the full complexity of the period's thinking on language or poetry, they do demonstrate the formation of an important and—as later chapters will show—persistent and politically implicated desire to renew the authority of poetic voice as mobilized in the practice of poetry recitation. Beyond this, my analysis as a whole demonstrates, not just how global ideologies can be creatively, if covertly, merged with autochthonous belief and practice, but also how, within this merger of the global and local, claims of ideological rupture can acquire force and legitimacy from underlying cultural continuity.

The Empire of Texts and the Voice of the *Dao*

Chinese life before the early twentieth century's agitation for nationalism and language reform was, of course, far from voiceless. We hardly need audio recordings from centuries ago to know that throughout China's multimillennial dynastic history people's ears were abuzz with the sounds of relatives and friends, neighbors and strangers, street hawkers, oral entertainers, and their own speaking selves. The more rarefied realm of the great foundational philosophical texts, too, are filled with accounts of spoken exchanges between sages and kings, while the *Analects* themselves claim to be transcriptions of Confucius' oral teachings. Indeed, the ideogram for "sage" (*sheng*) neatly comprises an ear beside a mouth set over the graph for "king." And yet, according to the civilizational ideal dominant for centuries, to be Chinese meant participating in shared script rather than shared speech. To be literate meant to possess "the mark of entry into the Chinese world," a place where "[g]eographic, political, racial, and historical considerations are secondary to that identification with its written language" (Allen 1992, 17-18). Writing was exalted because it belonged to a world of myth that constituted and preserved the institution of empire. As summarized by Mark Edward Lewis:

> the Chinese empire, including its artistic and religious versions, was based on an imaginary realm created within texts. These texts, couched in an artificial language above the local world of the spoken dialects, created a model of society against which actual institutions were measured. More important, they provided the basis of an educational program that embedded the vision of empire within the upper reaches of local communities. A shared commitment to these texts thus created the links between the imperial system and localities, links far more numerous and penetrating than those provided by a bureaucratic administration dwarfed by the realm it was supposed to

govern. The implanting of the imperial vision in local society in the form of
the written language and its texts also provided the mechanism by which the
institution of the empire survived the collapse of each of its incarnations.
It was the intellectual commitment of local elites to the text-based dream of
empire, and their economic dependence on its reality, that both secured the
longevity of the imperial system and led to the omnipresence of the written
graph in Chinese culture. (Lewis 1999, 4)

This textually generated imaginary realm, though anchored in an elaborate mate-
rial culture of ink, brush, paper, and print, depended upon the belief in something
quite abstract: that an underlying patternment, or *wen*, immanent in the reality of
the natural and human worlds gave form and meaning to the ultimate reality of
the Way or *dao*. Quite unlike phonocentric thinking's subordination of writing to
the immediacy of speech, the traditional Chinese myth of language valued writing
as "an independent system of signs directly derived from natural processes" (Lewis
1999, 278). Believed to function in organic correlation with the pattern of the cos-
mos and the institution of Chinese empire, writing embodied an ultimate truth
of the universe. As for the Chinese empire, it was as Lewis observes an empire of
texts, a political system whose authority was inseparable from mastery of writing,
because writing itself could not be separated from the incontrovertible, unchanging
substrate of reality.

Poetry was by no means excluded from this orthodox conception of writing.
Most notably, the verse gathered into the *Book of Songs* was read for millennia as
one of the Five Classics (Wu jing) forming the core of Confucian education. The
three hundred some verses constituting the *Songs*, believed to be products of the
Zhou dynasty (1027–770 B.C.E.) and later edited and compiled by the great sage
Confucius (551–479 B.C.E.) himself, span an array of perspectives on early agrar-
ian life in early China, from erotic love, to loyalty toward one's ruler, to court
verses and ritual chants. Because of its status as one of the essential classics meant
to foster moral development, interpretation of the *Songs* was guided by robust
rules for reading provided in the form of accompanying commentaries. The most
influential of these commentaries was the "Great Preface" composed during a
Confucian revival of the second century B.C.E. and eventually recognized as "the
most authoritative statement on the nature and function of poetry in traditional
China" (Owen 1992, 37).[1] The "Preface" powerfully framed this multivocal collec-
tion of ancient verse within the ambit of morally grounded civilizational ideology,
making the *Songs* not just a collection of poems but a model text on a par with
canonical philosophical works. Like the classics of philosophy, the *Songs* were be-
lieved to possess an immanent correspondence with the ultimate normative order
of the *dao* such that, when absorbed through reading and memorization, they

would guide and regulate the behavior of the reader in line with these ultimate norms.

Yet simply to equate the *Songs* with its counterpart classics by the likes of Mencius or Confucius would be a mistake. These were not sagely quotations or philosophical fables. They were poems, and as such were endowed with distinct generic properties. Perhaps the key feature attributed to poetry, and the one lastingly reinforced by the impact of the "Great Preface," related to how poetry *as poetry* transmits the *dao*. According to Steven Van Zoeren's analysis, the "Preface" insists that the poems of the *Book of Songs*—and by extension poetry in general—represent none other than a "perfect inscription" of their authors' authentic, heartfelt aims at the time of composition—aims that were without exception "paradigmatically normative" (1991, 114). By learning the *Songs*, typically through memorization and recitation, one would experience "in a direct, unmediated way . . . the feelings and impulses that originally gave rise to their composition" (14). It was through this transference of originary emotive experience that the student of the *Songs* would internalize, naturally and spontaneously, the ideal, normative values believed to have initially inspired the poems. This logic of reading and response did not represent the only ideology of poetic interpretation to be proposed in traditional China, but by the Han dynasty, "the promulgation of the Odes was claimed to be one of the privileged means by which the moral transformation of the empire could be achieved" (14). Or, as Stephen Owen remarks, after the canonization of the "Preface," the function of not just the *Songs* but poetry in general became recognized as "an instrument of civilization" (Owen 1992, 45).

But even as the "Preface" may have consolidated the *Songs*' place of honor among the written classics and the empire of texts, the early history of these poems was inseparable from the spoken voice, and especially voice that elicits response from its auditors within a situation of performance. According to Chow Tse-tsung's erudite speculations, the ideogram for poetry, *shi*, likely originated from symbolic elements related to the actions performed in sacrifice or religious ritual, *si*, and later took on the semantic element for "word" or "speech," *yan*, to emphasize the spoken or sung aspects of such ritual work (Chow 1968, 207). During the Zhou dynasty the *Songs* were performed by the nobility as verses set to music at banquets, rituals, and other gatherings (Lewis 1999). During the subsequent Spring and Autumn period (722–481 B.C.E.) they formed the core of oral political ritual for an elite ministerial class in the practice of *fu shi*—chanting from memory excerpts from the *Songs* as a convention of courtly and diplomatic rhetoric (Knechtges 1976; Lewis 1999, 155–163; Owen 1992, 39–40; Tam 1975).

Well before the "Preface" was written, then, the *Songs* participated actively in an elite oral poetic tradition practiced among the pre-Han feudal states. This rich courtly orality fell into decline with the overthrow of these feudal kingdoms during the Qin unification of the third century B.C.E. (Arbuckle 1994). But even as the practice of orally performed poetry diminished, the "Preface" indicates that the idea, if not the reality, of the spoken poem persisted to become a defining feature in the canonical understanding of poetic expression.

This oral imagination of the *Songs* receives its ideological force from a few seemingly simple phrases from the first section of the "Preface," phrases whose brevity belies their importance in Chinese literary thought: "The poem is that to which what is intently on the mind (*chih*) goes. In the mind (*hsin*) it is being intent (*chih*); coming out in language (*yen*), it is a poem" (Owen 1992, 40).

On the one hand, this part of the "Preface" rewrites an older formulation, that "poetry articulates aims" (*shi yan zhi*), so as to emphasize the *Songs'* ability to represent the perfect expression of the original intent of their authors (Van Zoeren 1991, 104–115). But in doing so the "Preface" here implies that poetry must be understood less as a thing than an action, or, as described by Owen, a "spatialization of poetic process" involving communicative movement from inner to outer, and by virtue of which "the essence of poetry resides in the situation of recitation and the immanence of the reciter's affections in the process" (1992, 41, 42). The canonical definition of poetry, then, not only assumes the spoken poem to be a unique means of transmitting interior truth, but also employs a metaphorical model based on the physical act of speech.

The intent of the "Preface," however, was not to sanction free, individual poetic expression. To the contrary, the emphasis on poetry's expressive authenticity supported conservative political aims. According to Van Zoeren, the "Preface" to the *Book of Songs* (which he refers to as the Odes) attempted to resolve the problem of mobilizing the emotions in the service of Confucian norms: "The Odes inscribed—preserved and made available for the student—the aims or *zhi* of their authors, and these aims are in every case paradigmatically normative ones. By "studying" the Odes—that is, by attending to their discursive exposition, by memorizing, reciting, and internalizing them—the student is able to "take on" those aims, at least temporarily" (1991, 114).

Lewis similarly observes, in his examination of pre-Han philosophical works and the logic of the "Preface," that the meanings of the *Songs* became affixed to the political realm in such a way that the significant emotional impact of the poems was restricted to "a manifestation of royal virtue, either of the present ruler or those in the past" (1999, 175). In short, early and lastingly influential definitions of poetry used a specific imagination of the poetic voice to recruit poetry into the political realm, with the result that for the next two millennia poetry, while primarily a written discourse, related to the "empire of texts" by virtue of an oral expressive dynamic.

National Auditions of the Spoken

By the turn of the twentieth century, it was precisely the Confucian civiliza-
tional morality voiced through the *Songs* that many of China's progressive reformers
hoped to move beyond. Confucianism, along with the ancien régime it was believed
to represent, came to be viewed as hopelessly incompetent and retrograde, a back-
ward system of thought and governance incompatible with an aggressive new world
of nation-states in competition. As individuals seeking new forms of literature,
politics, and society, this modernizing elite imagined a means of transcendence
assembled from a new global flow of ideas to which they had privileged access.
Most prominent among these elements were those related to conceptual models
of nationalist ideology, the "modular" forms of nationalist thought and practice
adapted and applied by intellectual elites around the world (Anderson 1991, 4).

Working subtly alongside and within these modular elements of global nation-
alist discourse, however, were the patterns inherited from the past—in fact, affini-
ties to the very system of native philosophical and aesthetic principles with which
China's new elite would claim to break. What came out of this mix was an amalgam
of the global and the local invented to resolve the crises at hand. Thus, even as
China's post-Imperial cultural avant-garde was raising a polemic chorus for the new,
the logic of existing patterns of thought was at work in the background. The inven-
tion of a new poetry was no exception.

As many have noted, poetry was entrusted with a special historical mission in
attempts to modernize and transcend the Chinese imperial regime, most notably
in Liang Qichao's turn-of-the-century "poetic revolution" (*shijie geming*), and in Hu
Shi's well-known proposal to write poetry in a modern Chinese vernacular, the 1917
essay "A Tentative Proposal for Reforming Literature" (1935a). In one respect this
attention to poetry can be attributed to the modernizing literati's own embedded-
ness in imperial China's scholarly tradition, one in which poetry had long occupied
a favored place in the hierarchy of literary genres. At work, too, was the orthodox
view of literature's ethical and political mission to shape and improve the human
subject in accord with a political order—precisely the belief forwarded by the "Great
Preface"—which persisted as an implicit but powerful assumption held by many
literary revolutionists. For an intellectual caste determined to change their society
for the better, the presumed power of literature, and poetry in particular, to exercise
transformative political influence over its audience was too alluring a belief to cast
off lightly.

On the other hand, even as such native traditions of literary ideology persisted,
China's modernizing elite drew extensively on forms of nationalist discourse. In the
case of poetry, the Chinese renovators of poetic discourse had a dual inheritance.
Along with the persistence of established thought in their own local tradition, they
also appropriated a newer tradition born of many nationalist movements—a global

tradition, as it were, and one readily available because it had preconstructed a modular imagination of poetry ready for adaptation to a variety of local contexts. This was the idea of poetry as literary representation of nationhood, an exalted mode of human expression believed to best exemplify the distinct features associated with the "character" of a particular nation's language and, by association, a particular nation's people as created and constituted by language. Especially in the European tradition, such promotion of nationally representative art-language, and especially the art-language of poetry, had been used to reinforce assertions of literature as the manifestation of national spirit or genius to be found in the works of their human authors, be they individual masters such as Homer, Dante, and Shakespeare, or an inchoate collective of folk poets.[2]

It was this last aspect of poetry—the Romantic-nationalist assurance of poetry's source in the human subject—that played a key role in the displacement of civilizational by nationalist ideology, as well as a corollary transition to a reimagined emphasis on the sounding poetic voice. For whereas the mainstream Confucian tradition imagined poetry as the vehicle for transmitting an abstract cosmic pattern reflecting timeless norms of ideal rule, nationalist ideology saw poetry as originating from the imaginary construct of the "timeless and perpetual Nation" (Gourgouris 1996, 18), one grounded not in the discredited Confucian *dao* but in the new, imported abstraction of the People. In both cases, the elite stewards of poetry—whether the Western Han Confucian literati who devised the "Great Preface" or the modernizing literati of the early twentieth century—sought to link poetry to a source endowed with political authority. Under the new, humanist ideology entering China in the early twentieth century, the source of this authority would be located, not in the morally edifying linguistic pattern understood as *wen*, but in the human, speaking subject. Or, to cite Michel Foucault's observations on nineteenth-century linguistic philology, language was now "'rooted' . . . in the active subject," such that "[i]n any language, the speaker, who never ceases to speak in a murmur that is not heard although it provides all the vividness of the language, is the people" (Foucault 1970, 290).

This idea of a language's source in the lived practice of the people is what Isaiah Berlin, in his classic study of Romantic-era German polymath Johann Gottfried Herder, describes as "expressionism": the assertion that "all the works of men are above all voices speaking, are not objects detached from their makers, are part of a living process of communication between persons and not independently existing entities . . ." (Berlin 1976, 153). Still prevalent to this day as a form of common sense, expressionism locates language in the spoken realm as the spontaneous and primarily oral creations of either the individual subject or the collective entity of the People. Among the many implications entailed by such a perspective, the one I stress is the belief that language be understood as the *sound* of talk, a living acoustic dimension of popular voices filling the national past and present. It was precisely this emphasis on voice over writing that animated the vernacular language reform movement of the 1910s, out of which came the invention of China's new vernacular poetry.

The Power of a Poetic Interior

The high tide of the movement to institute a modern vernacular and a modern poetry came during the ferment of intellectual activity during the latter half of the 1910s called the New Culture movement. Attempts to imagine a national voice of poetry, however, came at least a decade earlier. Most notable here is Lu Xun's "On the Power of Mara Poetry," perhaps the most compelling text of its time to introduce a nationalist imagination of poetic sound. The 1908 essay, typically read as a manifesto lamenting China's state of stagnation during the waning years of the Qing dynasty, recommends for emulation a pantheon of great national poets from Byron and Shelley to Pushkin, Lermontov, and Petöfi. But beyond content, Lu Xun also achieves a figurative impact in the essay. By combining auditory imagery with a nationalist ideology, he creates a renewed imagination of the sounding poetic voice, a voice that emanates from and resonates within the imagined space of a national interiority.

As I use it, the term "national interiority" describes a tendency to find the origins of poetry (and literature in general) in a spontaneous, emotional, sincere, expressive human interior. Though identified with the individual, this interior is also enlarged through the part-to-whole trope of metonymy to encompass a larger interior time-space of nation, one constituted by an imagination of the People as the authentic constituents of the nation.[3] Such assumptions derive from Romantic-evolutionist theories of literature, and of oral poetry in particular, which seek to establish "a continuity with the longed-for lost, other world of organic and emotional unity" (Finnegan 1992, 34). Chinese reformers, while on the one hand adopting these generic principles of linguistic and literary nationalism, were driven as well by local ethnopoetics guided by the definition of poetry supplied by the "Great Preface." In fact, the fundamental resonances between the two sets of concepts—especially the idea of origins in an idealized past and the spontaneous, oral transmission of authentic feeling and thought—made for a ready adaptation of nationalist thought among intellectuals favorable to literary modernization.

To return to "The Power of Mara Poetry," Lu Xun's essay prefigures the New Culture period's construction of a linguistic and poetic national interiority through imagination of the sounding voice. As Ban Wang notes in his perceptive reading of the essay, for Lu Xun the power of poetry is above all the power of voice (1997, 63). Be it the literary heritage of fallen civilizations or the vital and rebellious verse of European romantics, Lu Xun refers to poetry not as written text but as "voice of the soul" (*xinsheng*), a term that links him at once to the didactic tradition of the "Preface," with its emphasis on poetry's authentic source in the heart/mind (*xin*) and morally suasive effect through the voice (*sheng*). Yet at the same time Lu Xun expands this basic vocal ideology by invoking not only "the voice of the nation-people" (*guo min zhi sheng*; Lu 1996, 99; 2005, 67), but also rebel poets able to "bellow an audience to its feet" (*dong hang yi hu, wen zhe xing qi*; Lu 1996, 99; 2005, 68). Whereas today such invocations of voice would be regarded as dead metaphors, at the time Lu Xun was writing a new and powerful ideology energized such figures of speech. Voice above all meant the voice of the poet—here portrayed as a rebellious vanguard figure whose very reason for being is to find and express that latent interior identity without which a nation sinks into oblivion:

> It seems a small thing when poets become extinct, till the sense of desolation hits. To praise the true greatness of your native land takes introspection and knowing others—awareness comes from careful comparison. Once awareness finds its voice, each sound strikes the soul, clear, articulate, unlike ordinary sounds. Otherwise tongues cleave to palates, the crowd's speech founders: the advent of silence redoubled. (Lu 1996, 99; 2005, 67)

This passage suggests that it is the poet who identifies the inner truth of a nation, and that only by comprehending this national interiority can a nation, through its poets, find a voice. In other words, a nation unaware of its nationhood is a silent nation, and the awakening to awareness can only be mediated by the national poet's voice. For Lu Xun, then, the difference between coming into being as a self-aware national entity and remaining in a state of obtuse civilizational latency coincides with the difference between the sounding voice and the persistence of silence.

Working with this acoustic contrast, Lu Xun further describes poetry as a disruptive force, but only insofar as the poem, again imagined in auditory and in this case semimusical terms, replaces the stagnancy of an ancien régime with penetrating and resonant coming-to-awareness of a preexisting national interiority:

> Poets are they who disturb people's minds. Every mind harbors poetry; the poet makes the poem, but it is not his alone, for once it is read the mind will grasp it; everyone harbors the poet's poem. If not, how could it be grasped? Harbored but not expressed—the poet gives it words, puts pick to strings, mental chords respond, his voice pervades the soul, and all things animate raise their heads as though witness to dawn, giving scope to its beauty, force, and nobility, and it must thereby breach the stagnant peace. Breach of peace furthers all humanity. (Lu 1996, 102; 2005, 70)

According to this passage, the sound of poetry destabilizes the status quo, in this case a moribund imperial system whose ideal Lu Xun describes derisively as "Don't disturb" (Lu 1996, 101; 2005, 70). But this disruptive effect of poetry entails—and in fact prepares the way for—a positive, constructive force that arouses poetry's figurative auditors to awareness of a latent poetic presence—in effect, to an identity obscured until the poet's voice reawakens it. Lu Xun clearly attributes to the imagined sound of poetry an Orphic force that on the one hand disrupts the "stagnant peace" of the imperial era but also conveys a new and transformative energy, one that originates from the national interiority as accessed by the individual poet, but on the other also resonates with a national interiority constituted by a collective of human listeners. As Ban Wang writes in his exegesis of the essay, Lu Xun imagines poetry as an embodied, even warlike, force grounded in the affective power of a "heartfelt voice" able to awaken and elevate a long-dormant cultural spirit. The "aesthetic" of poetry in Lu Xun's essay, Wang adds, is the extension of "the private realm of emotion, spirit, bodily vitality, and impulses" into and continuous with "the collective vitality and well-being of Chinese culture as a whole" (B. Wang 1997, 65).

In one respect, Lu Xun treats poetry and the poetic voice as an instrument of national awakening. At the same time, however, he amplifies the poetic voice's transformative power to align its audience with the edifying order of its source, which brings his argument into correspondence with the logic of the "Preface"; only now, instead of exteriorizing the silent, written pattern of a politically normative *wen*, poetry assumes the task of orchestrating, through imagined audition, a collective initiation into national presence.

Language and the Popular Interior

If "On the Power of Mara Poetry" can be read as a Romantic manifesto exalting the voice of the poet as the expression of the awakened, individual national genius, the New Culture intellectuals who took the stage a decade later initiated a more systematic and even totalizing construction of a collective counterpart to the singular poetic voice of nation: the anonymous, communal voice of the popular.

To comprehend this impulse to define a collective subject of linguistic and literary origins, one needs to understand the linguistic and historical given of China's diglossic situation. Simply defined, "diglossia" refers to a dual language condition in which a formal, primarily written, linguistic register is superposed upon a largely spoken linguistic register used in everyday conversation.[4] Classical Chinese, the medium for the empire of texts Lewis describes, represented the superposed language. Meanwhile, the popular spoken language—which included the dialects and the unofficial lingua franca of Mandarin, or as it was known at the time, *guanhua*—constituted the register of everyday conversation.

Use of the written vernacular in fields such as journalism and education had in fact been progressing for several decades before the New Culture activism of the mid- to late 1910s (Doleželová-Velingerová 1977). The New Culture activists, however, polarized the linguistic field by radically opposing the classical and vernacular registers in terms of negative and positive ideological value. They smeared the written, classical register as a "dead" language incompatible with modern life and associated with a regressive ruling class believed responsible for China's declining, outmoded imperial system. The everyday spoken language of the common people, on the other hand, they celebrated as a "living" linguistic entity ideally adapted to the needs of modern expression and communication. As the outspoken New Culture activist Chen Duxiu famously and forcefully wrote in 1917, the "three great ideological tenets" of the "literary revolution" are "(1) Down with the ornate, sycophantic literature of the aristocracy; up with the plain, expressive literature of the people! (2) Down with stale, pompous, classical literature; up with fresh, sincere, realist literature! (3) Down with obscure, abstruse, eremitic literature; up with comprehensible, popularized social literature!" (D. Chen 1996, 141).

Just as the New Culture intellectuals were not the first to promote the vernacular, neither were they the first to interpret a diglossic language situation in these dichotomous terms. Such linguistic schemes are a classic example of modularity in nationalist thought. The metaphor of dead versus live languages dates at least to Johann Gottlieb Fichte's early nineteenth-century distinction between the Roman and Teutonic registers of German language (1922, 52–90). Since then, the practice of attributing positive and negative values to diglossic registers of a language has become a common nationalist tactic for expunging a presumably imposed and alien language in favor of an authentic, native language emanating from a national interiority located in historical time and generated by the everyday speech of the People. In fact, it is only by insisting on the inauthenticity of the dead language that one can claim an authenticity for the live one. In the Chinese case, essays by two of the leading New Culture advocates of vernacular reform, Qian Xuantong and Hu Shi, illustrate well how the period's intellectuals did the rhetorical work of relocating linguistic authority in the popular national subject.

Qian's essay—in fact written at Hu Shi's request for a preface to his groundbreaking compilation of modern Chinese vernacular poetry, Experiments (Changshiji; Jiang Tao 2005, 28)—appeared in the New Culture movement's flagship periodical New Youth in early 1918, during the height of the language reform controversy. Qian argues for a return to a pre-diglossic linguistic condition in which spoken and written Chinese were perfectly correlated. Spoken language, he writes, preceded the written language, so that in a long lost linguistic golden age, written ideographs were invented one for each spoken word. Thus for the spoken word lao (old) one ideograph was written down as its sign; likewise, for the different-sounding spoken word kao (examine or test) the ancients invented a different-looking written sign.

This matching of written ideographs to individual spoken words in a state of perfect correspondence Qian describes as "unity of the spoken and written" (*yanwen yizhi*). But, he adds, over historical time the Chinese language lost this originary unity due to two factors: first, China's "autocratic tyrants" (*dufu minzei*) committed centuries of linguistic depredations in order to fashion a private, elitist, and exclusively written lexicon that would enhance their aura of rulership. Second, over a period of over two thousand years, "literary devils" (*wenyao*) made a practice of emulating earlier writing styles rather than taking their vocabulary from contemporary life, thus violating the principle that "the people of each era use the language of that era" (Qian 1918).

Without doubt Qian greatly oversimplifies Chinese linguistic history. But more to the point, the tendentiousness of his scheme demonstrates the stark terms by which New Culture intellectuals saturated China's diglossic situation with political meaning. On one side of the linguistic coin, they demonized the Chinese script as an antidemocratic plot in violation of history, thereby excluding the old regime from participating in the making of a new Chinese nation; on the other, complementary side, they marked the language generated through speech of the common folk as an originary and authentic source of human expression inseparable from the human subject as subject of nation.

Such an appeal to the linguistic genius of popular speech appears again in a pair of essays by Hu Shi originally published in 1919 and 1920: "The National Language and National Language Grammar" (Guoyu yu guoyu wenfa) and "The Evolution of the National Language" (Guoyu de jinhua). The most prolific and certainly best-known advocate of vernacular reform, Hu extends Qian's lexical conception of language into the dimension of grammar. He argues that vernacular Chinese, as opposed to classical Chinese, is a living (*huo*), self-sufficient, self-perfecting entity that evolves over historical time. Like Qian, he assumes that both the classical and the vernacular languages have a shared origin. But according to Hu, while the classical language remained stagnant, the vernacular, a living mode of communication among the common folk, underwent a spontaneous and unconscious historical process of grammatical modification. The vernacular, he argues, evolved freely and naturally, sensing where changes were required and modifying itself structurally by either "complicating what ought to be complicated" or "simplifying what ought to be simplified." The former, according to Hu, refers to improving semantic clarity by increasing redundancy. Examples of this include replacing monosyllabic with bisyllabic lexical items, such as using *shifu* (teacher or master) in place of *shi*, a literary word easily confused with many homophonous characters; reduplication of morphemes in lexical items such as *mama* (mother) or *manman* (slow); and the addition of new words to the lexicon. As for simplifying the overly complex, Hu's examples include the elimination of unnecessarily fine differentials of meaning in the classical language's monosyllabic lexicon, such as six different words for "pig," each referring respectively to a pig at three months, one year, two years, and so on, and streamlining pronoun usage by doing away with subject and object forms of pronouns (1935e, 238–243).

One need not accept Hu's clear, though patently simplistic, reasoning to perceive the key element of his scheme: a strict class-based division of language. According to him, the inefficiencies of grammatical form have resulted exclusively from mechanical reproduction of inherited grammatical convention by "old-language literati" (*guwenjia*). The unlettered "common folk" (*xunchang baixing*), meanwhile, "were not afraid of offending the ancients," and altered the "difficulty" and "inconvenience" of classical grammar to make it easier to speak and remember (1935d, 232). Hu concludes that the grammar of the national language:

> is not something we can manufacture. It is the result of several thousand
> years of evolution, the expression and crystallization of China's "national
> common sense." . . . Complete credit for the evolution of the national
> language goes to the several thousand years of natural transformation per-
> formed by "common folk," with no input whatsoever from men-of-letters and
> grammarians. Our ancestors never purposefully changed grammar; it was
> grammar that unconsciously changed itself. But close inspection of where it
> did change shows it making perfect sense far beyond the ken of those count-
> less masters of the classical idiom! Thus, when faced with such marvelous
> changes, we can't help but doff our hats and declare it the "crystallization of
> national common sense"! (1935d, 232)

The lesson from all this, Hu concludes, is: "Don't look down upon the countless 'foolish farmers, village women and children!' They've taken on the task of innovation that was beyond the ability and courage of those famous masters of letters!" (1935e, 245).

For Hu, then, the grammatical dimension of the spoken vernacular reveals a collective unconscious, an interior national genius active through the centuries among the Chinese common folk. Like Qian, he sets value on the popular production of language as it evolves spontaneously and organically over historical time in a process mediated by precisely what Isaiah Berlin, in his definition of expressionism cited above, describes as "voices speaking" in "a living process of communication between persons." More, Hu's and Qian's reconstruction of lexicon and grammar reproduces in the Chinese context a patently nationalist linguistic ideology directly implicated in the construction of a national "people." To cite one of the originators of linguistic nationalism, J. G. Fichte, "we give the name of people to men whose organs of speech are influenced by the same external conditions, who live together, and who develop their language in continuous communication with each other" (cited in Kedourie 1993, 58). The "people" who develop this original language, do so in "direct connection between abstract ideas and immediate sense-experience, which allows for full experience"; derived languages, on the other hand, cut their users off from true sense-experience, leading to impoverished, mechanical existence (Kedourie 1993, 60–61). From this, concludes Fichte, and after him Hu Shi and Qian Xuantong, only those who speak an original, "live" language may be considered nations, as only they are linguistically in touch with the true and specific experiential conditions of a national interiority.

Liberating a Poetic Interiority

This impulse to return to a preexistent but obscured interior source of expressivist speech informed not just New Culture theories of language, but New Culture discourse on poetry as well. For Hu Shi, in his influential 1919 essay "On New Poetry," expressionism acts as the driving force and culmination of a historico-evolutionary narrative of Chinese poetic language. The essay, which I discuss in more depth in the next chapter, argues that, over the last two thousand or more years, Chinese poetry has undergone a series of formal liberations during its evolution toward an open-form ideal that corresponds ever more closely to the free flow of spoken language. The entire process, Hu argues, takes place as a "natural tendency" traceable through four liberations in line length: from the four-syllabic verse of the *Book of Songs* to five- and seven-syllabic Ancient Verse (*gushi*) and Regulated Verse (*lüshi*), to the Song dynasty (960–1279) *ci* or Lyric, on to the relatively more variable line lengths of the Yuan dynasty (1271–1368) *qu* or Aria, at which point Hu sees the further evolution of Chinese verse trapped by the formal demands of the accompanying music. The final step in this progression is the delivery, by present-day literary reformers, of a final push away from what Hu calls "written form" (*wen de xingshi*) and toward a modern free verse that conforms to patterns of "natural prosody" (*ziran de yinjie*)—an ambiguous term given that Hu does not define "natural," but one that points to the nationalist reformers' ideal of expressionist linguistic spontaneity (Hu 1935b).

Such a linguistic liberation of poetry, Hu adds, follows the model already seen in literary revolutions in any number of traditions, including the replacement of Latin by national literatures in Europe, the poetic innovations of poets in France and of Wordsworth in England during the eighteenth and nineteenth centuries, and, most recently, the "poetry revolution" (*shijie de geming*) in the West. With Euro-American counterparts as models, Hu urges a similar liberation of poetic form for the Chinese New Literature movement, because "Formal restrictions prevent the free development of the spirit and the full expression of good content" (Hu 1935b, 295). The "shackles" of the spirit must be broken, Hu writes, and

the recent new poetry movement in China is none other than "'a great libera-
tion of poetic form.' It is only by liberating poetic form that abundant material,
precise observation, high ideals, and complex feeling and emotion can enter into
poetry. Five- and seven-syllabic, eight-line Regulated Verse are absolutely incapable
of accommodating abundant material; the twenty-eight character *jueju* is absolutely
unsuited to the writing of precise observation; fixed-length five- and seven-syllabic
verse is absolutely incapable of subtly expressing high ideals and complex feeling
and emotion" (295).

As with Qian Xuantong's scheme of linguistic evolution, it would be easy to
discount Hu's narrative of poetic liberations as the arbitrary imposition of a linear
teleological scheme over what was in fact a long and complex tradition, one in
which poets could and did make flexible, creative, and simultaneous use of many
available forms at any given moment of history. But despite its oversimplification—
or perhaps even because of it—Hu's evolutionary history of Chinese poetry struck
a chord in its time to become "the touchstone for poetry creation and criticism"
during the early 1920s (Zhu Ziqing 1935, 2).

One reason "On New Poetry" exerted such strong literary-critical influence
was certainly Hu Shi's preeminence on the cultural scene at the time. He was,
and still is, regarded as one of the chief initiators of China's new culture and new
literature. Just as important, however, is the fact that Hu's scheme of poetic evolu-
tion links new poetry to the ongoing linguistic shift from civilization to nation. In
terms of poetry, Hu's narrative, and especially its end point in free and uninhibited
expression of content, lends logical historical structure to Lu Xun's earlier, heroic
call to recover the "clear, articulate" poetic voice that emerges from a stagnant
political system. In terms of language, the narrative structure of "On New Poetry"
corresponds to the narrative of evolutionary emergence that Qian Xuantong and
Hu Shi build around China's diglossic situation. Just as Qian and Hu describe the
popular spoken language as coextensive with an expressive national subject emerg-
ing victoriously from the repressive tyranny of a structurally ossified classical Chi-
nese, "On New Poetry" argues that new, vernacular poetry represents no less than
a liberation from the written classical form necessary to allow the human subject's
free and full poetic voicing of spirit, ideals, feelings, and emotions. From Lu Xun
to Qian to Hu, spoken emanations from a human interiority supersede a written
language now exiled to a detached, self-referential, and expressively sterile pattern-
ment of writing.

At the same time, however, the evolutionary narrative proposed in "On New
Poetry" and its counterpart narratives of language evolution differ in important
ways. First, where the active subject of linguistic evolution is a human collective, the
subjective agency of poetic evolution seems resident in poetic language itself; that
is, poetic structure (line length) evolves spontaneously, until the present-day reform-

ers, with Hu Shi at the forefront, arrive to consciously align poetry with its ultimate state of natural prosody. Clearly, such a narrative reserves linguistic agency for Hu and his contemporaries, making it a move that lends historical legitimacy and literary preeminence to those inventing a new Chinese poetry. At the same time, the essay gives historical foundation to the notion of "literary creation" (*chuangzuo*), the idea prevalent among new poets in the early 1920s that "literature has to struggle free from the conventions and accumulated habits of tradition so as to express a unique, true, and richly imaginative inner experience" (Jiang Tao 2005, 36). Put differently, where linguistic evolution would derive from a collective national interiority—that of the People—the new poetry made possible by Hu's poetic liberation finds its source in the individual national interiority, that of the contemporary Chinese literary genius.

Yet this scheme creates a problem even as it solves one. Insofar as nations are imagined as unities, how to manage the split between two separate and distinct linguistic national interiorities? Hu Shi offers a resolution to this dilemma in his seminal 1918 essay "On the Constructive Literary Revolution." The essay centers upon the slogan "a national language literature, a literary national language" (*guoyu de wenxue he wenxue de guoyu*), which Hu explains as: "The literary revolution that we advocate seeks only to create for China a national language literature. Only when there exists a national language literature can there be a literary national language. Only when there exists a literary national language can our national language be considered a true national language. Without literature, the national language has no life, no value, cannot be established, and cannot develop" (Hu 1935c, 128).

According to this formula, national literature and national language function interdependently; literary language draws upon and refines everyday language, and this newly refined art-language then acts back on and improves everyday language. Thus two distinct and linguistically constituted national subjects—the popular collective on the one hand and the individualized literary elite on the other—achieve a constructive and progressive unity in the course of ongoing linguistic exchange. But more important, at least for the makers of literature, is the exalted status Hu confers upon them. Given the assumption that a nation cannot properly exist without a national language, and that a national language cannot be generated without a national literature, those who produce national literature are essential to the very making of the nation.

There was more, however, to the issue of dissolving the class boundaries between the people and the literary elite than Hu's mechanism of linguistic exchange. When it came to the reinvention of poetry, the need to convert the civilizational to the national meant a return to the more mystic realm of poetic voice. Below I focus on attempts to link new poetry to the collective subject of nation—specifically, how interest in "folk" and "commoner" poetry during the early 1920s drew upon the trope of the national interiority as shaped by the local imagination of expressionism.

Constructing Poetic Origins: Folk Song and Commoner Poetry

By the early 1920s, new poetry had begun to appear regularly in a number of progressive publications, and indeed writing it became both a gesture of support for China's fledgling New Literature movement and a token of membership in its forward-looking literary project. But even as new poets assumed the role of literary pioneers, they also gazed back into nation-time for ways to link their new and fragile genre to authoritative origins. Foremost among such theories were efforts during the early 1920s to tie new poetry to a collective national subject through the categories of folk song (*geyao* or *minyao*) and commoner poetry (*pingmin shi*).

Before looking at the specific—and, as we shall see, already familiar—strategies used to articulate new poetry to folk song and commoner poetry, it must be said that when individual poets and critics recommended these as sources for new poetry, their statements constructed—and were constructed by—positions within the bifurcated discourse of the collective and individual linguistic national subject. When invoking the Chinese folk and commoners as the authentic origins of poetry, these poets and theorists took the position that poetic authority derives from a national interiority to be found in the collective, anonymous subject of the people. The short life span of the interest in commoner poetry speaks to the fluidity of such discursive arrangements. For, no sooner had the commoner camp of poets begun to advocate a return to a populist fountainhead of poetry, than others took the opposing position that true poetry was distinguished by an individualistic, "aristocratic" (*guizu*) essence. Before long, many who had originally called for commoner poetry—including the key initiator of the movement, Zhou Zuoren—retreated from their original claims, and most in fact gave up on writing new poetry altogether.[5] The call for commoner poetry, as well as the early 1920s efforts to connect poetry and folk song, ought, then, to be understood as a discrete moment in the history of Chinese new poetry, though one whose defining tension between individual and collective sources of poetry—the very same tension Hu Shi's literary sloganeering aimed to resolve—was bound to reappear in different guises through the decades to come.[6]

However short-lived the early 1920s discussion of folk and commoner poetry may have been, the arguments and oppositions therein assume a larger significance for how they adapt modular nationalist concepts to local poetics. In one respect, by invoking terms like "folk" and "commoner," these poet-intellectuals aligned themselves with well-founded and readily adopted precedents among other nationalist movements.[7] That is, their approach to folk song and commoner poetry reflected Romantic-nationalist views of folklore prevalent during the nineteenth and early twentieth centuries, and in particular the belief that national literature in its indigenous forms "springs up of itself from deep, mysterious roots which can be traced far back in the history and inner depths of mankind" where it offers contact with a lost or obscured ideal of "organic and emotional unity" (Finnegan 1992, 34). At the same time, however, such generic nationalist concepts resonated with a powerful literary common sense shaped by traditional literary thought. As already discussed, the traditional poetic principle of the "Great Preface"— the emphasis on imagined vocal projection of spontaneous, authentic, interior thought and feeling originating from a normative pattern dating from a lost golden age—entered into correspondence with nationalist ideas of poetic voice as expressing a national interiority constituted by the speech of the ultimate legitimator of nation, the People.

The discussions of folk song and commoner poetry reproduce these conceptual patterns with great fidelity. Proponents of both—and the two categories of poetry are often only loosely distinguished—describe the accumulation over time of exterior linguistic form associated with an antipopulist, aristocratic class and argue that the accretion of this exterior form blocks the necessary return to an interior domain of truth and reality resident in the creations of an oral folk tradition belonging to the commoners. In this sense, the advocates of folk song and commoner poetry not only reproduced the schemes laid down by Qian Xuantong and Hu Shi in their narratives of linguistic evolution and poetic liberation, but in fact merged the two. That is, they transferred the popular linguistic subject of language constructed by Qian's and Hu's narratives of language to the center of Hu Shi's narrative of poetic liberation. Remaining in the medium of language, they made the popular subject of nation the very source of poetry's authenticity.

One of the most well-known and influential intellectuals to construct linkages between new poetry and folk song was poet, critic, translator, folklorist, and brother of Lu Xun, Zhou Zuoren. Zhou's writing on folk song provides an important and, given its relatively early date, foundational example of the facility with which Chinese intellectuals conjoined local concepts of voice with the imagination of a national interiority. This merger is especially apparent in an essay simply entitled "Folk Song" (Geyao; Zhou 1923). Here Zhou builds upon perceived points of resonance among local and nonlocal sources: Frank Kidson's English Folk Song and Dance, the "Great Preface" to the Book of Songs, and the Italian folklorist Guido Vitale's Pekinese Rhymes (Kidson and Neal 1972; Vitale 1896). The connections demonstrate how native and imported concepts were fashioned into an ideology of a poetic voice emanating from an expressionist national interiority centered on the human collective subject of the People.

First, citing Kidson, Zhou writes of folk song in general as a variety of poetry "born of the people and used by the people as an expression of their emotions" for which "we have no definite knowledge of its original birth, and frequently but a very vague idea as to its period" (Kidson and Neal 1972, 10). From Kidson's patently Romanticist assertions, Zhou moves easily to principles of naturalness and expressionism attributed to the poetry from the *Book of Songs*. After observing that the origin of poetry is "most likely spontaneous songs from primitive society," Zhou adds that such songs can be likened to the origins of poetry as given in the "Great Preface," and in particular the description of the poem as a process whereby "the affections are stirred within and take on form in words" (*qing dong yu zhong er fa yu yan*) (1923, 7).[8] Here Zhou forges an apparent correspondence between global and local theories of poetic expression: the imported concept of poetic expressionism from nationalist ideology, and the indigenous psychological-expressive idea of poetry from Confucian civilizational ideology. In effect, he reconciles disparate ideological systems through an imagined relation between different constructions of poetic voice.

Such a move not only indigenizes nationalist ideology, it also roots the freshly arrived concepts of nation in an autochthonous theory of poetry dating back several millennia. The joining of the two is certainly aided by the shared idea that the emotion expressed by folk song, like the affections expressed by the *Songs*, both emerge from the depths of historical time; or, as Zhou phrases it, "folk song is poetry that is primitive—and yet not old" (1923, 7). Put differently, the spontaneous, natural ideal of poetic expression may originate from the depths of the nation's history, but its essential expressivity remains timelessly available in pure, unadulterated form through access to the popular voice. Working from this assumption, Zhou asserts that poets of today can and should make use of folk song precisely because it carries an authentic expressivity—or in Zhou's terms, "good faith and sincerity" (*zhenzhi yu chengxin*)—that emanates from a national interiority constituted by the People:

> The relation between folk song and new poetry, though it may be doubted by some, is in fact a quite natural one, because the strongest and most valuable characteristics of folk song are its good faith and sincerity, which are the shared soul [*gongtong jinghun*] of works of art and of great benefit to the cultivation of artistic taste. Kidson writes, "The maker of a folk-song did not produce his work for professional reasons; he sang because he must, and sometimes he was very ill-fitted for the task. Yet the work, being done in good faith, has not only the power of appeal [*ganrenli*] to the class for which it was made, but also to a higher culture." This is the power most essential for new poetry to absorb (Zhou 1923, 8; Kidson and Neal 1972, 36).

Here again we see an emphasis on the emotional authenticity of folk song, but with enlarged significance. Purity of expression becomes not just an essential feature of folk song, but functions too as an inner force that defines art in general while improving the cultivation of the artist. It is in this stress on the presence, projection, and suasive force of poetry's authentic inner emotion that Zhou's understanding of folk song draws upon the expressionist and pragmatic principles of the "Great Preface." Going further, Zhou's citation of Kidson in the passage suggests how, by virtue of expression emanating from a national-popular interiority, folk song can impart to new poetry the ability to cross class boundaries. At this point Zhou moves into the realm of modern nationalist thought, and specifically the idea that literature can function to "designate and codify a national consciousness" by creating a sense of shared identity that transcends class boundaries (Jusdanis 1991, 40). It thus follows that when Zhou turns to the "Preface" of Vitale's 1896 *Pekinese Rhymes*, a book that deeply impressed Zhou and other early Chinese folklorists as a forerunner to their own project, he cites a passage recommending Chinese folk song as a possible source for a reinvented national poetry[9]: "One can find in Chinese folk song a little true poetry. . . . These things, although created by people who don't understand classical Chinese and who are uneducated, nonetheless possess a poetic regularity much akin to that found in European countries, and almost identical to Italian poetics. A new national-popular [*guomin*] poetry could grow out of these folk songs and the true feelings of the people" (Zhou Zuoren 1923, 8). Zhou comments that this passage is "exceptionally insightful." While he does not spell out the nature of this insight, the contour of his argument suggests agreement with Vitale's assertion that the "true feelings of the people," this popularly voiced expression of a national interiority, can and should be incorporated into a new national poetry.

The transfer of authentic voice from folk song to poetry that Zhou Zuoren gestures toward receives detailed development in Yu Pingbo's 1922 essay, "Return to Origins in the Evolution of Poetry." As its title suggests, "Return" was embedded in the Romantic-evolutionist project that shaped the thinking of the writers discussed above. Like them, Yu imagines the recovery of a pure, popular voice obscured by the historical accretions of external rhetoric. At the same time, Yu envisions poetry as a morally constitutive force for society at large, a belief that again demonstrates the powerful influence of local poetic concerns on the reinvention of China's new poetry.

Yu's essay deserves attention, too, for its prominence in literary discussion and debate of the time. "Return" appeared in the first issue of the first literary journal specifically devoted to new poetry, *Poetry Monthly* (*Shi*), which ran seven issues from January 1922 to May 1923. First, as the only lengthy theoretical piece in this inaugural issue, the essay assumes a manifesto-like status. Second, the essay was published in the midst of heightened discussion on the role of literature as mediator between intellectuals and the people, a concern that inspired an ongoing series of articles written by Yu and his literary associates regarding the nature and significance of *minzhong wenxue* or "mass literature."[10] Third, within debates focused on new poetry, the essay represents one of the most substantial contributions to a series of polemical statements that Yu and his associates had been directing against what they saw as another literary group's dangerous and reactionary advocacy of old-style poetry.[11] Finally, the essay participates in the "commoner" versus "aristocratic" position taking then animating the literary scene. "Return" responds directly and at length to a piece by a fellow new poet, Kang Baiqing, asserting that poetry is by nature aristocratic, and in turn elicited a series of oppositional responses attacking many of Yu's basic premises.[12]

As for the category "commoner literature," which figures centrally in Yu's argument, the term was not his invention but had entered the period's literary critical currency several years earlier with the appearance of Zhou Zuoren's 1919 essay "Commoner Literature." A brief piece, and one that does not deal with poetry specifically, "Commoner Literature" deserves attention for its authoritative introduction of key concepts guiding Yu's treatment of new poetry. In short, Zhou argues that "commoner literature is the precise opposite of aristocratic literature" in terms of "a distinction in literary spirit: whether it [the literary spirit] is or is not held in common [pubian], and whether it is or is not in good faith [zhenzhi]" (Zhou 1935, 210). That which is "held in common," according to Zhou, refers to the recording of generally shared and commonplace "thought and fact," as opposed to supernatural tales of heroes, scholars, and great beauties. The term "in good faith" refers to the attributes of unadorned poetic sincerity and honesty, the "expression of my true thoughts and actual experiences, without, of course, attending to polished compositional rules and ornate phrasing" (211). Zhou's commoner literature, then, falls in line with the class-inflected stress on content over form, inner sincerity over outer invention, running throughout progressive literary thought of the time.

As one of Yu Pingbo's mentors at Peking University during the May Fourth period, Zhou's influence on Yu cannot be overlooked. In fact, "Return" extends to poetry the basic premises Zhou had introduced several years previously. Specifically, Yu argues for an evolutionary reemergence, through commoner poetry, of an original poetic essence (zhisu) of emotionally authentic expression. Drawing explicitly from a Chinese translation of Leo Tolstoy's What Is Art? but making unmistakable reference to traditional poetic theory, Yu writes that poetry should be judged for its ability to move people morally and emotionally rather than for aesthetic qualities only appreciable by an aristocratic few.[13] While Yu does not reject this aristocratic nature of poetry, he believes it unsuited to the times. What the current era requires, he maintains, is poetry able to influence a much broader range of people. By this standard, "good poetry" is the sort able to "deeply move a majority of people toward goodness [xiang shan]" (Yu Pingbo 1922, 33). He thus recommends poetry that can "transmit sincere, natural, and commonly held feeling among people while uniting person with person in proper relations" (32).

Yu's unmistakable emphasis here on the suasive, socially constructive, moral force of poetry clearly echoes the traditional Confucian poetics of the "Great Preface." In his stress on the need of the times, however, he leans toward the demands of nationalist ideology, and in particular the desire to imagine into being a popular unity. This unity is for him grounded in "commonly held feeling" (*pubian de qinggan*), an emotional bond unifying all members of a social group, which he describes as "the most valuable stuff [*cailiao*] of poetry" (34). Further solidifying his adaptation of traditional poetics to modern nationalist thought, Yu locates this unifying "stuff" in "people's feeling and will" (*renmen de qinggan he yizhi*), which he insists may be found at the core of either commoner folk song or aristocratic poetry. Borrowing the logic of Qian's and Hu's evolutionary arguments, Yu argues that the only difference between the two is that of the accretion of exterior differences over time:

> The separation of poetry and folk song in literary history has been due to several thousand years of change in which the two have become distinct objects—one orthodox literature and the other nonorthodox—which cannot be forcefully united, however one may wish them so. If you were to take those "boudoir lyrics" or "Western Kun poems" and sing them alongside peasant songs, you would certainly cause an uproar. But from the perspective of literary essence, they are indistinguishable from folk song, for their differences lie only in outer appearance—truly just in outer appearance! (38–39)

Folk song and poetry, Yu continues, differ only in that the former "rolls in coarse diction" while the latter "puts on gentlemanly airs," a distinction that he claims "has not the least importance, as neither can be considered "literary essence" (*wenxue de zhisu*) (39).

Yu then proceeds to locate this true literary essence shared by what he calls "author poetry" (*zuojia de shi*) and "popular poetry" (*minjian de shi*). In either case, this essence resides in poetry's ability to "express feeling and speak the will" (*shuqing yanzhi*). Author poetry, while it has the potential to express the author's interior feeling and will, typically relies on "description" and "imagination" for its content, a tendency that Yu sees as blocking "natural, deep, and clear" expression, the reason being that "depth" goes hand in hand with "obscurity," while clarity leads too easily into shallowness, resulting in a lack of naturalness. Author poems can attain all three of these qualities—naturalness, depth, and clarity—only with the greatest difficulty, and such poems are in Yu's opinion "one in a million" (39).

Popular poetry, on the other hand, achieves these qualities with ease. Although falling far short of author poetry with regard to precision and propriety of diction, in poetry created by the people one can still on occasion discover places where the poetic content surpasses the ordinary in its expression of "primitive will and feeling, almost free of bizarre description and imagination," making this poetry "in all respects ordinary and true" (39). As to why the people are able to produce such poetry, Yu explains:

> In their attitude toward making poetry, they know only to speak what is on
> their minds, to say things how they want to say them, and to describe directly
> the feelings in their breast, free of so-called constraints. Where it is good
> it can express deeply, clearly, and naturally; even where it is not good it is
> always plain and clear, direct and forthright, without affectation, disingenu-
> ousness, or the unseemly. The reason for this is that they regard themselves
> as unrefined sorts, not as poets who, while producing poems, hold to the no-
> tion that "I am making poetry." If it's good, fine; if not, so what? Why worry
> about it!? This valuable quality is shared by all popular literature. (39–40)

From this Yu concludes that "art was originally of the commoners" (40). He then establishes the main point of the essay: that Chinese poetry can return to its com- moner essence by "evolving" into a state free of excess ornamentation:

> Basically what I'm saying is that commoner quality is the very essence of
> poetry, while aristocratic features are what were added on later so thickly
> that they obstructed the universality of poetry. Thus we should try another
> tack, that is, "return to purity and simplicity" [huan chun fan pu], to reveal the
> original face of poetry from beneath the piled-on rouge and powder. I believe
> that not only ought the poetry of the future be commoner, and that primi-
> tive poetry was originally commoner, but that good, aristocratic-style poetry
> of today also contains the commoner essence within, only covered over and
> thus not visible. Poets need not exert superhuman effort to open up a "new
> land" [xinbang], but only clear away a patch of thorns. (47)

In his appeal for an authentically expressive poetry of the People—variously referred to as pingmin, minjian, or minzhong—Yu, like the other writers discussed in this chap- ter, relocates the source of poetry in the humanistic history of China's national interiority. Internal poetic content is timeless, persisting over evolutionary history beneath the exterior accretion, only awaiting the right historical moment to re- emerge from obscurity. This content, moreover, Yu locates within a popular subject of history, the unlettered pingmin, with whom the present-day, intellectual creators of poetry are expected to merge once the essence of poetry is freed from external en- cumbrances. The exterior of poetry, meanwhile, Yu associates with the aristocracy, such that releasing poetry from the constraints of form cuts away retrograde monar- chist tendencies to reveal a true, but previously obscured, national interiority.

For all its detours into imported literary theory and fashionable terminology, at the core of Yu's argument lies the logic of the "Great Preface." Or as Yu plainly states: "The ancients said it well: 'poetry speaks the intent' [shi yan zhi], and: 'The poem is that to which what is intently on the mind goes' [shi zhe, zhi zhi suo zhi ye]. Zhi is something everyone possesses, so why is speaking the intent so difficult, so highly valued? It mystifies me" (41). It is the expressive substance of the zhi upon which Yu's entire argument rests, and it is the recovery of zhi as expressive national interiority upon which the future of modern, national Chinese poetry depends. Yu writes in conclusion: "The poetry of today's and of future poets, if it can overthrow the kingdom of poetry [shi de wangguo] and recover the republic of poetry [shi de gongheguo], will mark a further return to origins. I call this proposition *the return to origins of poetry*" (47; italics in original). Thus to recover the essence of Chinese poetry is to disclose the essence of modern nationhood: both are less a matter of constructing the new than of stripping away the old to manifest a timeless, authentic interior originating from that abstract, but all-important entity, the People.

To be sure, Yu's recommendations for new poetry offer little in the way of concrete, practical approaches to actually writing a modern commoner poetry. He does, however, demonstrate the shaping force of local poetics on the modular import of national literature. First, by deploying this dichotomy in terms of poetic content and form, Yu allows himself simultaneously to reject certain elements of the past, namely the accretion of aristocratic linguistic devices in poetry, and to retain others, most notably the timeless but obscured commoner essence of poetry, its "purity and simplicity" or "primitive will and feeling." By defining this poetic essence as generated in and among the commoners, Yu aligns the substance of poetry with the history of the People, the abiding folk who constitute the national subject and who have, in his view, unconsciously carried the essence of poetry forward from primordial times to the present. Finally, and not least, Yu confirms the place of modern Chinese intellectuals in this nationalist history of poetry by arguing that a new poetry, the very poetry then being invented by Yu and his cohort, can and should evolve to where it "returns" to the timeless poetic essence stretching back to the beginnings of Chinese poetry itself.

Yu Pingbo ends his lengthy essay with a poetic couplet of his own:

Return, my heart!	*wu xin guilai ya!*
From the people, return!	*cong minjian guilai!*
	(48)

Short, straightforward, and patently exclamatory, it would be easy to conclude that these two lines are none other than Yu's heartfelt outcry, the sudden and spontaneous poetic expression of his desire to become one, on the plane of emotion, with the Chinese common folk. Yu's summoning of his heart—the very source of his interior being—from the people seems tragically driven by an intersubjective gulf: the one separating the authentic subject of nation, embodied by the common folk, and the inventors of that subject, found in the persons of Yu and the modern literary elite. Here, of course, lies an irony. For by imagining into being the domain of a linguistic national interiority grounded in the common folk, Yu and others run the risk of excluding themselves from the very nation they themselves promote.

Yet more important than the message of alienation expressed by Yu's couplet is the form he adopts to express it. At one level, Yu mobilizes the ideology of expressionism by shifting from the register of prose to words marked as new poetry—a genre preconstructed as the medium for voicing the poet's authentic interior state. But more interestingly, Yu enhances the effect of vocal projection by symbolically transforming the written poetic word into the sounded poetic voice. Exclamation marks, the expletive *ya*, the pauses implied by line breaks, and even the rhetorical stance of direct address—all indicate that Yu's concluding couplet is meant to be heard more than seen. In short, Yu applies techniques of print to give voice to writing, thus projecting his written poem into the realm of imagined sound, and his subjective interior into the realm of the People, where his own true interiority, his heart, presumably resides.

CHAPTER 2

Poetry Off the Page

Sound Aesthetics in Print

THERE CAN BE no "pure voice," cautions Michel de Certeau, because orality is always determined and codified by a "scriptural economy" (1984, 132). China's new poetry is surely no exception. For one thing, the imagination of a pure, originary voice of poetry drew its positive ideological value less from the actual practice of oral literature than from its deliberate opposition to its negative Other, the written classical language. Equally important in determining and codifying poetic voice were two intersecting, highly politicized, and non-oral modalities, each established in canonical texts: the local ethnopoetics of the expressionist, morally suasive force, enshrined in the "Great Preface" to the *Book of Songs*; and the global poetics of Romantic-nationalism that emphasized the human source of poetry. And not least, for all the oralist assumptions built into the construction of Chinese new poetry, it was of course introduced and popularized as a printed rather than a recited or otherwise orally propagated discourse.

The point here is not to prove that in their attempts to write voice into their poetry early new poets misled themselves, or worse, acted in bad faith to further their social self-interest. Refashioning poetic voice has been an essential aspect of poetic invention for most any tradition. In the case of China's new poets, their attempts to conjoin speech and poetry were not an isolated literary scheme, but marked their participation in a much wider twentieth-century trend of experimentation with free verse and spoken language (Perkins 1976, 232–233). As for social self-interest, the vernacular language movement, with new literature and new poetry at its cutting edge, was indeed a political act intended to create an autonomous space of socially committed activism for intellectuals in the wake of the failed 1911 Republican Revolution (Gunn 1991, 38–39).

The preceding chapter explored this intersection of art and politics in terms of a new poetry produced in tune with the vocal imperatives of local and global ideology. This chapter moves on to the effects that the vocal imagination exerted on new poetry through the 1920s and up through the beginning of the War of Resistance against Japan in 1937. The chapter is divided into four parts. First I return to Hu Shi's 1919 essay "On New Poetry" to unravel a pair of conflicting

aesthetic strands in his notion of "natural prosody" (*ziran de yinjie*)—one stress-
ing new poetry's communication of interior content, and the other encouraging
self-orientation of the poetic text. "Hu's contradiction"—my shorthand for this
poetic tension—would reconcile the desire to legitimate new poetry by construct-
ing a voice-mediated link to a national interiority beyond the poem, but at the
same time create for new poetry a domain of autonomy by stressing its distinct
self-orientation. This split, I argue, is emblematic of the political fault lines later
to emerge in new poetry, and especially in the later emergence of poetry written
specifically for recitation.

Parts two through four explore how these two strands played out from the
1920s into the 1930s as the idea of performing new poetry gathered a certain mo-
mentum. On one hand, we find a desire to articulate national interiority through
poetic voice by imagining a movement of vocal sound traveling *through* the poem,
with relatively little self-conscious regard for poetic form; on the other, we find
poets who deploy the sounded poem as a means of enhancing prosodic effects.
Part two explores the former tendency by examining poems of the 1920s that use
specific devices to inscribe a sounding voice in poems not intentionally written for
actual oral performance. Part three of the chapter then turns to the first attempts
at producing a metalanguage for this sort of poem, specifically, efforts made in the
early 1930s by the left-wing China Poetry Society (Zhongguo shige hui) to legitimate
recitation through theoretical discourse. Part four shifts to the first poets who in
fact regularly experimented with reading aloud and reciting modern poetry in the
1920s and 1930s. These were not poets of the leftist camp, as one might expect, but
the frequenters of literary salons in cosmopolitan, academic Beiping, a group that
emphasized speaking and listening to poetry as a way of refining poetic language.
For them, the voice of poetry flowed in a closed circuit, from the recited text to the
listening audience and back into the text through revision. Recitational practice of
this sort made for a dynamic of the sounding voice that contributed to the inner
orientation of the visually present poetic text. The last portion of the chapter shows
how the tensions embedded in Hu's contradiction peaked as war loomed, poets
dueled, and the voices of recitation reached a crescendo.

Hu's Contradiction

Given the underlying ideologies of sound and voice in early twentieth-century
discourse on Chinese new poetry, one might assume that open public recitation
of these poems was common practice. Unlike, for instance, the Anglo-American
tradition, this does not seem to have been the case.[1] Writing in 1927, Zhu Ziqing
speculates that the rarity of such oral performance might have been because of the
way the poems were phrased and rhymed, or because no one knew how to read
them, or simply due to a prejudice against reading them aloud. But Zhu's use of

the term *yinsong*, which refers to the tonal chanting of traditional poetry, suggests that at this early stage poets were still unable to imagine an independent, modern vocal mode for their infant and almost exclusively written genre (1996a, 222).[2] Yet a certain imagination of oral performance has been present in new poetry since its invention. Based on the ideologies of expressionism discussed in the previous chapter, poets began to emphasize poetry as something more than just words on the page. "Creating poetry," writes Hu Shi, in a 1916 diary entry, "is much like talking" (*zuo shi po ru shuo hua*; 1977, 3, 838). Three years later, in his seminal essay "On New Poetry," Hu developed the link between talk and poetry when he recommended a "natural prosody" based in part on the "natural rhythm of spoken tone" (*yuqi de ziran jiezou*; Hu 1935b, 304). Hu's call for a natural poetics based on the aesthetic features of speech, innocent enough on its surface, in fact highlights a defining tension in the imagination of new poetry: is poetry "poetic" for an expressionist orientation originating from the emotive and affective voice, or for an aesthetic self-orientation constructed from textual surface features? Due to the strong presence of an expressionist ideology linked to a national interiority, this question lay at the center of conflicts over the ideal voice of new poetry. Hu's 1919 recommendation for natural prosody represents an early effort to reconcile this issue. Should new poetry be based on a dynamics of speech or a dynamics of text? It was in the framework of this question that the recitational aesthetic emerged in the 1920s and 1930s.

As discussed in Chapter 1, Hu's evolutionary narrative of poetic liberation assumes new poetry's ability to communicate the content of a national interiority. New vernacular poetry, which represents the end point of this process, is for Hu the final stage in a millennia-long relaxation of line-length restrictions in Chinese classical poetry, a slow, unconscious process that gradually allowed the significant "content" of "abundant material, precise observation, high ideals, and complex feeling and emotion" to be expressed through poetry (Hu 1935b, 295). Such a narrative—in effect a linear evolutionary history of poetic form—implies two things: first, that poetic language, like the modern vernacular, mediates a connection to lived thought and experience so as to express personality, life, vitality, and liberating power, in other words, the content of national interiority; second, that any deliberate return to the formal intricacies that knit together classical Chinese poetic lines—such as rhyme and tone schemes as well as phonological, grammatical, and semantic parallelism—may be viewed as not only counter to the natural historical progression of Chinese poetic form but ideologically retrograde because it threatens to override and thus obscure the poetic projection of national interiority. Hu's poetic liberation thus encourages poetry oriented more toward communication of meaningful content than formal aspects involving self-orientation of textual surfaces. The implications are clear: poets should concern themselves primarily with content over

form, signified over signifier, source over surface, psychology over prosody, and ul-
timately, interior over exterior. Anything less runs the risk of betraying a national
identity.

Hu's emphasis on the communicative function of poetry may help to resolve
the problem of the legitimating source of poetry; but at the same time it makes for
aesthetic problems, especially when viewed from the perspective of Formalist and
Structuralist criticism. According to Czech Structuralist Jan Mukarovsky: "Aesthetic
effect is the goal of poetic expression. However, the aesthetic function, which thus
dominates in poetic language, concentrates attention on the linguistic sign itself—
hence it is exactly the opposite of practical orientation toward a goal which in lan-
guage is communicative" (Mukarovsky 1976, 4). Hu's narrative of poetic progress,
like his corresponding narrative of linguistic evolution, tends toward just this prac-
tical, communicative orientation: the expression of content defined as "abundant
material, precise observation, high ideals, and complex feeling and emotion." Hu
thus leans toward the opposing linguistic pole of what is, in Mukarovsky's view,
required to create a distinct, poetic language.

Hu responds to this apparent imbalance by introducing the idea of formal tech-
nique. But he does so cautiously, under the rubric of "natural prosody." According
to Hu, natural prosody has two primary components: sound (yin) and grouping
or segmentation (jie). Sound refers to two subcomponents: "natural accent" (ziran
de qingzhong gaoxia) and "natural rhyme" (ziran de yongyun). Grouping refers to the
rhythmic parsing of the poetic line into units based on "natural semantic group-
ing" and "natural grammatical grouping" (Hu 1935b, 305). Perhaps not surprisingly
given the lack of existing and accepted conventions for modern Chinese vernacu-
lar poetry, Hu has trouble defining "natural" except in opposition to the classical
poetic conventions on tone pattern and rhyme. The examples he provides of word
groupings are largely arbitrary, while natural cadence and rhyme elude explication
beyond the assertion that they are "in the bones" (zai guzi li) of new poetry (Hu
1935b, 306). Hu does, however, provide an example of natural prosody, and it is
here that we see his contradiction take shape. Hu extracts several lines—those itali-
cized below—from Zhou Zuoren's poem "Snow Sweepers" (Liangge saoxue de ren):

> Dark, gloomy weather,
> Powdery white snow fills the sky and covers the ground.
> Outside Heavenly Peace Gate, on the snow-hazy road,
> No sign of horse or cart,
> Only two figures out there, sweeping snow.
> *So they sweep, so it falls:*
> *When the east side's swept clean, again the west side's snowed over;*
> *When the high spots are cleared, again the low spots are level.*

A layer of snow lies on their coarse, hempen overcoats,
The two of them sweep without pause. . . .
(Hu 1935b, 306; Zhou et al. 1927, 29)

Once restored to their original accompanying text, the three lines Hu cites immediately stand out as the only part of the poem that makes significant use of parallelism. According to Roman Jakobson, parallelism is a fundamentally important category of the "recurrent returns" that constitute "the essence of poetic artifice," and as such functions crucially to differentiate the more internally oriented language of poetry from the language of communicative prose (1987, 145–179). Granted, the three lines Hu selects do not depart widely from colloquial spoken diction, and in fact illustrate how spoken-language diction can be turned to poetic effect. But at the same time, it is intriguing that Hu should specifically designate as natural the one portion of the poem so clearly marked by formal artifice. His idea of the natural is thus a conflicted one in that he proposes that new poetry be naturally spontaneous *and* carefully structured. Or, as he puts it, poets should strive for "internal organization and arrangement of words and phrases" because "only then can there occur harmonious natural prosody" (Hu 1935b, 306). On the one hand, then, Hu calls for new poetry to break with formal restraints and freely transmit thought and feeling. But at the same time, under the sign of the natural, he implicitly condones a formalist aesthetics of self-oriented poetic artifice.

This contradiction is by no means unique to Chinese new poetry. "There is," Mukarovsky observes, "a constant struggle and a constant tension between self-orientation and communication so that poetic language, though it stands in opposition to the other functional languages in its self-orientation, is not cut off from them by an insurmountable boundary" (1976, 6). Hu engages this tension. He asks that new poetry, as a part of "national language literature," communicate broadly to its audience by retaining the naturalness residing "in the bones" of the spoken vernacular, the authentic, popular source of linguistic expression; at the same time, however, he responds to the need for new poetry to establish its difference from natural language, to stand in linguistic relief against the eminently functional modern national language.

Hu's natural ideal, then, can be understood as a national ideal. As discussed in Chapter 1, his formula for "a national language literature and a literary national language" requires that the art-language of literature and the functional language of people's everyday discourse build one upon the other. The two must be able to interact, not just to mutually improve both literature and language, but to ensure a linguistically mediated unity between the elite, individual makers of the literature and the popular, collective creators of the national language. Hu's cautious insistence upon "natural" artifice reveals the conflicting double duty he requires of new poetry. His call for naturalness indicates a desire to affirm and maintain new poetry's affinity with the popular spoken language. Here Hu aligns himself with a Romantic attitude toward language and poetry, the same logic that Gerald Bruns discerns in nineteenth-century Romantic ideas of poetic language, that poetry "is not to be dissociated from the dynamics of speech, for to do so is to dissociate word and man—to isolate the word from human reality whose life is revealed in the immediacy of thought and feeling" (Bruns 1974, 51). This is the reality of the national interiority, the human space of lived experience and linguistic production that, according to Qian Xuantong and Hu Shi, make the vernacular (*baihua*) the stuff of a viable national language. But Hu's attention to poetic artifice also intends to define an alternative space, one that equates aesthetic autonomy for poetic language with social autonomy for the makers of new poetry. Such autonomy would elevate them to the status of innovative creators filling the distinct role of a socially progressive vanguard. Hu's contradiction, this desire to simultaneously efface and maintain linguistic difference in the field of new poetry, is symptomatic of this double bind. To no small degree, too, Hu's contradiction speaks to the modernity of Chinese new poetry by defining a multiform but persistent conflict—that which exists between poetic texts marking out a detached domain of aesthetic autonomy and the countervailing demand for a poetry that is socially involved by virtue of its ability to access and communicate the substance of a national interiority. Poetry recitation, because of its inevitable links to expressionist speech, became a key battleground for this poetic tension.

Spoken Emotion

Writing poetry that would "naturally" express the essential prelinguistic thought and feeling that constitutes a national interiority comes up against an intractable problem: gesturing toward an inner world requires its own set of formal conventions. As the example of "Snow Sweepers" already indicates, these were conventions that constructed voice as an immediate expression of emotional interiority. The most strongly emphasized and notably preeminent category of expressionist content during the early days of new poetry was emotion (*qingxu*). Why this was so has everything to do with the emergence of new poetry from the conjoining of two discourses: a local ethnopoetic tradition that stressed the power of poetic voice to express cosmically grounded civilizational norms, and a Romantic-nationalist ideology that emphasized the vocal mediation of a shared national interiority grounded in the expressionist capabilities of the human subject. For both systems, emotion served as the ultimate ground of interior human truth, a belief that, as Haiyan Lee asserts in her study of sentiment in modern Chinese fiction, "the modern nation is . . . a community of sympathy" (Lee 2007, 7). An insistence on emotional authenticity, then, became one of the key legitimators of the new poetry as well as an unshakable assumption in the definition of what makes poetry *poetry*.

A characteristic statement on the place of emotion in poetry appears in the preface to the 1922 anthology of new poetry by eight new poets, *A Snowy Morning* (*Xuezhao*), where poet and critic Zheng Zhenduo writes:

> Poetry is the product of human emotions. When one experiences strong feeling, be it bitter or glad, or sorrowful and angry, we invariably wish to make it known: poetry is the very best instrument for expressing this sort of emotion.
>
> Rhyme, meter and all other formal fetters of poetry—we want to smash them, because emotion will not be contained by metrical restrictions. Once held back it becomes despondent and denatured, or at the very least reduced from its original strength.
>
> We demand "sincerity," speaking what comes to mind, without concealment or pretense. We demand "plain simplicity," no more than the frank unadorned expression of what our hearts feel. Ornament and cosmetics are no more than a refuge of "falsity" and the destroyer of "sincerity."
>
> Although we know the poetry that eight of us have published here is quite immature, it still counts as "sincere" expression of emotion; although unable to express the spirit of the age, we can say that it is the reflection of each of our characters or personalities.
>
> If these frail voices of ours can leave a slight impression on the heart of a sympathetic reader, can arouse in them a fuller and more sonorous resonance, then our wishes will have been completely fulfilled. (Zhou et al. 1927, no page number)

In a few short paragraphs Zheng invokes all the main components informing the ideology of new poetry: the opposition between free expression and formal restriction, the metaphor of voice, the dichotomy between collective ("spirit of the age") and individual ("characters or personalities") literary expression, and the imagination of a sound-based resonance with an imagined audience. At the root of all these elements, Zheng implies with his first sentence, is the idea of poetry as conveyor of authentic inner emotion.

Given that the new poetry Zheng refers to here was almost all written, how in formal terms does a poet construct emotional presence? What is the rhetoric of poetic emotion? One approach, frequently noted in studies of this period's fiction (Lee 2004; Anderson 1990), is how poets and other writers generate emotional presence by positioning an implied speaker in sympathetic relation with various representatives of the oppressed classes, a generic nationalist technique based upon "a new degree of imaginative sympathy and community with countrymen more directly oppressed and affected" (Trumpener 1997, 32). Zhou Zuoren's "Snow Sweepers," with its observer's expression of sympathy for two common laborers, represents just one example of such an attitude as it appears in early new poems. A prominent feature of this sympathetic expression in these poems is the inscription of the sound of voice on the page, of writing poetry that would conduct the substance of sympathy to an imagined auditor through the medium of imagined sound. "Snow Sweepers" in fact rehearses this vocal inscription in its second half with the line, "Bless you, snow-sweepers!" (zhufu ni saoxue de ren; Zhou et al. 1927, 29). This line marks the dramatic climax of the poem: a moment of recognition and contact between the poet and the commoner. It is a moment, too, produced by the poem's shift from detached observation of the commoner subject to an imagined speech act, one enacted grammatically through direct address, and visually by the use of the exclamation mark. Zhou's interpolation of virtual speech, foregrounded by grammatical variation and amplified by punctuation, has an important function in his poem; it indicates the formalization of the sounding voice in new poetry, a voice that would exceed simple visual observation of its human object to project a vocally mediated emotive resonance. One can even say that it represents, in poetic form, the same idea of vocal projection of an emotive interior that Zheng Zhenduo describes in his prefatory remarks to Snowy Morning.

Given that "Snow Sweepers" appeared in the anthology prefaced by Zheng's statements, such a correspondence might seem less than surprising. It is interesting to note, then, that the same belief in the emotional, expressionist, and ultimately vocal nature of poetry appears in the writing of someone outside the literary field and who regarded new poetry with outright disdain. In an article published in the The Chinese Journal of Psychology (Xinli) in 1924, pioneering Chinese psychologist Y. C. Chang (Zhang Yaoxiang) published a statistical analysis of emotion in new poets. His scientific analysis—in fact a thinly veiled critique—of recent new poetry demonstrates the prevalence of the expressionist paradigm. But more intriguingly, his statistical method foregrounds the period's poetic imagination of sounding voice as inscribed in print.

The stated purpose of Chang's study is to measure emotion scientifically just as one would test vision, hearing, or taste. Those senses, he remarks, can be objectively observed using light, sound waves, and chemicals. Emotion, however, presents difficulties because it cannot be consistently stimulated and stably maintained in the laboratory. Poetry, according to Chang, can provide data in such a project because it represents "writing specially for the purpose of expressing feeling" (1924, 2). Chang is led to new poetry because his research interests focus on emotion in Chinese youth, and new poetry is popular primarily among Chinese young people. His data, consequently, come from nine recent poetry volumes: seven collections by individual poets and two multiauthor anthologies.[3]

What makes Chang's study interesting in terms of visual inscription of the sounding voice is that, rather than gauging emotional content based on readers' responses to the poems—an approach he discounts as subject to the vagaries of individual interpretation—Chang turns instead to the "new punctuation symbols" used in these poems, and in particular the exclamation mark (*gantan hao*). He explains: "To learn the degree of a person's dejection, passivity, pessimism, and world-weariness, you can add up the number of exclamatory phrases in his writing; to add up the number of exclamatory phrases in a piece of writing, you can add up the number of exclamation marks. This is what is known as objective research methodology" (Chang 1924, 3).

From today's perspective, it is difficult to grant Chang's method either objectivity or scientific validity. Quantitatively analyzing punctuation can certainly produce a set of statistical results, but to correlate the quantity of printed exclamation marks with the quantity of emotion resident in a poet at the time of writing violates currently accepted literary critical principles that insist on the many levels of mediation between a writer's interior psychological state and his or her textual production. Chang does acknowledge this disjuncture to some degree when he recognizes the subjective nature of literary interpretation, but he insists all the same on the ability to objectively measure emotion through numeric measurement.

His approach, however, makes perfect sense in the context of contemporary literary thought; that is, according to the formula that poetry directly conveys not just the inner emotional state of the author but also, as we shall see, the condition of a national interiority. Chang's analysis, for all its appeal to scientific method, is ultimately driven by literary and nationalist rather than scientific principles. But what makes his study relevant to the writing of early new poetry is how he links devices used in the visual realm of the printed new vernacular poem—the exclamation mark and exclamatory particles—to emotion, voice, and the national condition, which for him point to a crisis among Chinese youth.

After tabulating data from the nine poetry collections, Chang finds that the Chinese poems in his sample average one exclamation mark every 4.3 lines (see Table 2.1). This figure he compares to the ratio of one exclamation mark per 25.5 lines in a control group of "universally recognized good poetry" that, among other works, includes Shakespeare's "Sonnets," Milton's *Paradise Lost*, Browning's *The Ring and the Book*, and the classic Victorian-era anthology of English poetry, Palgrave's *The Golden Treasury*.[4] China's new poets, he notes with dismay, are "six times more likely to sigh or exclaim than major foreign poets" (1924, 14). Here Chang clearly identifies the use of the printed exclamation mark with vocalization. This vocal imagination he asserts even more plainly when he writes, "If someone were to read these [poems] out loud, with a sigh or a shout every four lines, listeners would surely cover their ears and leave, cursing the reader as a lunatic" (10). Extending

TABLE 2.1 Exclamation Marks per Line in New Poetry Collections

Book title	No. of stanzas	No. of lines	No. of exclamation marks	Average no. of exclamation marks per stanza	Average no. of lines
Experiments (Changshi ji)	68	615	105	1.5	5.8
The Grass (Cao'er)	158	2,659	394	2.5	6.7
The Goddesses (Nüshen)	238	1,517	918	3.9	1.6
Winter Night (Dongye)	289	2,767	455	1.6	6.1
Myriad of Stars (Fanxing)	164	695	108	0.7	6.4
Spring Waters (Chunshui)	164	709	151	0.9	4.7
Spume (Langhua)	57	320	41	0.7	7.8
Annual Selection of New Poetry (Xinshi nianxuan)	123	1,511	321	2.6	4.7
Vernacular Poetry Study Collection (Baihua shi yanjiuxuan)	82	546	137	1.7	4.0
Totals	1,261	11,339	2,630	2.1	4.3

Source: Chang Y. C., "Xin shiren zhi qingxiu," Xinli 3, no. 2 (April 1924): 10.

this point, he adds that young authors of new poetry, "upon seeing a bird, riding in a rickshaw, strolling to a brook, or climbing a mound of earth, burst forth with dozens of successive exclamations" (11).

Chang also ties this vocalized sound to emotive expression by claiming that new poets frequently use the new punctuation symbol "to indicate an exclamatory emotion" (2). He reinforces the connection between voice and emotion when he locates, and again tabulates, the words most frequently preceding the exclamation marks. Along with le, which he identifies as a "past particle," these include a set of monosyllabic interjections, including ya, a, he, aiyo, ba and ne. Several of these interjections—ya, a, he, aiyo—are sound words performing paralinguistic functions, while the others—le, ba, and ne—perform definite grammatical functions. Except for *le*, which Chang equates with an old person thinking of the past (whereas young people ought to think of the future), each of the other interjections Chang relates to spoken sound, from a baby's babble to a porter's grunt (*a* and *he*), the groans of an invalid, the act of giving up, and rude country dialects, respectively. For a new poet to use these exclamations, Chang observes, means that his or her identity becomes "affiliated with that of the elderly, infants, coolies, the infirm, rustic locals, and world-weary pessimists, and not with generally healthy, happy, cultured youth" (12).

Obviously Chang was no friend of the new poetry. But more to the point, his critique derives from the same conventionalized aesthetic assumptions held by new poets. First, he regards poetry, new or old, as a clear and direct conduit of emotional expression. Emotions, in turn, correspond to the moral condition of the nation. For Chang the condition of the nation is grounded in the human subject, in this case new poets, who by his reckoning represent the sad moral condition of Chinese youth in general, especially when compared to representative foreign poets.

The significance of Chang's article thus lies less in his pseudoscientific method than in his reaction to the appearance of early new poetry in print, or what Edward Gunn refers to as the "dramatic visual impact" of the printed vernacular during that period (Gunn 1991, 39–40). The innovation of typesetting poetry in the Western style certainly figures here, but it was the exclamation marks—one of the set of punctuation symbols introduced at about the same time the first new poems were being published (Gunn 1991, 305n24)—that caught Chang's eye, as well as his poetic imagination. The space for this imagination comes from how punctuation, and the exclamation mark in particular, typically lack "a precise value or exclusive specifying function," so that interpretation is frequently arrived at pragmatically, that is, based on readers' behavioral experience (Parkes 1993, 114, 1–2). The interjections Chang singles out represent another important and striking visual element in the modern reinvention of written vernacular, and one that also leads Chang to import specific meaning. In both cases, exclamation marks and interjections, Chang draws upon existing literary convention to interpret new poetry as the visual inscription of the sounding voice, and the sounding voice as an emanation of emotional content. His study gives evidence for the tendency to reify the links between interior emotion, the visual realm of print media, and a typographic imagination of the sounding voice.

If the prolific use of exclamation marks indicates one aspect of the visual inscription of sounding voice in early new poetry, then according to Chang's calculations the poet most committed to imagined sound would be Guo Moruo with his 1921 collection *The Goddesses* (*Nüshen*).[5] The effect of unrestrained vocalization these exclamation marks create is, assuredly, one reason that, since its publication in 1921, critics often mention *The Goddesses* in the same breath as they acclaim these poems for their significant content, typically described as a new "spirit of the age" (*shidai jingshen*) (Sun 1996, 264; Tang 1993, 155; Zhu Ziqing 1935, 5). But rather than turning to *The Goddesses* itself, I want to consider instead a poem that singles out Guo's collection in a manner that speaks to additional dimensions of a latent recitational aesthetic of the early 1920s. It is a short poem, written by a little-known poet and entitled "Poet's Joy" (Shiren de huanxi):

> Passing through the market one afternoon, I saw a vendor of copper and
> brassware reading *The Goddesses*. Happily astonished, I gasped in admiration.
>
> You are able to hear the sound of poetry,
> You are the one whom the goddess seeks!
> If you, for all your care and toil,
> Seek consolation from her,
> I believe she is able truly to give it to you.
>
> The sound of poetry spreads through the markets;
> The sound of poetry spreads through the fields;
> The sound of poetry spreads through the factories;
> The sound of poetry spreads everywhere.
>
> The sound of poetry releases the souls of all from purgatory.
> This is the poet's joy.
>
> (Chen Nanshi 1922, 23)

An obscure poem by an obscure poet, "Poet's Joy" deserves attention not for its influence upon the literary scene (it had none) but for how it realizes in print a poetic imagination of orality. To comprehend the significance of Chen's poem requires a specific strategy of reading, one that recognizes its participation in an emergent recitational aesthetic that inscribed voice into the printed poem.

This reading strategy is needed because of the poem's situation within the ongoing discourse of new poetry. "Poet's Joy" was published at the height of the agitation for "commoner" and "mass" poetries able to articulate a connection between the general Chinese populace and elite writers. It is not accidental, then, that "Poet's Joy" appeared in the very same issue of *Poetry Monthly* as Yu Pingbo's exposition on the theoretical possibility for such poetry in his "Return to Origins" essay. Both Chen and Yu, as literary affiliates, were at the time writing from a distinct, though provisional, ideological position: that of using poetry to consolidate and integrate an imagined national community.

What makes Chen's poem worth returning to is how it realizes the imagination of such a community by activating the "sociocorporeal" nature of oral performance. According to Paul Zumthor, sociocorporeal refers to the social "nonlinguistic forms" produced by the active, physically present bodies, both individual and collective, that distinguish oral performance from written text (Zumthor 1994; 1990, 60–62). "Poet's Joy," though obviously a written text, functions at several levels to reproduce in print the forms of a physically present oral performance. In doing so, it creates a virtual poetry recitation, and one that emphasizes the existential presence of a national community mediated by the poet's sounding voice.

The performative situation of the poem begins with the way its epigraph frames a real-world, first-person setting—on the street, face to face with a genuine commoner—ripe with potential for imagined oral performance. This sets the stage for the virtual direct address in the poem's first three lines, which insistently repeat the second-person pronoun "you" (ni). By placing the speaking self of the poet on stage in this impromptu, imaginary theater, Chen creates a virtual sociocorporeality of the orally performed poem. The poet is the performer, the commoner is the listening audience, and conjoining the two is none other than new poetry, or more precisely, the "sound of poetry" (shisheng) identified both with a copy of Guo's *The Goddesses*—here elevated from print to sound—and Chen's own implied vocal address to the vendor.

The poem further reinforces this virtual sociocorporeality by its use of repetition. In one respect, repetition characterizes oral poetry in its practical ability to overcome the ephemerality of the spoken word (Finnegan 1992, 129). The reliance—some might say overreliance—of "Poet's Joy" on repetitive phrasing thus marks the text with a certain oral character. But Chen's poem also deploys "discursive recurrence," a form of repetition that, according to Zumthor, "constitutes the most efficacious means to verbalize a spatiotemporal experience, to make the listener participate in it" (Zumthor 1990, 112). As just mentioned, the poem's first stanza, by repeating "you" three times, gestures toward the real-time effect of oral performance. The second stanza continues and extends this virtual oral modality by adopting the form of a litany, a characteristic technique of oral poetry marked by "an indefinite repetition of a single structure, be it syntactic or partially lexical, some words being modified on each repetition in such a way as to mark a progression by slippage or gaps" (Zumthor 1990, 112). Chen constructs his litany with four lines that begin with the same four characters, *shisheng sanbu* (the sound of poetry spreads [through]), but end with bisyllabic compounds for spatial locations: markets (*shishang*), fields (*tianli*), factories (*gongchang*), and everywhere (*gechu*). Finally, the strong, definitive closure of the line endings, especially when coupled with the anaphoric phrasing just discussed, partake of an "oracular" free-verse technique reminiscent of public speaking (Fussell 1979, 80–81).

All these formal techniques for constructing a poetic voice in the poem come together in an emphasis on the auditory dimension of space—in this case, Chen's use of imagined poetic sound to define and integrate the space of nation. We "hear" this happening in the second stanza, where formal recurrences deliberately amplify the sound of the poetic voice so that it pervades a linguistically defined territory, one comprising all commoner members of the national community within imaginative earshot of the Chinese new poem. Chen exploits several features of auditory imagination here. First is the ability of sound not only to appropriate space but also to realize a "mutual envelopment of aurality" that "predisposes an exchange among presences" (Barthes 1985, 247; Kahn 1999). Chen's construction of voice also corresponds to what Steven Connor calls the "Romantic idealization of sound, which stressed the capacity of sound both to pervade and to integrate objects and entities which the eye kept separate." Unlike visual, perspectival space, writes Connor, "auditory experience" of this sort defines "a self imaged not as a point, but as a membrane; not as a picture, but as a channel through which voices, noises and musics travel" (1997, 207). Chen's emotion-driven voice, then, would transcend the textual presence of new poetry by imagining into being a grand theater of auditory experience that integrates all hearers into a mutually shared, sound-based presence.

"Poet's Joy" may be obscure, but it is not insignificant. Its importance resides in how, from a specific and, as we shall see, durable discursive position in the field of new poetry, it uses poetry itself to imagine into being a national theater of the sounding poetic voice. Through a combination of formal devices, the poem would exceed its presence on the printed page to enter the domain of vocalized sound, and from there national space, a space it must enter and fill in order to perform its ultimate salvational mission.

Chen Nanshi's poetic career extended no further than the early 1920s, and his "Poet's Joy" faded quickly from literary memory. But the idea that new poetry should transcend the medium of print in order to reach the imagined ears of its audience persisted in poems of the mid- and late 1920s, especially those written by poets whose leftist orientation committed them to the mission of national salvation. The poet I discuss, Jiang Guangci, did not actively practice or advocate recitation. But as I will show, his poems are distinguished by devices that inscribe the sounding voice to simulate the projection of emotion-bearing sound.

One of China's first self-proclaimed revolutionary writers, Jiang accrued his revolutionary credentials by studying in the Soviet Union, where he joined the Communist Party, and then entering China's leftist literary circles, first as a poet and later as a writer of fiction. Even though he is not known to have actually recited his poetry, Jiang represents one among the earliest forerunners of the socialist era's political lyric (zhengzhi shuqing shi), a "public square poetry" (guangchang shige) often purposefully written for recitation (Hong and Liu 2005, 97). His use of oratorical devices certainly suggests such an association. Jiang's poetry, according to T. A. Hsia, seems to come from someone "choked with emotion," who sounds "like a soapbox orator at a loss for the right words but straining his voice to rouse his audience" (1968, 75). Though clearly a negative appraisal, Hsia's critique responds precisely to the imagined aurality of the visual inscription of sound, a feature carried by an identifiable set of linguistic apparatuses that, like those in "Poet's Joy," suggest a recitational aesthetic. Jiang employs direct address, parallelism, interjection, and punctuation to amplify the written words of his poems. Together these devices seem to will his inner voice out into national space, where it would awaken the populace by sheer volume and purge the national shame through association of vocal sound with cataclysmic floods and purifying flame. "Sorrow for China" (Ai Zhongguo), Jiang's most frequently anthologized poem and the title work of his 1927 poetry collection, displays these features prominently:

Look East: there is oppressed Korea;
Look South: there is trodden-down India;
Aiyou! I cannot bear to repeat the miseries of conquered nations!
I fear that China shall fall to myriad plunderings and not recover.
I would run to the summit of Kunlun's high peaks
To shout awake compatriots lost in dreams;
I want to release the torrential flood of the East Sea
To wash away the sloth of the Chinese people.
I . . . ah! I am shamed by this silence stretching back an eternity! . . .
(Jiang Guangchi 1983, 143)

Even more direct in its imagined vocal force is Jiang's "Burst of Blood-flowers" (Xuehua de baolie), a poem elicited by the notorious May Thirtieth Incident of 1925, when British police opened fire on a crowd of protestors in Shanghai, killing twelve Chinese. The poem in turn vociferates against Japanese capitalists and the British police ("You foul bandits of imperialism!"), exhorts the Chinese people ("Hasten to awake from boundless pipe-dreams!"), and exalts the martyred protestors ("Bless the sacrificed vanguard!"), before concluding with the unsubtle command, "Kill, kill, kill, kill, kill . . ." (Jiang Guangchi 1983, 160–162). Also, and much like Chen Nanshi before him, Jiang uses his poetry to create an imagined theater for his words by setting his poetic persona in the street to shout his fury to all who would hear:

I am but a crude and outraged singer,
Not a softly droning ivory-tower poet.

From now on let others listen to that exquisite music,
Let others write those exquisite stanzas, I care not;
I am merely a crude and outraged singer,
I wish only to spend my life crying out at the crossroads! . . .
(Jiang Guangchi 1983, 181–182)

Here Jiang takes the step of moving from the implication of sounding poetic voice
to the explicit, though still hypothetical, installation of the poet himself perform-
ing poetry in a public space. Significant, too, as we shall see, is how at the same
moment Jiang defines the revolutionary poet in contrast to the "ivory-tower" poet,
the former spatially enclosed and reciting in a low drone, the latter in open, public
space and vocalizing at a high emotive pitch.

Theorizing Interior

However prominent the recitational impulse may appear in Chen's and Jiang's
poems, the actual practice of recitation remains implicit. What we see in their po-
ems is more a politically informed aesthetic bent than a deliberately conceptualized
category of literary practice. Before long, however, the recitational aesthetic moved
from poetic rhetoric to theoretical pronouncements. This shift came about with the
founding of the China Poetry Society (Zhongguo shige hui) in Shanghai in 1932.
The society was a branch of the League of Left-Wing Writers (Zuoyi zuojia lian-
meng), an organization founded in 1930 to unify various radical literary camps un-
der the banner of writing and propagating anti-imperialist proletarian literature. In
accord with this overarching goal, the China Poetry Society proposed the creation of
new poetry whose political content would be accessible to the general, uneducated
populace through readily comprehensible and easily propagated oral forms, such as
popular song, folk melodies, and recited poetry. Rather than poetry for publication
on the printed page, this was poetry created with actual performance in mind. As
the editors wrote in the journal's inaugural issue, poems ought to be "taken among
the popular masses and recited" "to see if others can understand them" (Tongren
deng 1933, 8).

While the society took the forefront in theorizing poetry recitation, the idea
of reciting to the masses came from the acknowledged leader of the League of Left-
Wing Writers, Qu Qiubai. In the context of adapting existing popular forms of oral
literature to his program of creating revolutionary proletarian literature and art,
Qu wrote in 1931 of creating a "popular-language poetry (*suhua shi*) that doesn't
need to be sung to musical notation, but can be recited or read aloud with a very
moving and entertaining tone and rhythm" (Qu 1953, 863). For Qu, this rather
sketchily conceived form of poetry recitation represented one among many genres
of reformed oral literature that could potentially come out of existing genres, like

storytelling, songs, or local opera, all of which would be based on an emergent, living "proletarian common speech" (*puluo putonghua*) able to mediate revolutionary consciousness among the unlettered masses.

The China Poetry Society followed up Qu's proposal with an article spelling out the agitational principles behind what they optimistically described as a "poetry recitation movement." In response to the question, "Why is poetry recitation (*shige de langdu*) necessary?" poet Ren Jun, writing under the pseudonym Sen Bao, stresses the sounds of the poetic voice, in contrast to the visuality of the written, as a powerful means of projecting emotion generated by national interiority. First, recited poetry possesses a "direct affectivity" (*zhijie de gandongxing*) superior to that of visible, written discourse:

> It hardly need be said that the spoken and written languages both constitute signs representing a person's intent, thought, feeling, etc. The difference is that written language is visible while spoken language is not. However, in general spoken language is more highly concretized [*juxianghua*] than written, and thus better able to move people emotionally than writing. This is especially so in the case of poetry filled with the rise and fall of emotion [*qinggan zhi qifu*], which when recited, presents content with greater vividness. (Sen 1933, 1)

Emotion, according to Ren Jun, is the affective vehicle of content. As for the kind of content to be included in poetry, the society provides a catalog of preferred subject matter: anti-imperialist and antiwarlord zeal; the suffering of the masses under natural disaster, civil war, or heavy taxation; China's past revolutionary struggles; the lives of peasants and workers; "meaningful" news of society; the wretchedness of war; and adaptations of international poetry (Tongren deng 1933, 8). Except for the last item, which insists on sinification of poetry from outside of China, all these topics represent the experiential condition—emotional, political, historical, and geographic—of an interior national space.

Next, Ren stresses another advantage of the spoken over the written: its potential for "mass circulability" (*dazhong de pujixing*) among a largely illiterate audience to whom visually perceived written texts are, quite simply, inaccessible. In such a situation, Ren argues, "spoken language [*yanyu*] perforce becomes the most important means of expressing one's intent," so that "we should pour our poetry into and among the masses through their ears" (Sen 1933, 1). Third, and also favoring the aural over the visual, is his notion of "collective agitation" (*jituan de gudongxing*). Here Ren states that visually presented writing, even when posted large on a wall, can only exercise its effect on a limited number of people at a single time. At a recitation, however, poetry can simultaneously reach "large groups of several tens, hundreds, thousands, and even tens of thousands, thus achieving an organizational effect" (1–2). Lastly, Ren turns to the question of emotional content in his discussion of *how* to recite: "In brief, we should assimilate the overall rhythm [*yinlü*] in the work we want to recite. What sort of thing is this so-called rhythm? In plain language, it is the emotional flux [*qingxu de boliu*] constituting a poem. The better we can properly internalize [*shequ*] the rhythm of the poem we are reading and project it during recitation, the better able we are to transmit the feeling and thought of that poem to the audience" (2).

For Ren, rhythm *is* emotion, and vice versa. The emotive affect of a poem does not proceed from the disposition of quantifiable phonetic or semantic units, but from the immediate presence of emotional content, content channeled through the reciter but drawn from the condition of the national interiority. This interiority, centering on the oppression and suffering of the national populace, is mediated by the body of the reciter, who internalizes it, or, more literally, "absorbs" (*shequ*) it as the body absorbs nourishment. Thus when reciting the poet does not so much engage a text through reading as unmediatedly assimilate a raw emotional force that can be vocally projected into the mass consciousness. Thus, for Ren Jun the primary advantage of poetry recitation is its presumed ability to bypass the presence of a poetic text by communicating the "realities" of a geographic national interiority through an emotive interiority and projecting it outward again through the affective and agitational powers of voice. Clearly, Ren adheres to an expressionist imagination of poetry, and one that would disavow the aesthetic function of a poetic text in favor of an invisible auditory aesthetics of the emotive voice.

If we may take Chen Nanshi, Jiang Guangci, and Ren Jun as representative of an identifiable strain of aesthetic thought, what we see taking shape in the 1920s and early 1930s is a notion of new poetry as a primarily communicative discourse. Instead of focusing on the linguistic sign itself, they locate the "poetic" beyond the poem and in the imagined emotional reality of a national interiority, an interiority transmitted through a speaking subject by the emotive voice. In the terms of Hu's contradiction, they would locate the defining presence of poetry in the signified rather than the signifier, in the invisible domain of emotional presence entering the world through the audible voice.

Voicing Text: Salon Recitation of the 1920s and 1930s

Although Ren Jun and the leftist poets of the early 1930s were the first to call for a program of poetry recitation, they actually did very little actual recitation. In an essay from 1938, cofounder of the China Poetry Society Mu Mutian writes that until the 13 August 1932 Japanese attack on Shanghai, it was not possible to recite among the "masses," nor did they actively practice recitation within their small poetic circle (Mu 2000, 221). Instead, the first poets to make a regular practice of reciting new poetry belonged to two groups of writers whom many leftist poets described derisively as "elite men of refinement" (Mu 2000, 225): the Beijing-based, academically inclined poets affiliated with the Crescent Moon Society (Xinyue she), led by Xu Zhimo; and the Poetry Reading Society (Dushi pekhui), founded by Beijing University professor Zhu Guangqian. New poetry recitation as practiced in Beijing courtyards and salons from the mid-1920s until 1937 among this "Chinese Bloomsbury" had in fact preceded leftist poets' call for a poetry recitation movement by at least seven years.[6] A closer look at this alternative lineage of recitation reveals something more: that for these academic poets poetry recitation was primarily and most effectively a means of working closely with language as an aesthetic object in and of itself, and not as a way of transparently expressing emotion emanating from a national interiority.

In an article published in the autumn of 1938, writer and sometimes poet Shen Congwen describes his experience with the poets of these two literary societies. Shen writes that his first encounter with Xu Zhimo, one of the leading experimenters with form and meter in new poetry until his untimely death in 1931, took place at a poetry reading in the Crescent Moon Society's courtyard off the city's Pine Tree Hutong. There one autumn day the bespectacled Xu, seated on a stone bench beside an ivy-covered wall, enthusiastically read aloud his latest poems to a small gathering of guests. Shen also visited poet-painter Wen Yiduo's black-walled bohemian apartment in the mid-1920s, where Wen and a circle of young poets— including Xu Zhimo, Zhu Xiang, Liu Mengwei, Sun Dayu, Rao Mengkan, Yang Zihui, and Zhu Da'nan—would read aloud and comment on their own and others' poems (Shen 2002, 244–245).

According to Shen's account of the latter session, these early salon poets discovered and worked with the interdependence of a poem's written and recited versions. In part, this interdependence was due to the semantic density and opacity of the poems themselves. Listeners, Shen observes, typically had to have read a poem, encountered it visually, in order to "more fully appreciate its finer points in a live reading by apprehending the success of its diction."[7] In contrast, poems the audience had not seen in print were "difficult to understand, much less judge for quality" (245). A large number of poems, Shen adds, were composed through this practice of combined visual and oral "reading," including Wen Yiduo's "Stagnation" (Sishui), a landmark in the consolidation of Formalist and Symbolist aesthetics in new poetry during the late 1920s and into the 1930s.[8] These early experiments in new poetry reading, he concludes, prove a point: "the composition of new poetry relies upon verbal form (xingshi) and internal prosody (yinjie) as a means of conveyance" (245).

Continuing the practice of salon-style poetry recitation into the following decade were the participants in the Poetry Reading Society, an informal grouping of poets and writers that met once or twice a month at Zhu Guangqian's Beiping residence from 1933 to 1937. Zhu, then a professor of literature at Peking University, writes that the idea of starting the society came from his experience in London, where he frequented the Thursday poetry readings at Harold Monro's Poetry Bookshop, though according to Zhu Ziqing, Zhu Guangqian had broached the idea as early as 1927, before his travels abroad (Zhu Guangqian 1987, 324; Zhu Ziqing 1996a, 222–223). Participants in Zhu's poetry salon included practically all the major and minor new poets living in or passing through the city: Liang Zongdai, Bian Zhilin, Feng Zhi, Sun Dayu, Luo Niansheng, Fei Ming, He Qifang, Lin Geng, Cao Baohua, Yu Pingbo, and the woman poet Lin Huiyin. Foreign writers also attended, including Harold Acton, then teaching English literature at Peking University, as well as the nephew of Virginia Woolf, Julian Bell, who visited in early 1936. The editor of the American journal *Poetry*, Harriet Monroe, figures tangentially in these activities, too. During a visit to China in 1934, Monroe, who received many invitations to read modern American poetry in and around Beiping, delivered poems of Vachel Lindsay, Carl Sandburg, Wallace Stevens, Edna St. Vincent Millay and others at Tsinghua University and Beiping Normal University "in halls packed with vividly appreciative faces." At Beiping's Hotel du Nord she was also witness to the informal custom of postprandial poetry recitation, where "[t]wo or three Chinese bards chanted classical lyrics and recited some of their own poems in the vernacular, translating them beforehand as a friendly concession to our ignorance"[9] (Monroe 1935, 32–33). But literary tourism aside, one goal of Beiping's 1930s parlor poets was, according to Shen Congwen, to explore whether new poetry could in fact be successfully recited. To this end the attending poets took an eclectic approach, experimenting with new, classical, and foreign poetry in vocal styles ranging from casual spoken diction to traditional intonation, and employing local dialects from all over the map (Shen 2002, 247–248).

According to Shen Congwen, a frequent participant in Zhu's salon, these four years of oral experimentation proved that "free verse is unable to achieve any sort of surprising effect through recitation." Rather, the success of orally performed poetry depends on several factors, including the skill of the performer, the atmosphere of the performance, and above all, attention to linguistic art. "Asking for extreme 'freedom' in new poetry," Shen reminds his readers, "entails completely abandoning the hope of a certain formal success that is obtained aurally"; or, more simply, "if one wants to succeed aurally, one must sacrifice a little 'freedom' and attend to ornamentation (*cizao*) and form" (Shen 2002, 248).

Shen's article, published in late 1938 at the high-water mark of wartime recitation, was meant as a corrective to the vociferous extremes he saw in the recent spate of hyperpatriotic recitation poems, a phenomenon to be discussed in the following chapter. But more to the point, he founds his argument on the importance of textual self-orientation in the sound of the orally performed poem. Just as much, if not more, than the written poem, the success of the spoken poem relies on the aesthetic over the communicative function. The performed poem, in other words, is not a conduit for pure emotive force emanating from a national interiority, but a concrete, if invisible, aesthetic object in itself. The impresario of the later Beiping salon, Zhu Guangqian, echoes this idea of reading as a means of foregrounding poetry's orientation toward the verbal beauty of the poetic word. The motivation for establishing the Poetry Reading Society, Zhu recalls, came from his sojourn in London, where he realized that "poetry must be recitable—have meter and rhythm— in order to be good poetry" (Shang 1995, 91-92). Recalling his aural experience at London recitals given by actors and by poets, Zhu writes of English poets who believed that during a recitation, "the function of rhythm [yinlü] is to lull to sleep all associations with real life, to create an inviolate mental state where we can lose ourselves absolutely in the imagery and music of poetry" (Zhu Guangqian 1987, 324). Zhu himself leans toward a balance of spoken and musical rhythm when he insists that "when reciting, many aspects of poetic expression need to be made apparent through variation in pitch and pacing" (247). In this respect, Zhu asks that recited poetry maintain a definite autonomous distinction from natural language. Or, as he puts it, "recitation must possess an independent prosody [yinjie] apart from that of natural language [yuyan]; it cannot resemble spoken language [shuo hua]." "Poetic prosody should," he adds "have a certain mesmerizing effect which leads the listener to forget the real world and focus intently on artistic beauty" (246-247).

For a more concrete sense of the poetic effect to which Shen Congwen and Zhu Guangqian refer, it is instructive to take a close look at one of the poems that emerged from the Beiping poetry salons: Zhu Xiang's "Lotus-picking Song" (Cailian qu):[10]

A boat gently drifts,	*xiaochuan ya qingpiao,*
The willow tree nods in the breeze;	*yangliu ya feng li dianyao;*
Lotus leaves green,	*heye ya cui gai,*
Lotus blooms at winsome ease.	*hehua ya ren yang jiaorao.*
Sun dipping,	*riluo,*
Fine rippling,	*weibo,*
Gold threads sparkle o'er the stream.	*jinsi shandong guo xiaohe.*
Left gliding,	*zuo hang,*
Right poling,	*you cheng,*
From the lotus boat songs are lifting.	*lianzhou shang yangqi gesheng.*
	(Zhu Xiang 1935, 296)

The poem, which comprises five stanzas formally matching the one translated above, makes careful use of the visual geometry allowed by modern typography to foreground the structural patterning among short lines of seven, five, and two syllables. The brevity of these line lengths also maximizes the effect of the terminal full and slant rhymes, which in each stanza occur according to the pattern: aabacccddd. Zhu's use throughout of relatively short, rhyming lines, as well as the insertion of caesura with the expletive *ya*, compensate for the weak syllabic stress patterns in vernacular Chinese by enforcing regular pauses when reading the poem. The two-syllable rhyming couplets stand out most in this respect. According to Zhu's own commentary on the poem, the stress pattern of these very short couplets ("Left gliding,/Right poling") attempt rhythmically to re-create "the sensation of the rise and fall of the wake made by a passing lotus-gathering punt" (Zhu Xiang 1983, 51). The regular interpolation in each stanza of such two-syllable lines produces at the level of the poem's material surface—both visual and aural—the effect of a small boat being rhythmically poled through water. When comparing Zhu's poem to those of Chen Nanshi and Jiang Guangci, we find that instead of orienting his text toward a direct, voice-based appeal to the subjectivity of a presumed audience, Zhu builds a poem that relies upon self-oriented poeticity activated by the surface features of the poetic text.

Returning now to Shen Congwen and his 1938 article on recitation, we find him rebutting the leftist poets' critiques by pointing out that "where they [leftist critics] might simply mock them as ideologically retrograde (*yishi luowu*), they go too far and turn this into formally retrograde (*xingshi luowu*). These people are completely unaware that at the time the revival of the issue of stressing language and form was precisely an effort at popularization" (Shen 2002, 246). Revolutionary poets' fixation on the communicative function of recited poetry, suggests Shen, in fact stands in the way of achieving their very goal of communication with a broader audience, a task that demands attention to the concrete elements of language and form. Indeed, he adds, if the ranks of those experimenting with formal aspects of new poetry had not been severely thinned by the untimely passing of so many maturing poets, there might have come into being a body of poetry able to influence popular consciousness on the strength of its "suitability for recitation, ease of memorization, and affectivity" (246).[11] Shen, in short, recommends that poets work in and on the material medium of poetry, its written or oral presence as text, instead of simply presuming a pretextual fullness of meaning in poetry. He suggests that attention to textual self-orientation does not of necessity impede popularization, but that on the contrary, the ideology that calls for an awakening of national consciousness may be better served by a closer attention to how new poetry could develop the linguistic resources of modern vernacular Chinese.

Anti-poetry and Its Discontents

For all its insight, Shen's plea fell on deaf ears. His article was, in fact, a rear-guard action launched well after the outbreak of war in July 1937, a time when polemic attacks from leftist poets polarized the literary field to a point where the slightest suggestion of poetic aestheticism could draw accusations of treason.[12] Enmities among poets can be attributed to personal, institutional, and regional factors, but in this case the terrain of their sparring lay in the political aesthetics of language. Most notable in this regard was what we might call an "anti-poetry," anticipated by Jiang Guangci's self-portrayal as "a crude and outraged singer" some ten years earlier and now produced by the leader of the "poetry recitation movement," Ren Jun. Just as Jiang distanced himself from the "softly droning ivory-tower poet," Ren's satirical poems flaunted their opposition to the work coming out of the Beiping salons. One example is the verse preface to Ren Jun's 1936 collection of satirical verse, *Lengre ji* (Hot and Cold), a poem entitled "Not a Poem" (Bu shi shi):

This is not a poem,
Because there are no elegant words here,
And no fancy phrases.

This is not a poem,
Because there are no gentle rhythms here,
And no placid mood.

This is not a poem,
Because it doesn't extol soft silky hair,
Nor praise lively eyes.

This is not a poem,
Because poetry is high and pure,
While this just sings of "vulgar" events and politics.

Fine, if it's not a poem, so be it.
Good thing I'm no "poet,"
I want only to sketch a bit of truth in the times and its people.
(Ren 1936, 1-2)

The irony is heavy-handed, but Ren's point is clear, and not without a certain aesthetic bearing. For in writing a poem that labels itself "not a poem," Ren lampoons the aesthetic principle implicit in the poetics Shen and Zhu supported: that poetry is "poetic" because it foregrounds the linguistic sign by means of those visual and aural potentialities of language that draw attention to the words themselves. Ren's "anti-poem," whose primary reason for being is to decry "poetic" poetry in favor of verse that communicates the extratextual real world of people and events, attacks this aesthetic of autonomy head on. Similarly caustic is another poem in the same volume, Ren's "The Poet Lost His Dictionary" (Shiren de cidian diao le):

> The poet is deeply grieved,
> For no longer can he write poetry;
> > Why can't he write?—
> Because the poet lost his dictionary!
>
> > Perhaps you didn't know:
> > This dictionary was—
> A sole-surviving volume!
> A magic charm for versifying!
> > In it are—
> Many fresh words,
> Many lovely phrasings:
> > Be it "seven-stringed zither," "seasonal winds" . . .
> > Or "lilac melancholy," "autumn dream" . . .
> > Or "rosy allure" . . .
> You can look them up here in a jiffy. . . .
> > > (Ren 1936, 46)

One hesitates to read too deeply into Ren's poetic pasquinade. Still, it may be observed that to lose a dictionary is to lose the material presence of words themselves. This "dictionary," moreover, represents what may be construed as an enclosed, isolated poetic lexicon divorced from the language of "real life" as spoken by the popular masses.

Behind this poem and many others by Ren and his circle of poets immediately prior to the war was the call for National Defense (guofang) Poetry[13] that featured satirical poems in particular as weapons to resist the Japanese invaders. As Ren himself wrote in 1935: "Poets of China! Arise! Arise, let us prepare our bayonets and carry our special weapon—poetry—up to the heroic front lines of National Salvation, assume your post and hold it firm" (Ren 1948, 178).

However sincere their efforts at the literary salvation of China, or perhaps because of their single-minded patriotic utilitarianism, the poets of National Defense came in for criticism as well. One of the telling ironies confronting the revolutionary poets of the 1930s was the fact that the new poetry they wrote in order to awaken and inform the masses was in the main as opaque and unappealing to the average Chinese as the ivory-tower lyricism of their academic counterparts. While the revolutionary romanticism of leftist poets like Ren Jun and his cohort may have found an audience among restive high school and college students, the average Chinese commoner, if he or she even bothered to read it, would find little if any pleasure therein.[14] It took poets with resolute aestheticist affinities to point this out with any forthrightness, as for example did Dai Wangshu in his April 1937 polemic "On National Defense Poetry." In the article, Dai supports his position with an account of what in fact happens when the "masses" are presented with a National Defense poem:

> On my way back to Hangzhou at the end of the Lunar year, I was leafing
> through a copy of a so-called progressive magazine I had by chance bought
> there on the train, and which contained two "National Defense Poems."
> Struck by a poetic impulse, I thought I would find out how the average
> person might apprehend this "National Defense Poetry." I proposed to a
> laborer type (I afterwards found that he was a laborer in a Shanghai construc-
> tion facility) sitting next to me that I read a poem aloud to him and that he
> tell me what he thought of it. He was taken aback, but agreed. He listened
> in amazement as I read. When I had finished he shook his head and said, "I
> don't understand it, and it sounds terrible." A soldier sitting across from me
> had been looking on with curiosity. I handed the magazine to him and asked
> him to take a look at the poem I had just read. He was holding a newspaper
> so I knew he was literate. He received the magazine and with furrowed brow
> pored over it, reading aloud from time to time. When he had finished I
> asked his opinion. He replied, "What a bore—a load of rubbish. What's this
> 'strike the enemy'? What's the point of shouting when what you really need
> is our guns!" He then uttered an uncouth phrase. (Dai 1937, 85)

In the politicized climate of Shanghai literary circles, Dai's impromptu acid test of National Defense Poetry did not go unremarked by that movement's exponents: rebuttals from Ren Jun and others were immediate and acrimonious.[15] But before long the outbreak of war with Japan in July 1937 all but silenced the public expression of aesthetic views like Dai's. The mood had shifted abruptly and in a way that, for the time being, powerfully supported the poetics of emotive expressionism. The degree to which some poets now attributed the "poetic" of poetry to the presence of pure emotion is demonstrated vividly by Mu Mutian, who wrote that when suffering the ravages of invasion, "the cry of 'fuck his mother' [*cao ta mama de*] sometimes has great power to move people emotionally. Can you say such a cry of rage is not poetic? Passion-filled slogans are the only truly fervent poetry" (Mu 1937,

113). The arrival of war also brought with it a powerful impetus to communicate the realities of wartime, awaken the masses, and once again liberate poetry from formal constraints through the production of long poems (*chang shi*), street poems, report-age poems (*baogao shi*), postcard poems (*mingxinpian shi*), and "live report" poems (*huobao shi*). Yet it was this desire to communicate not only information but the intersubjective stuff of pure emotion that made recitation poetry the most widely practiced and discussed of all these wartime poetic subgenres.

CHAPTER 3

Inventing Recitation

Poetry and the Idea of the Sounding Voice
during the War of Resistance

"If WE LET STAND this new term 'recitation poetry,'" averred poet Liu Qing in late 1938, "then singable songs, performable drama, and edible food each can stand alone and apart from song, drama, and food" (61). By the time Liu wrote these words over a year into the War of Resistance, something labeled "recitation poetry" had begun to proliferate in the pages of literary journals, newspaper supplements, and at least one poetry collection. Beyond those printed pages, too, one could hear poetry recited at war-related meetings and rallies with a frequency and publicity far beyond anything attempted in the past. You could see it, and you could hear it, but, as Liu Qing prompts his reader to ask, What *is* it?

This chapter does not answer that question, at least not at its face value. Instead, it builds upon the foregoing discussions of language, poetry, and recitation to trace the imagination of the sounding poetic voice into the critically formative period of the War of Resistance against Japan. The previous chapter's analysis of an emergent recitational aesthetic may seem to anticipate the formation of a definite type or category of poetry, a poetic text distinguished by identifiable textual features that construct the sense of a soundful voice originating from the inner springs of a national emotional experience. The recitation poetry we see in print from the war period's early years does in some ways follow from the new tradition of poetry as voice. Yet to harden the boundaries of recitation poetry into a distinct genre is hardly possible. This is because the limits of any literary genre are the constructions of interested historical actors—primarily critics and anthologists—rather than the result of a priori, ontologically stable defining criteria. As Mark Jeffreys notes in his study of the generic boundaries of the Anglophone poetry, "lyric poetry" refers to "that set of texts that identify themselves or that have been identified as lyric" (1995, 203). Much the same can be said for Chinese recitation poetry. Better than trying strictly to define recitation poetry as an actually existing literary genre, one can learn more by looking to the historical contingencies of how recitation poetry came into being as an accepted, if debated, category of literary practice. Examining the making of recitation poetry as a discursive object helps to unfold the persistent but mutable motivations, assumptions, and contradictions as they play out at any historical moment.

Before entering into the actual performance of new poetry during wartime—the task of Chapter 4—here I continue to explore those written poetic texts as well as writings about recitation that contributed to the imagination of a recitational voice in modern China. Because the period's attempts to define or deny this thing called recitation poetry were fraught with tension, I begin by discussing what this poetry was not. To do so I analyze one of the war period's most prominent critiques of poetry recitation, Liang Zongdai's 1939 article "On 'Recitation Poetry'" for its position on the nature of poetic sound and vision. Liang's article helps set the terms for understanding the very different aesthetic features that one finds in the recitation poetry of the early wartime period, and it is in contrast to Liang's position that I gather and read texts specifically labeled "recitation poem" (*langsong shi*) when they appeared in print during the high tide of recitation in 1937 and 1938. Read as a set, these poems inherit and elaborate on features distinguishing the poems of Chen Nanshi and Jiang Guangci in the 1920s. Most notably, they construct a poetry that not only foregrounds the sounding voice, but that also seeks to voice sound, making them texts that privilege auditory poetry of the ear over silent poetry of the eye. The assumption is that this poetry not only can and should achieve resonance with an imagined audience in need of this poetic sound, but that the wartime nation is a vast soundscape filled with this poetically generated sound. I then approach recitation from the metatextual level—that is, writing about recitation—in the form of wartime articles and recitation manuals. Here we find notions of national interiority—historical, emotive, and even physiological—familiar from the invention of new vernacular poetry and Ren Jun's early conception of recitation but elaborated to a much finer degree. This increased level of attention to poetry recitation, especially its history and practical method, not only consolidates it as a cultural practice, but also determines the meaning of the vocalized poem.

In the final portion of the chapter I contrast the confident poetics of sound, voice, and awakening found in recitation poetry and writings about recitation with long poems written by two of the most prominent figures in the wartime recitation movement, Guang Weiran and Gao Lan. Guang's "Thunder at Midnight" (Wuye de leisheng) and Gao's "Weeping for Lost Sufei" (Ku wangnü Sufei), both written four to five years into the war, demonstrate how, even as the orientation toward sound and voice remains, poems concerned with the sounding voice can also subtly undermine the imagination of poetic sound as an effective call to arms. Thus, where authors of early wartime sound poems sought to address and awaken their implied audience, these poems undercut or qualify the presumed power of the poet's voice by either rendering it mute or imagining the disappearance of its audience. Muteness and loss, I argue, indicate vacillating belief in the power of poetic voice and the ability of the reciting poet to articulate a national interiority.

Questioning a Category

Poetry recitation only began to achieve a certain prominence when mobilization for full-scale warfare erupted in the latter half of 1937. As other studies have documented (Gunn 1993; Hung 1994; Mackinnon 2008), national crisis motivated writers and artists of all stripes, poets not excluded, to support the wartime propaganda effort. Dispersed to the interior cities and towns, and frequently organized into traveling cultural performance troupes, urban literary intellectuals turned their talents to orally mediated forms—including street drama, patriotic song, and adaptations of folk and popular performance genres—as the most effective means of rapidly disseminating wartime awareness to a minimally educated rural population (Hung 1994). The many poets swept up in this minor explosion of cultural reinvention, and especially those with established leftist-populist leanings, began to write and perform what they called recitation poetry. As they saw it, such work represented one among many wartime literary movements aimed at producing and disseminating mass forms of art and literature, and with few inhibitions they channeled their enthusiasm for the war effort into promoting and creating poetry for oral performance. Recitation activists like Gao Lan, Guang Weiran, Ke Zhongping, Pu Feng, Jiang Xijin, Mu Mutian, and Xu Chi each made a concerted effort to write poetry intended to be read aloud in public performance. Gao Lan, by far the most active in the movement in terms of both writing and performing, published at least four volumes of his own recitation poems during the war. Many others made a practice of publishing verse under the rubric "recitation poem" in journals and literary supplements to newspapers.

As the quotation from Liu Qing attests, however, not everyone was ready to accept the creation ex nihilo of a new poetic subgenre, least of all other poets. Recitation poetry, wrote Paris-trained poet and literature professor Liang Zongdai in early 1939, is just another in a series of fashionable literary terms that initially cause "much ink to fly" but "in the end come to naught." Liang found illogical the assumption that recitation poetry could be "an actively promoted and unique category of poetry with a special function." He argued instead that "recitation" referred not to an identifiable genre of poetry, but to the oral performance of poetry by "recitation poets" who—quite naively given the cultural tastes of the general populace—desired above all "mass effect and collective response" (Liang 1939).

Liang's critique was not off the mark. As discussed in Chapter 2, mass effect and collective response were from the start the main goals of left-leaning proponents of poetry recitation, precisely the group Liang takes to task. But it must also be kept in mind that in 1939 most of the collections and handbooks able to lend an institutional reality to recitation poetry had only begun to appear, and recitation performance, as we shall see in Chapter 4, was at the time only beginning to establish itself as a cultural form. This is not to say that Liang's critique was premature. On the contrary, it was as incisive as it was constructive. More important, Liang's essay is worth highlighting for how its oppositional aesthetic position helps define the terms of recitation poetry's de facto existence.

Underlying Liang's argument against recitation poetry are ideological criteria that stress poetic value as located in the self-oriented, textual features of poetic language rather than in the actual production of poetic voice. Liang does not say that poetry should not be recited. On the contrary, he points out that, unlike traditional Chinese poetry, whose strictly formalized "musical" nature is suited to vocalization through "a sort of semi-sung 'chanting' (yin) or 'intoning' (yong)," Western poetry, and by implication Chinese new poetry, resemble a musicalized prose that "not only has a ringing sonority pleasing to the ear, but possesses as well a prose-like suppleness and intimacy suited to tracing the rise and fall of thought and feeling, making it best read aloud in a manner akin to speaking [shuo hua], but which heightens speech to the level of recitation [langsong]." Liang then asserts that "an affinity with spoken language is a requirement for all recitable poetry." However, his use of the musical metaphor warns the would-be poets of spoken language, the promoters of recitation, that it is the inner workings of the poetic text, its in-built tones, rhythms, and harmonies, that guide the deployment of voice, not the other way around (1939).

A problem with wartime "recitation poetry" (a term Liang insists on confining within scare quotes) is how the desire for instantaneous effect on the broadest audience compromises this musicality. The poems, Liang continues, "cater to the comprehension of the average person, and their work is extremely prose-like and extremely talky, or as they say, 'plain as speech' [mingbai ru hua]" (1939). For Liang, a believer in the need to refine the accumulated crudities of the Chinese vernacular through the redeeming influence of individual literary invention (1936a, 63–73), this modeling of poetry on quotidian speech rather than on poetic principles disqualifies recitation poetry as poetry per se. For recitation poets, however, a straight-talking style was essential to the recitation poem and exerted a powerful transformative effect on the writing of poetry. Recitation activist Jiang Xijin, for example, records that in the process of writing his 1938 "My Hometown—Yixing" (Wo de jiaxiang—Yixing), a poem prepared specifically for a poetry recitation program in Hankou's Guangming Theater, "I had to take into account 'aural comprehension,' so I altered many portions to maximize the use of colloquial diction and idiom" (Xi Jin 1938a, 61). Poets also felt it necessary to revise their existing poems when rehearsing for recitation events. In order to prepare for a performance in Chongqing in the spring of 1939, woman poet and playwright An E spent a sleepless night in the spring reworking her verse drama "The Gaoliang Has Turned Red" (Gaoliang hong le). Gao Lan records her remarks at the time: "It didn't occur to me that it would be recited when I wrote it. It absolutely must be changed, because any which way I recite it I discover all kinds of flaws" (Gao 1942).

Here, however, it must be observed that the attempt to shift poetry into the register of the spoken, to calibrate it more closely to the readily apprehended linguistic patterns of everyday speech, was typical not only of recitation poetry, but of a great quantity of wartime poetry. The ideal of such poetry, as described by well-known poet Ai Qing, was an unadorned and expressive "prose-style beauty" close to the masses' language of daily life (1939, 48–49). While the attempt to reproduce common and comprehensible speech in recitation poetry cannot, then, suffice as a defining stylistic feature for recitation poetry, it does stand as an aesthetic by-product of the project of committing poetry to the register of sound.

For Liang, however, the public rendering of printed poetry into speech dooms the poem. Here Liang draws on his expertise in French neo-Symbolist aesthetics to claim that excessive focus on the art of recitation "frequently harms the essence of poetry" (1939). This "essence," the aesthetic sine qua non that for Liang makes poetry *poetry*, entails foregrounding an internalized musicality tied to the visual register. A devotee of the *poésie pure* (*chun shi*) of Paul Valéry (with whom he was personally acquainted) and Stéphane Mallarmé, Liang recommends a voice of poetry that does not betray the aesthetic qualities built into the poetic text. In support of this view, he cites Valéry's complaint against those who presume to transform the poetry of print into the poetry of externalized sound: "I can seldom bear the professional readers of poetry who claim to bring out or interpret when actually they are overemphasizing, debauching the author's intentions, corrupting the harmonies of a text, and substituting their own lyricism for the intrinsic melodies of the linked words" (Liang 1939; Valéry 1972, 308).

While Liang's citation of the French poet does not exclude recitation from its poetic ideal, he understands the dimension of the heard—here couched in the musical terminology of harmony and melody—as intrinsic to the written text of a poem. Quite unlike the boosters of recitation, but in accord with fellow academic Zhu Guangqian's aesthetic sensibility, Liang's is a hermetic conception of poetic sound, one that he elsewhere describes as an otherworldly aural quality that produces "an incantatory suggestiveness that arouses our senses and imagination, transporting our souls to an illumined, paradisaic, metaphysical realm"—an effect quite different from the stark and sudden awakening to national awareness and crisis consciousness desired by the recitation poets (1936b, 6). Liang's notion of the proper sound of poetry, then, positions itself in opposition to the agitational, externalized sound valued by Chinese proponents of modern poetry recitation discussed in Chapter 2. Liang also distances himself from the primacy of vocalized sound through an implied stress on visuality as the aesthetic dominant of poetry. We detect this dimension of Liang's critique from the source of the above passage on poetry recitation. It comes from Paul Valéry's description of his first encounter with Mallarmé's enigmatic work of diagrammatic visual poetry, "Un coup de dés jamais n'abolira le hasard" (A throw of the dice will never abolish change). In that essay Valéry champions the visual dimension of the poetic text. Liang's citation of this text suggests in turn the Chinese poet's affinity with the French neo-Symbolist ocular paradigm.

Turning now to the recitation poems themselves, we find poets working from a quite different premise: that the visual dimension of poetry must be subordinate to the aural, because sound and voice provide the best and most direct means of arresting people's attention and awakening them to enlightened awareness of their participation as individual subjects in the plight of that larger, collective subjectivity, the nation. As Xu Chi in his wartime *Poetry Recitation Handbook* instructs the would-be reciter, "The best opening phrase is 'Listen!'" (1942, 49). And in the end it is only by "listening" to the recitation poems produced during the war that we may locate and trace their appeals to sound and voice.

Voicing Soundscapes: Early Wartime Recitation Poems

A survey of early wartime recitation poems finds them dominated by many of the same aesthetic features already discussed in the poems of Chen Nanshi and Jiang Guangci, only more so. Oratorial forms of repetition in the form of direct address and litany are used extensively, and in Gao Lan's early wartime recitation poems in particular, the poetic voice is amplified to resonate throughout an imagined auditory space, enacting what Leonid Cherkassky (Cherkasskii) suggestively describes as an "invasion" of a very concrete territory comprising wartime cities and population centers (1989, 107). At a more thematic level, these poems also construct an opposition between sound and silence, the heard and the seen, with the former terms in these pairings given absolute preference over the latter.

In the earliest of these poems, the technique of apostrophe—the poetic address of imagined auditors—is most prominent in recitation poetry addressed to the poetic community itself. At this stage, wartime recitation poets took on the role of the avant-garde's avant-garde: poets entrusting themselves with the task of awakening other poets into national consciousness and in effect recruiting them into the ranks of reciters. These poems for poets were marked, not only by their emphasis on projecting the sound of the poet's voice, but by the construction of a strict opposition between "active" sound and "passive" silence, a pairing that frequently aligns with the opposed registers of the heard and the seen. Zang Kejia, who was closely involved with recitation activities in and around Hankou in 1938, recalls the opening four lines of a poem inspired by the heady first rush of wartime fervor. Even in this brief excerpt we discover a contrast between the resounding voice of the wartime recitationist and the silence of any other variety of poem:

Poets,
Open your throats,
Aside from spirited singing of songs of war,
Your poetry shall be dumb silence.
(Zang Kejia 1985, 1)

For Zang, the difference between sound and silence reigns absolute. The former, here linked to the wartime salvation project, overwhelms the latter, which recedes into mute oblivion. Or as Gao Lan, the most prolific recitation poet of the war, wrote in his own poetic address to poets in 1937:

Poet!
Only recited poetry,
Is our poetry.
Only recited poetry,
Leaves behind sighs over flying petals and falling leaves,
Only recited poetry,
Leaves behind murmuring self-analysis,
It is
The roaring voice of slaves.
(Gao 1937)

Following Zang, Gao first hails the poet, and then contrasts the externalized poetry of pure volume with the soft utterances of sentimentalism and the barely audible speech of reflective self-doubt. In another of these calls to poets, Jiang Xijin's 1937 "Go and Recite" (Langsong qu), this sound–silence, active–passive opposition goes a step further by aligning these two dichotomies with a qualitative distinction between sound and vision, which as we have seen was prevalent in the recitation theory of the time. Here is the refrain to Jiang's poem:

Go, go and recite!
No more sit in your rooms blankly staring.
(Xi 1937)

Jiang directs his poem toward awakening the Chinese poet from a state of artistic catatonia. He imagines sound—the sound of his own recited poem—as an active, positive, outwardly directed medium of awakening. Meanwhile, vision, the poet's blank stare into nothingness, Jiang associates with enclosure, voicelessness, immobility. Beyond its refrain, the poem also voices a command to poets to immerse themselves bodily among the masses of people who, like the "blankly staring" poet, dumbly await the vocal tocsin of national awakening:

> Arise,
> Step out the door.
> Outside the innumerable masses wait,
> Wait for you,
> To open your throat.
> . . . .
>
> Ah! Where have your voices gone?
> You should run into the streets and alleyways.
> There the people have slept soundly for generations.

Jiang's "Go and Recite" intends to awaken poets to a sense of national mission and turn them out into the streets. Mu Mutian, who worked closely with Jiang early in the war, seems to have taken his cue from Jiang's poetic call for mass awakening in the recitation poem "Go Wage Guerilla War" (Qu da youji zhan), where he imagines his poetry already ringing out along the "streets and alleyways." Assuming the role of a resident of an imagined village, Mu in fact addresses the constituents of the Chinese masses by name:

> Zhang Number Five!
> Wang Number Three
> Let's go!
> We're off to wage guerilla war!
> . . . .
> Sister-in-law Zhang!
> Mama Li!
> Zhao Number Six!
> Li Number Three!
> Everyone must rush to mobilize,
> To protect our home.
>   (Mu 1938, 140–141)

The imagined auditors for these poems were not limited to poets and villagers, but extended to a diverse mix of peoples, places, and even times. For the most active and dedicated wartime recitation poet, Gao Lan, the sheer range of direct address stands out as one of the defining features of his work during the first two years of the war. Among the twenty-one poems comprising Gao's 1940 volume *Poems for Recitation* (*Langsongshi ji*), we hear him urging the city of Wuhan to erupt like a volcano, persuading the toiling masses of Japanese soldiers to lay down their arms, calling on Taiwan to arise and free itself from foreign occupation, exhorting Manchurian refugee children to spread word of enemy depredations, encouraging air-force pilots to take to the skies, and welcoming the years 1938 and 1939 as new stages in the war effort.

Gao reinforces the imagined impact of these poems by inventing for them a poetics of pure volume. One of Gao Lan's earliest recitation poems, the 1937 "Now Is the Time, My Countrymen!" (Shi shihou le, wo de tongbao!) is typical for its use of a variety of devices—including end-rhyme, metaphor, typography, and imagery—to amplify the sonic urgency of his vocal address. Most of the poems in *Poems for Recitation* make extensive use of highly repetitive end-rhyme, most often on open-throated vowel sounds *-a, -an, -ang*. The desired effect is not the subtle harmonies Liang Zongdai recommends; rather, Gao's rhymes make the poems easier to project vocally, give them an immediately audible unity of sound, and assist recitation from memory—a skill Gao Lan was known for. In "Now Is the Time," thirty-one of forty-eight lines terminate with the open-vowel phoneme *ao*. Such high frequency of recurrence at times strains Gao's powers of invention to a degree that would dismay more restrained poets, as in the couplet, "If you haven't forgotten (*wangdiao*) the humiliation / If you never again want to live as an ignominious suppuration (*nongbao*)" (line 1). At the same time, however, the single-minded repetition of the same bellowing end-rhyme helps produce a certain sound symbolism, akin to a verbal carpet bombing, well suited to an agitational, wartime poem.

The devices of metaphor and typography.Gao links in a manner that likens the poet's voice to a fuse able to detonate an explosive awakening to national crisis. After declaring his "comrades" to be "gunpowder on the verge of a blast" in the first stanza, Gao, with a calligrammatic flourish, ladder-steps up the three short lines:

>   Explode!
>   Explode!
> Explode!
>   *baozha!*
>   *baozha!*
> *baozha!*

By incrementally elevating each line (from right to left, bottom to top in the vertically typeset Chinese text), Gao's typography prompts the reciter to bring this repeated imperative to a vocal crescendo that would function as an aural detonator for his combustible compatriots. In addition to such typographic gymnastics, Gao also fills the poem with imagery suggesting a landscape alive with sound. It is a place where people "bellow with anger" (*nuhou*), horses neigh (*sijiao*), and even the realm of the inanimate joins the chorus when "ancient border towns" voice their "final cries of sorrow" (*zuihou de beixiao*), the earth "madly roars" (*kuangxiao*), swinging sabers "howl" (*paoxiao*), and the town of Wanping "sounds the first bugle call" (*xiangqile di yi sheng junhao*; Gao 1940, 1–2).[1]

When "Now Is the Time" is read along with Gao's other early recitation poems, it becomes apparent that the orchestrating voice of the reciting poet in fact constructs a soundscape of war. Not only are these poems filled with bloodthirsty battle cries and fervid exhortation, they also range multidimensionally across the national landscape. As described above, laterally Gao's recitation poems address the peripheral regions of Taiwan and Manchuria but also the "heart" of the nation, Wuhan, a city from whence the Yangtze River stretches like "intestines" from west to east, and the "steel arms" of the railway reach north and south to extend its "fingers" into the ten major cities (Gao 1940, 9). Vertically, his voice extends upwards with the poem "The Sky of the Motherland Has Blossomed" (Zuguo de tiankong kai le hua), a text that asks the reciter to imitate the rattle of wing guns (*da da da da da*) as it celebrates a victory of the Chinese air force. Downwards and into the earth, the poem "Natural Gas Flame from an Artesian Well" (Ziliujing de tianran wasi huo) likens the release of subterranean gas reserves—a task of wartime national construction—to "mouths of flame / roaring triumphant songs of liberation" (21).

In addition to the saturation of national space with vocalized sound, Gao's recitation poems also define a gendered space for wartime poetic sound. "Farewell! Young Miss!" (Zaihui ba! Xiaojie!), written in November 1937 (Zhang and Lu 1989, 25), remonstrates with a young woman reluctant to give up a personal love interest in favor of selfless immersion in the collective national struggle:

> Farewell! Young Miss!
> The enemy has raised
>   Such fierce, sharp blades!
> So many of us sons and daughters of China,
> Have whipped up a great war!
> A roar of rage,
> Charges toward the enemy battle line,
> And with blood, flesh, and skulls,
> Builds our new Great Wall! . . .

But you,

Young miss!

Your passion runs strong,

For those rosy sunsets and autumnal pools,

The foxtrot,

You dance so jaunty and carefree,

At times airing your delicate feelings,

In a light song,

A few lines of new poetry,

So subtle and sorrowful,

So like the chirping of swallows and orioles,

Hazy as a dream!

Empty as dream.

I hasten to close my eyes to it all. . . .

(Gao 1940, 7–8)

Significant here is how Gao juxtaposes two extremes of sound aesthetics: the "roar of rage" versus the "chirping of swallows and orioles"—the former ideologically marked as the domain of hard, combative, and masculine poetic subjectivity; the latter the product of the soft, passive, sentiment associated with the feminine qualities of new poetry.[2] The poem suggests, too, a rejection of visuality for its affiliation with the snares of individual desire. The poet monkishly renounces the young miss, and the feminized sounds of her poetry, by shutting his eyes—all the better to single-mindedly immerse himself in the rousing and all-encompassing resonance of a nation unified by crisis.

Wartime Recitation Theory: Sources of the Sounding Voice

The same year Gao Lan published *Poems for Recitation*, the woman poet Guan Lu orated the following "Opening Remarks" at a poetry recital held in Shanghai:[3]

Ladies and gentlemen, poetry recitation is nothing new. Rather, it is so ancient that we have forgotten it. In the beginning, where there was poetry there was recitation, because long before humankind wrote poetry, anyone at all could produce poetry orally. But because poetry came to be recorded in writing, poetic composition came to be the exclusive domain of the written word. Poetry and the living language went their separate ways. Poetry, drawing its last dying breath, was practically eliminated from people's lives. Many came to regard poetry as little more than a vainglorious display of written words. This is most unfortunate. But now we shall recite poetry, and from this poetry recitation movement, from the reunion of poetry and the living language, shall come new life for poetry. (Shu 1941, 20–21)

In 1940, Guan Lu's ideas on poetry recitation were nothing new either. By then, well over two years into the war, extensive discussion of poetry recitation had appeared in newspapers, journals, and books published out of Chongqing, Chengdu, Guilin, Yan'an, and other wartime cultural centers. An overview of this accumulated body of writing reveals another level of the discursive construction of poetry recitation during these key wartime years. A review of what these poet-theorists had to say finds them adding specificity and sophistication to very much the same ideas we saw in Yu Pingbo's "Return to Origins" essay, Ren Jun's initial discussion of poetry recitation in 1933, and even Hu Shi's seminal narratives of linguistic and poetic evolution: that reciting poetry represents a return to a lost ideal of poetic communication, one where silent writing gives way to sound, and sound to an underlying and emotional presence. Guan Lu's compressed story, ending in recitation's gift of "new life for poetry," was typical of these histories. All of them imagined poetry as a medium able to communicate as directly and transparently as possible a fundamental subjective experience of emotional presence. Although none of these theorists of recitation expressed such ideas in quite the same way—and practically none, with the exception of Liang Zongdai openly challenged such logic—wartime theories of recitation were unmistakably variations on the theme that poetic language should be inalienably linked to expressive recovery of a national interiority.

Two years before Guan Lu's "Remarks," one of the most active proponents of poetry recitation during the war, Jiang Xijin, had looked to legitimate recitation poetry by explaining that "poetry was originally an oral art" meant to "popularize the most precise feeling and understanding" (Xi Jin 1938b, 259). When poetry came to be written, however, it could no longer express "new emotion" (xin de qingxu). This emotional-communicative blockage occurred twice in the history of Chinese poetry: first with the formal excesses of classical poetry, and again with the arrival of those new poets who "gladly hide in their corners to arrange foolish devil's ranks of written words." According to Jiang, a second liberation of poetry from writing was necessary in order to "bring poetry back to the path of recitation" (Xi Jin 1938b, 262). Liberation from script naturally implied a turn to sound, and in the following year Jiang wrote that, because the spoken language is transmitted by sound, expression through that medium "is more direct, more rapid, and livelier" than through "silent written characters" (Xi Jin 1939, 56). The current state of poetry, he adds, is one of dependence on the written, a situation that some "formalist" poets who "never had the desire to sing aloud" have already, and quite mistakenly, accepted as the fate of poetry (58).

Echoing Guan Lu and Jiang Xijin's narratives of spoken and written poetry, Wang Bingyang, in an article that was in fact paired with Liang Zongdai's, argues that "poetry has gone from recitable to unrecitable, and again from unrecitable to recitable." Wang favors poetry with narrative structure and concrete, realist content, such as massacre, pillage, rape, wartime construction, and so on, because he believes such poems to be congruent with the wartime psychology of the laboring classes, whom he describes as having "an unnameable explosive coursing through their blood." Wang believes this realistic content is communicated most effectively to this mass psychic state by sound. A recitation poem, he argues, "truly comes alive and reaches completion when the mouth and lips recite it aloud to the ears and into the hearts of a mass listening audience." Unlike Guan Lu and Jiang Xijin but in line with a prominent doctrine of wartime literature, Wang recommends adapting traditional forms for recitation poems. At the same time, however, he also makes the distinctly modernist recommendation that recitation poetry, because it is a product of the war, "should strive to mimic sound images that are specific to the War of Resistance, such as heaving, concussion, explosion, howling, groans of pain, surging and other such 'sound imagery,' for only in this way can it achieve a powerful resonance" (Wang 1939). Much like F. T. Marinetti's Futurist experiments reciting the sounds of war, Wang asks for a poetry of vocally generated sonic mimesis, a mode of realist representation that stretches the expressive capabilities of the written word into the realm of sound symbolism.[4] While Wang does not offer examples of such combat poetry in his article, they can, as already noted, be found in Gao Lan's poetry. An additional example of such vocal sound effects appears in Gao's depiction of enemy bombers in the poem "Japan's 'King of Bombardiers'" (Riben de "hongzha zhi wang"):

Humm . . . humm . . . humm . . . [hong . . . hong . . . hong . . .]
From far to near
In the north, in the east,
The beautiful blue sky of the motherland,
    The beautiful white clouds,
Moving beneath the white clouds,
A dozen or so black specks. . . .

                                        (Gao 1949, 21–22)

A more kinetic effort is Zhang Zhezhi's "Ha! I'm a Bomb!" (Ah! Wo shi zhadan):

Ha! I'm a bomb,
Blast! Blast! Blast! [zha! zha! zha!]
Blast! Blast to oblivion the cruel dwarf devils!

Blast! Blast from the water the fierce enemy warships!
Blast! Blast Tokyo flat!
Blast! Blast Osaka flat!
Blast! Blast Kobe flat! . . .

(1937, 20)

To be sure, the bellicose excess that inspired poems like Zhang's faded some-
what several years into the war, but attempts to consolidate the genre of recitation
poetry continued with the publication of longer and more detailed tracts on poetry
recitation. In a lengthy article from 1945, Gao Lan himself elaborates on the earlier
accounts of oral versus written poetry. Asserting first, like other commentators on
recitation, that poetry originated as an oral art, he then finds precedents for recita-
tion in China extending through the *Book of Songs*, Qu Yuan, Li Bai and Du Fu,
and on into the Song dynasty. In the West, Gao traces a lineage of poetry recitation
from Homer, Plato, and Sappho on through Shakespeare and up to Vachel Lindsay,
Carl Sandburg, William Butler Yeats, Federico García Lorca, and Vladimir Maya-
kovsky. But, Gao notes, whereas poetry recitation consistently flourished in the
West, it all but disappeared in China until the recent arrival of the war (Gao 1987c,
1–7).

Regarding the reasons why poetry should be recited, Gao, like Guan Lu, Jiang
Xijin, and Wang Bingyang, stresses the priority of sound and emotion. Citing an
unnamed source, Gao writes:[5] "The art of printing has done much to dull our liter-
ary perceptions. Words have a double virtue—that which resides in the sense and
that which resides in the sound. We miss much of the charm if the eye is made to
do duty also for the ear. The words, bereft of their vocal force, are but half alive on
the printed page. The music of verse, when repeated only to the inward ear, comes
as a faint echo" (Gao 1987c, 8). Gao strongly recommends training oneself to recite
to an audience so that "the poem can pass through your feeling and understanding
and, in an elevated, complete, and artistic manner, move others with all the emo-
tional rhythm and meaning that the poem contains and must express, thus unifying
the pulse of the reciter, the author, the audience, and the poem itself" (9).

Recitation poetry also inspired several book-length tracts, one by the poet and
critic Xu Chi, and another by the American-trained dramatist Hong Shen. Xu, after
writing his *Poetry Recitation Handbook* in Hong Kong, smuggled the galley proof in a
hot-water bottle through Macau and the Japanese-occupied coastal regions to the in-
land wartime cultural center Guilin, where it was published in July 1942 (Xu 1942,
7). A cosmopolitan Shanghai modernist in the 1930s, Xu was one among many
poets whose view of poetry, as he puts it in the *Handbook's* preface, "changed" with
the arrival of the war (7). The *Handbook* covers a total of forty-seven separate topics
relating to poetry recitation, from Guan Lu's assertion that recitation is the revival

of poetry in its original state, to a history of recitation in Greece, Europe, America, and the Soviet Union (from which Gao Lan later borrowed), and on through the issues of poetry and singing, recitation and folk song, poetry and film, individual and group recitation, individual and collective recitation, how to analyze recitation poetry, rehearsal for recitation, and stage effects for recitation performance, to name a few. Such a breadth of coverage reflects Xu's cosmopolitan tastes as well as his practical experience. By the time Xu wrote the *Handbook*, he had recited to large audiences in Hong Kong, and poetry recitation events had become common all over China.[6]

A consistent theme runs throughout Xu's many topics: the subordination of poetry's materiality in writing and sound in favor of abstract emotional presence. For example, in the section "Poetry and the Colloquial" (Shi yu kouyu) he writes: "The reason Chinese new poetry has become so frightfully hard to understand, or such a mess that it can please no one is because it hasn't courageously, forthrightly, and frankly spoken [shuo hua]. Instead, for the sake of maintaining refined literary affectation and polish, it plays about with word surfaces [zimian]" (Xu 1942, 57–58). The only way "to return poetry to its proper track," Xu concludes, is through poetry recitation. Xu's target here is again the Chinese Formalists and the Symbolists, whose poetry, he observes, "had no sooner escaped from five-character and seven-character classical lines than it slipped into fourteen-line sonnets, and which, after advocating free verse (ziyou shi) immediately took up obscure difficult poetry" (57).

Complementing Xu's disposition against written surfaces of language is an emphasis on emotion, and in particular the mind's-eye images that he sees as the vehicles of emotional affectivity. In two adjacent sections, "Poetry Recitation Is the Reigniting of the Poem" and "Imagization and Fantasy," Xu first explains that poems "contain" the fiery emotions the poet experienced at the time of writing. Xu, however, gives his own inflection to this Romantic cliché, adding that these emotions remain in the poem when it is published ("like canned food" is his simile) until a skilled reciter "fully expresses the feelings of the author at the time of writing" (Xu 1942, 17). Poetic emotion, Xu adds, can only be "reignited" by poems that present "images" (xingxiang). He then writes that since the advent of printing, poetry in the West has moved from concrete imagery to abstraction, from feeling to thought, and from the heart to the mind. Abstractions, he adds, cannot be recited. Now, however, with "the world returning to the road of recitation," the nature of poetry will change once again such that "poetry cannot but become imagistic [xing-xianghua]" (18).

Concrete imagery here represents less a return to the visual register than a manifestation of the human emotional interiority as visualized by the mind's eye. Xu makes this point clear in the section "The Eyes of the Reciter," where he advises

would-be reciters to "[l]ook up from the book! Because the eyes—they are the win-
dows of emotional expression. The reciter's eyes must be bright and flashing. From
the mouth comes speech, but inner meaning is all in the eyes." He then urges the
reciter to "(1) Envision the images you wish to recite; (2) attend closely to the eyes
of the audience, search out their eyes, talk to the audience's eyes, make the audience
see with their own eyes the images you recite" (Xu 1942, 46–47).

Such advice is more than a lesson in stage presence. For Xu, recitation is trans-
duction from text to mental image to emotion. Arousing emotion is the end goal of
poetry recitation, and Xu devotes a chapter specifically to this topic, writing:

> It is a matter of course that there be feeling during a recitation. But one must
> understand that such feeling refers to the feelings aroused in the audience
> by the reciter, not the feelings of the reciter himself. Many reciters become
> emotionally overwrought—personally overwrought, that is, even to the point
> of bursting into tears. But the audience, rather than being aroused to grief
> and indignation, simply thinks that the reciter has made a fool of himself.
> This sort of thing has happened many times. The reciter himself can be
> either cool-headed or excited, as long as he maintains control. He frequently
> observes the audience. When the audience becomes visibly moved, his tone
> and feeling can be unrestrained. If the audience is not yet visibly moved, it is
> better to read more slowly and carefully so that the audience can apprehend
> every word. (Xu 1942, 49)

Xu's call for emotional restraint in recitation would be the exception that proves
the rule. That is to say, his warning against unfettered feeling responds to what was
apparently a very real tendency among reciters to let emotion overcome them on
stage. The goal of recitation, Xu suggests, is not to demonstrate a personal excess
of sentiment and performative "noise," but to communicate an originary emotion
from "within" the poem to as many people as possible.

The desire to communicate such emotion to the largest audience leads Xu
into the very real issue given China's linguistic situation—that of dialect—and he
proposes overcoming such linguistic barriers through a specific mode of transla-
tion. Translation for Xu refers not to translating foreign languages into Chinese or
vice versa, but to transposing "print poetry" (yinshuapin shi) into recitation poetry
and "national language poetry" (guoyu shi) into dialect poetry. Xu reasons that a
dead language cannot communicate live images, which to him represent the pre-
ferred vehicle for emotional expression. "Dead language" here refers to words used
in print rather than the spoken language, and in particular to the linguistic regis-
ter of classical poetry. While Xu readily admits that the language of classical poetry
can present live imagery, he asserts that when performed orally such condensed

language cannot be readily understood, nor the images be "seen" by the audience (40).

One cannot argue with Xu that for the general audience a vernacular rendering would be easier to understand in oral performance. But due to his preoccupation with interiorized meaning and the accompanying emotional presence, he fails to consider the dependence of the immaterial psychic phenomenon, the signified, on the material medium of discourse, the signifier. Transposing from classical to vernacular Chinese is not a neutral act, as both "languages" are distinct linguistic registers with different semiotic correspondences. The point here, however, is not to take the theoretical high ground in criticizing Xu's conception of language. It is rather to show how the idea of poetry at the time, and in particular recitation poetry, was governed by an ideology of representation focused on emotional presence to a degree that denied the surface materiality of language. In Xu's view, the signified concepts (images, emotion) have an a priori existence independent of the language that brings them into consciousness. The poet need only recalibrate the language of the poem to make it accessible to the audience, and the original images will follow of themselves.

Xu's second mode of translation is from the national language into local dialect, which for him must include not only what he calls the major dialects of Cantonese, Shanghainese, and Sichuanese, but also more localized variants, such as the regional speech centered in cities like Chongqing, Chengdu, Suzhou, Hangzhou, and Guangzhou, as well as the Hakka dialect (Xu 1942, 58). Xu's reasoning is again grounded in the idea of emotional presence, for to him dialect represents an enhanced medium for the transmission of prelinguistic content. He writes: "Only local dialect [difangyan] is refined language, for it has the special properties of resonant pronunciation and profound content, so that whenever we hear a phrase of dialect we feel a sense of solid, transparent power" (55). In discussing dialect, Xu may as well have stressed the opacity of a particular regional speech to those Chinese who do not understand it. Instead, while not wholly disregarding the sound aspect of dialect, he locates its value in its transparency. In other words, he falls again on the side of voiced poetry's presumed ability to create an unencumbered flow of meaning to the nation as a whole.

The culminating discussion of new poetry recitation is to be found in dramatist Hong Shen's ambitious *Dramatic Speaking and the Recitation of Poetry (Xi de nianci yu shi de langsong)*, published in 1943. By far the most theoretically sophisticated commentator on recitation poetry, the Harvard-trained Hong cites an array of English-language authorities on poetry, acting, and voice training to fashion an at times highly technical explication of recitational method, one that Guo Moruo describes in the book's preface as "the first step towards making a science of this field" (Hong Shen 1950, 3). Scientific method notwithstanding, Hong's analysis of poetry recitation still rests upon the premise that "poetry" resides in emotional presence, with the corollary that the fundamental surface effects of poetic discourse, rhythm and meter, are but secondary products generated by emotion.

We find this tendency most readily in Hong's discussion of metrical pattern (*yunlü*), where he writes: "Metrical pattern alone does not make poetry. Poetry must have 'poetic content,' a beautiful and great something that cannot be expressed without the use of metrically patterned language" (49). The "something" that Hong refers to here is not simply emotion, but a "communal emotion" shared by members of a social collective. Hong's source for this idea, Francis B. Gummere's *The Beginnings of Poetry*, constructs a wide-ranging comparative-historical, ethnographically grounded, and fundamentally Romantic-nationalist argument identifying rhythm as the result of human emotional response and the "main factor" distinguishing poetry from prose. Hong cites Gummere: "but the poet is still essentially emotional, and just so far as he is to utter the great joys and the great pains of life, just so far he must go back to communal emotions, to the sense of kind, to the social foundation. The mere fact of utterance is social; however solitary his thought, a poet's utterance must voice this consent of man with man, and his emotion must fall into rhythm, the one and eternal expression of consent" (Gummere 1908, 115; Hong Shen 1950, 51).

In drawing authority from Gummere, Hong aligns himself with a school of thought on poetry that can be traced back to the seminal cultural nationalist and expressionist ideas of J. G. Herder. Significantly, Gummere himself praises Herder as "the prophet of the faith in communal poetry" and the chief progenitor of his own thought on poetry, explaining: "Full of scorn for closet verse of the day, he held up the racial or national, the 'popular' in its best sense, against the pedantic and the laboured,—poetry that beats with the pulse of a whole people against poetry that copies its exercises from a dead page and has no sense of race. He sundered poetry for the ear from poetry for the eye, poetry said or sung from poetry that looks to 'a paper eternity' for its reward" (Gummere 1908, 131).

The correspondence of these ideas on poetry with those shared among the Chinese recitation theorists I have discussed could not be closer and demonstrates their alignment with Romantic-nationalist thought on language and poetry. Hong, following Gummere, inflects these ideas in his own way by focusing on the relation between metrical pattern and emotion: "Metrical pattern is neither accidental nor supplementary. Given the presence of content that incites song or weeping, there will be, and must be, a corresponding metrical pattern. When poetic phrases of such metrical pattern are recited, the listener is in fact invisibly involved in a shared singing, which indicates 'communal emotion' and 'social consent'" (Hong 1950, 52).

Hong does not ignore metrical patterning as an element of poetic discourse,

TABLE 3.1 Emotion and Rhythm in Different Modes of Utterance

Poetry			Drama		Talk	
Highly metrical poetry	General poetry	Free verse	Emotional prose	General prose	Unorganized spoken utterance	
← Emotion gradually increases					Chaotic	**Emotion**
← Rhythm gradually more distinct					Chaotic	**Rhythm**

Source: Hong Shen, *Xi de nianci yu shi de langsong* (Shanghai: Zhonghua shuju, 1950), 61.

but he subordinates it to the prediscursive force of emotion: "Emotion [*qinggan*] drives rhythm; the stronger the emotion, the more pronounced is the rhythm. When a person feels strong emotion, the rhythm of the pulse and breathing are particularly apparent and powerful—the two are intimately related to human physical and mental activity. Thus of all modes of utterance [*huaju*], *poetic form is most suitable as a language of emotion* . . ." (59; italics in original).

According to this logic, the metrical regularity of language varies proportionately with the intensity of the emotion motivating it. The technically minded Hong illustrates this with a table diagram (see Table 3.1).

According to Hong's scheme, forms of speech from regular talk to drama to poetry lie along a continuum where, "As emotion gradually increases rhythm becomes gradually more distinct" (60). Thus while Hong differs from the other wartime theorists of recitation by recognizing presence of form (metrical pattern) in the visual and sonic dimensions of poetry, he subordinates these to the presence of interiorized emotion. Poetry might be distinguished by its regularity of metrical pattern, but such patterning exists only as the effect of a shared, underlying, communal consciousness of kind, an imagined union of subjectivities. Behind Hong's science of recitation lies a mystical inner presence, a fullness of feeling that corresponds to the emotional "real" of a national interiority.

Late War Poems: Dream Sound and Death of the Auditor

Turning now to poems written during the middle and later years of the war, we find the imagination of the sounding voice of poetry undergoing a certain modification. In contrast to the sanguine, high-volume projection of voice in early wartime recitation poems, by the later years of the war one finds that, while voice and sound still dominate, the poems themselves dwell upon the loss of both the poetic voice and its listening audience. The two poets I will analyze in this regard are Guang Weiran and Gao Lan, both leading figures in new poetry recitation throughout the course of the war. The poems that demonstrate this variation in poetic consciousness are Guang's "Thunder at Midnight" (Guang 1985, 403–409), written in Kunming in 1943 (Guang 2002, 5, 293), and Gao's most famous recitation poem, "Weeping for Lost Sufei," written in 1942 to mourn the death of his young daughter (Gao 1949, 120–130).[7]

Although recognized primarily for his landmark patriotic anthem of 1939, *Yellow River Cantata* (*Huanghe dahechang*), Guang Weiran was one of the most active poets of recitation during the War of Resistance. Indeed, the *Cantata* itself began as a poem. After a year and a half of contributing to wartime street theater and song lyrics in Shanghai, Hankou, and Shanxi, Guang began work on a long poem entitled "Yellow River Chant" (Huanghe yin) in January 1939 while recuperating in Yan'an from a broken arm. At Xian Xinghai's suggestion, Guang revised the poem (orally due to his injury) as the libretto of the *Cantata*. He also recited portions of the *Cantata*, reportedly in an impassioned and resonant voice, at a Chinese New Year's Eve party in February 1939, at the *Cantata*'s debut in Yan'an two months later, and in 1941 in Chongqing (Guang 2002, 5, 288; Zang Yunyuan 1979, 76; Chen 1941).[8] Read without the score, *Yellow River Cantata* does share certain features with early wartime recitation poetry. Most notably, each of the seven sections of the 1939 version opens with a brief introductory recitation, which in several instances directly addresses the audience as "Friends!" (Guang and Xian 1956, 40–55). These recitational interludes provide a unifying vocal frame to an otherwise polyvocal piece that features in turn the rhythmic chant of hardy boatmen, the exalted register of a male panegyrist, the folksy call and response of a refugee farmer and merchant, and the operatic female soloist's "Yellow River Lament." In the climactic seventh section, "Roar! Yellow River," all voices join in a resounding chorus that commands the major rivers of China, from the Pearl in the south to the Sungari in the north, to raise a collective and bellicose hue and cry.

After leaving Yan'an, Guang traced a path south and west. After further recuperation in Chengdu, he arrived in Chongqing in September 1939, where in November 1940 he participated in the founding of the Poetry Recitation Team (Shige langsong dui), a group formed under the auspices of the wartime cultural organization All-China Resistance Association of Writers and Artists, or ACRAWA (Jiang Guipu 1940).[9] Not long afterwards, he was dispatched by the Chinese Communist Party to engage in cultural resistance work with the overseas Chinese community in Rangoon and Mandalay, where he frequently recited poetry before fleeing overland to Yunnan in 1942 in the face of the Japanese advance (Guang 2002, 5, 291–292). After a period of illness, he taught middle school in Kunming, but could often be heard reciting at political meetings at Kunming's Southwest Associated University and Yunnan University, and at "culture salons" held at the home of democracy activist Li Gongpu (Guang 1990, "Preface," 2 and passim; 2002, 5, 292–294).

It was also in Kunming in 1944 that Guang published his first poetry collection, *Thunder* (*Lei*), which included the two-part, 148-line poem "Thunder at Midnight." Although I have been unable to verify whether Guang ever recited this particular poem, as a text written by an active recitation poet and intensely concerned with the thematics of sound and the poet's voice, "Thunder at Midnight" participates in the aesthetics of recitation constructed by wartime poetry and theory. It does so, however, in a way that subtly contravenes the principles driving the wartime poetry of voice that had come before it. Guang alludes to the unusual nature of the poem in the 1944 collection's epilogue, which reads as a disclaimer for "morbid poems," described as "groans of illness, ravings of a madman, a voice unhealthy and inharmonious" written during a period of "loneliness and nervous anxiety" when he had "lost the power of self-restraint" after arriving in the cultural backwater of Kunming. The only positive value of the poems, he adds, is their therapeutic value as a psychological release for himself and any young readers similarly caught up in the "pestilence of individual feeling" (Guang 2002, 4, 42-43).

There is more to such a statement, I believe, than conventionalized self-deprecation. A close reading of "Thunder at Midnight" shows it to be a text that mobilizes the acoustic clichés of the war: a sleeping populace, sudden explosions, cataclysmic storms, and a roaring poet portrayed in the first person. The poem, however, works with these elements in a different way, giving them an added level of complexity that creates an uneasy distance from any straightforward confidence in the positive impact, or even the very presence, of the poet's sounding voice.

The two-part poem opens with the poet being awakened by a thunderclap at midnight:

> Your thunder at midnight
> Rolling from beyond the sky
> Crossing high peaks
> Penetrating the clouds
> Exploding outside my window
> Jolting me awake from a nightmare. . . .
> (Guang 1985, 403)

To the wartime reader, imagery of darkness and passivity preceding a storm was inevitably associated with the idea of war's arrival awakening a somnolent nation. Especially in the early years of the conflict, China's poets and writers had welcomed Japan's all-out assault on Chinese territory, as they saw the fury of pitched battle bringing relief from the stultifying atmosphere of political compromise that weighed upon the national psyche during the 1930s. Wartime literati-at-arms embellished this sentiment with a set of metaphors—raging tempests, tidal

waves, conflagrations, and so on—meant to suggest a sweeping, salvational purga-
tive. For Guang, a poet committed to the aesthetics of recitation, war assumes
the metaphorical guise of sound or, more specifically, of thunderclaps, pressing
down upon the poet with crescendoing urgency, "Rolling towards me/As roar
upon roar you/Hurl bombs packed with fury/At the world of men" (404). In the
following stanza, these elemental forces inspire doomsday terror among all living
creatures as they wreak devastation on land and water, "causing the cowardly to
pale/The young to wail," "knocking to flinders masts on the river" and "drop-
ping sand like red clouds/burying armies in their midnight advance" (404–405).
Part One of the poem concludes as the poet imagines countless others like him,
sitting up dumbly in bed in the midst of the storm, "Enduring the long night's
sleeplessness/Dully awaiting the daylight" (405). In a manner distinctly unlike
the roaring sounds of warfare one finds in early wartime poetry, here cataclys-
mic noise not only wreaks pure destruction but fails to stir its auditors beyond a
passive, unresponsive state.

In Part Two, Guang sets up an equivalence between the sound of thunderous
explosions and the sound of language in two short, parallel stanzas:

I hear
Your resounding
Steely bombs
Fiery bombs
Like raindrops cast upon the world of men.

It seems that
Your resounding
Steely speech
Fiery speech
Earnestly calls to me. . . .

(406)

The parallelism of these two stanzas foregrounds a transformation from inanimate
to animate sound. On the surface, the second lines of both stanzas are identical
(ni yi sheng jiezhe yi sheng). In the first stanza, however, "sound" (sheng) refers to the
inhuman noise of bombs, while in the second this inanimate "sound" has become
instead the sound of human speech (yuyan). A form of vocal address takes place
here, and one that thematically links this text to the early wartime recitation po-
ems discussed earlier. We note, however, that this address is contained within the
poem's narrative and is not, as was the case with the early sound poems discussed
above, a "live" externalized address to a listening audience. For Guang, the poet is

still the privileged carrier of war's powerful language, but already stylistic differences
have begun to emerge.

After reflecting on the paralysis of the imagined soundscape up until that
moment, the poet then leaps from his bed to experience an ecstatic moment:

Though it comes on ever stronger
Though the driving rain pierces my body like arrows
I seem to feel
After a flash of your lightning's cold brilliance
The blood of my body
Like lightning surging to my heart
Your voice rouses my voice
Your fury excites my fury
And from my bursting heart
From the depths of my heart now aflame
From my long years of pent grievance
Erupts
A soundless roar. . . .
(407)

This ecstatic—but strangely silent—roar matches the potent fury of the storm, for it
"Penetrates the black clouds/Answering your/Thunder of the skies/Ah ha" (407).
Next the poet envisions those around him awakening one by one and "Rubbing
their fogged eyes/Opening their astonished eyes" (408). In denouement, Guang's
poet invites the people to use "fiery speech/steely speech" and "fiery voices/steely
voices" to banish the "night specter" (408-409). The poem concludes on a note of
confidence and unity, with the poet crying out to the people:

Ah ha Come
Be brave
Follow me
I shall lead you
Lead those just awakened
Lost in pleasant dreams
Suffocated by nightmares
Neighbors on all sides
To go forth as one
And conquer him
The tyrant of midnight. . . .
(409)

From beginning to end, "Thunder at Midnight" replays the devices and themes that dominated recitation poetry from early on in the war. We have the poet as voice of the salvational vanguard, an emphasis on the resounding fury of the elements and their metaphorical relation to the national wartime situation, and the call to awaken a passive, somnolent populace to the need for salvation. But why, then, does Guang insist that the poet's initial roar be "soundless"? The reason for this moment of curious reversal lies, I believe, in the poet's subtle but persistent attachment to his own dreamlike state. In this condition of reverie, the poet is free to imagine sound as an all-powerful force of awakening. To break this reverie is to destroy the dream and return to a waking world in which the sound of the poet's voice is but a feeble echo of its transcendent ideal. Because the roar is soundless, the dream may persist. That it does so beyond this critical moment is evidenced by the poem's repeated use, *after* the mention of the "soundless roar," of the phrase *fangfu*, "seems," or "as if"—a simple expression, but one that gently and persistently destabilizes what would otherwise appear to be a standard recitational representation of sound-mediated resonance with a listening national audience. The expression *fangfu* is notably absent in the poem's Part One, where Guang describes the pre-awakening, benighted condition of himself and his national surroundings. Its absence there suggests that the condition of sleep and darkness depicted in Part One are perhaps more real to the poet than the subsequent condition of wakefulness. Corroborating this is the disposition of the four instances of *fangfu* in Part Two. In each location we see it undermining the belief that any awakening has or will take place outside of the poet's imaginary construct.

The first instance of "seeming" occurs in the second stanza of Part Two, at that critical moment where Guang depicts the transmission of sound from the inanimate, elemental storm to a humanly intelligible voice calling to the poet. The second occurrence Guang places at the onset of the climactic flash where the poet finds his voice and "erupts" in his curiously soundless roar. Guang then immediately reinforces this moment of ambiguity by relating that his awakened I-narrator only *seems* "to sense/The furious sound/released from the bottom of my midnight's heart" (*Wo fangfu juede/cong wo wuye de xindi fachu de/fennu de shengyin*; 407). Finally, Guang drapes the veil of "seeming" over the effect the poet's voice has upon his audience:

I *seem* to see
All around me
All those around me
At another of your thunderclaps
At another of my thundering roars
One by one jolted awake in their beds at midnight.
(408; italics added)

In contrast with the early wartime sound poems that unequivocally assert the power of poetically mediated sound to awaken their audience, "Thunder at Midnight" shifts the project of such awakening into the domain of dreaming. Does the poet truly find his voice and arouse those around him, or does he only *seem* to do so? Can the sound of poetry truly awaken a nation to a sense of imminent crisis, or is this but the idle dream of the wartime poet? Guang asserts the former but implies the latter. The slippage that ensues indicates a corrosion of faith in the power of sounded poetry to fulfill its salvational mission.

"Weeping for Lost Sufei": Death of the Audience, Loss of the Voice

If there is one poem from the war period that achieved a relatively wide and lasting popularity, it is "Weeping for Lost Sufei," Gao Lan's elegy to his seven-year-old daughter who died of malaria in March 1941. I have selected "Sufei" for detailed treatment here, first, because it has acquired something of a legendary status among wartime recitation poems, and second, like Guang's "Thunder at Midnight" it treats the aesthetic components of sound and voice in a manner that suggests how poets' imagined relation to their audience had changed since the beginnings of the wartime poetry recitation movement.

If for no other reason, "Weeping for Lost Sufei" commands attention because it is the one wartime recitation poem with a record of consistently stirring audiences' strong, if lachrymose, emotions. The poem gained a following first in Chongqing where, after appearing in the *L'Impartial* (*Dagongbao*) literary supplement *Battle Line* (*Zhanxian*) in March 1942, it was disseminated quickly and spontaneously by people who recited it, wrote out copies by hand, or memorized the entire poem or long sections of it (Zhang and Lu 1989, 52). Given such popularity, it should not be surprising that accounts of "Sufei" recitations far outnumber those of any other wartime recitation poem. These accounts fit into one of two modes—maudlin tearfulness or cool defiance of authority. As for the former, poet Zang Yunyuan recalls the following wartime performance of "Sufei" by actress Zhang Ruifang: "The moment the recitation began she was touched by emotion, her tone became sincere and lovely, and her teardrops fell like flower petals. Aroused to sympathy, the listeners felt the emotion and wept" (Zang Yunyuan 1979, 77). Gao Lan himself relates that during his first two attempts publicly to recite the poem he broke down in tears midway through and was unable to finish. Later, after a conscious effort to steel himself emotionally, he managed to complete a reading of "Sufei" at the Central University Student Union near Chongqing. Gao was pleased to see "not a few listeners wiping away tears or quietly weeping, as well as several students who wailed aloud when the reading ended" (Gao 1987b, 146). Even after 1949 the poem apparently maintained its popularity as a sentimental favorite: a broadcast recitation of "Sufei" in 1957 allegedly drove listeners to outpourings of vicarious grief (Zhang and Lu 1989, 52).

The dimension of political defiance in accounts of "Sufei" readings is almost as strong as its reputation for eliciting sentimental effusion. Gao tells a story of how the poem found its way into prison during the winter of 1942, where an underground Communist Party member incarcerated at the Guomindang's notorious Wuyunshan concentration camp in Chongqing made a practice of fluently reciting "Sufei" to his cellmates, thus "bringing their sense of outrage to a climax" (Gao 1987c, 16–17). The poet also tells how at an evening reading of "Sufei" in May 1946 on a windy, rain-swept athletic field at Beiping Normal University, Guomindang secret police cut the lights in an attempt to shut down his performance. Gao reportedly carried on to the poem's end by the light of two candles, bravely held high by a pair of college students (16). More than twenty years later, during the Cultural Revolution, fans of "Sufei" are said to have quietly recited the poem under their breath "to ease feelings that had been repressed in the suffocating atmosphere" (Zhang and Lu 1989, 52).

The two modes of response to "Sufei," the lachrymose and the defiant, would seem to stand in opposition: the former suggesting an almost morbid desire to immerse the self in a sense of deep personal loss, and the latter inhabited by a larger, collective will to resist political oppression. The poem certainly can accommodate both dimensions. However, commentary on the poem in the decades after it was written attempts to reconcile these two threads by subsuming the poem's expression of private loss, Sufei's death, into the Chinese Communist national narrative. Thus, in 1979 Zang Yunyuan writes of "Sufei" as "a masterwork of accusation against the old society" (77). Gao Lan, writing in the 1980s, claims that "mourning the death of a little girl reflects the suffering the broad masses of the people were forced to endure at the time, and raises an accusation against the brutal rule of the then-current Guomindang reactionaries" (Gao 1987c, 16). Gao relates, too, that at his first complete public reading of the poem at Central University, he avoided emotional breakdown only by reminding himself that he was "reciting to the masses," and thus had to arouse the audience against "reactionary rule," rather than succumb to "a pointless display of personal sentiment" (Gao 1987d, 146).

Such construals of the poem no doubt register a certain actuality. They do so, however, in a manner delimited by the narratives of injustice and victimization that orthodox Chinese Communist history has imposed on the immediate pre-1949 period. By aligning the powerful sentimental appeal of "Sufei" with issues of party politics, such accounts of the poem's performance foreclose the production of alternative meanings from what was the most important and influential recitation poem of the war. Moreover, they do so in a manner that, much like the theoretical writings on recitation poetry maintain, insists upon voiced poetry's ability to tap into the shared emotion constituting national interiority. The poem can certainly be understood as a poetic evocation of underlying emotive presence, but not without a certain diminution of meaning. What political boilerplate readings like Zang and Gao's obscure is how "Sufei," when understood as a recitation poem, in fact narrates a retreat from wartime recitation poetry's dominant features. This retreat can be detected, not only in how the poem depicts the failure of the poet's voice to act as a sound-based mode of direct address, but in how the poem oscillates between investing in the emotive power of voice and that of the visual image. This shift in aesthetic priorities attests to a loss of confidence in the register of sound and, indirectly, in the accompanying ideology of new poetry as an instrument of national awakening.

Formally, "Sufei" is typical of many recitation poems of the war period. Like many of these it runs rather long, though at 138 lines it falls short of other works by Gao Lan, not a few of which stretch out heroically to the several hundreds of lines. Also, like most poems written for recitation, line lengths are irregular, rhyme is employed frequently, though without fixed pattern, and there is no regular stanzaic structure. Gao uses this extended free-verse form to detail the remorse, loss, and self-recrimination that alternately overcome the I-narrator as he opens a chest of Sufei's old belongings, collapses from grief at the memories aroused by the sight of her clothes and toys, and then awakens in the depth of a cold and rainy night to set off, lantern in hand, on a vain attempt to call back Sufei's departed soul.

Although "Sufei" differs greatly from Guang Weiran's "Thunder at Midnight" in terms of mood, the two poems share a basic narrative sequence. In both the sleeping poet, upon awakening into a dark, restless night, cries out to be heard. But more important, both poems also subtly betray the "awakened" poet's ability to, in turn, arouse others with the sound of his voice. Guang portrays a mass awakening prompted by the poet's roar, yet this roar is both soundless and relegated to the unsure domain of poetic seeming. In "Weeping for Lost Sufei," the poet speaks to a listener who will never and can never awaken, suggesting that the poet's address may not be directed to an audience at all, but to absence itself. We see this in the poem's opening line, "Where have you gone? My Sufei!" (Gao 1949, 120), an utterance that cries out to an audience that is, in fact, long lost. One might read this line, and the many more like it in the poem, as a standard poetic apostrophe articulated in the face of irrevocable death, or even as modernized enactment of zhaohun, the traditional rite of calling the soul back from the dead. But when we consider the poem in the context of the poetics of wartime recitation, we can detect in Gao's outcry the beginning of a poetic subtext expressing the loss of faith in sound, and in particular the sound of the poet's voice, to reach its intended audience.

As the poem moves on from the initial invocation of loss in the first line, we encounter a series of passages from sound to silence—one in each of the first three stanzas. In the first stanza, Gao follows up on the apostrophic first line with an image of absence framed as the loss of a defiant voice:

> This day last year
> You were still on stage singing "Drive Out Japan to the Last Breath"!
> Today, this year, ah!
> The grass has grown green on your grave mound so desolate! . . .
>
>   (Gao 1949, 120)

Even as these four lines introduce the poem's primary theme of anguish over the loss of a loved one, they also inscribe a movement from the public performance of patriotic song—the close cousin of wartime recitation—to an image of deserted, unpopulated stillness. Following closely upon this imagery of silence, the second stanza shows the grief-stricken narrator continuing his address to the absent audience. Now, however, he discovers his own voice hesitating on the brink of silence as he struggles for words:

> Child, ah!
> You have in hard times
> Given me seven happy years, and I thank you.
> But the sorrow you give me
> Will it stretch on endlessly?
> What is it I should say to you? . . .
>
>   (Gao 1949, 120)

In stanza three Gao, in a mood of almost gothic melancholia, stresses the narrator's temporal and spatial distance from the object of his longing, before closing again on the subtheme of sound:

> A year!
> Spring grasses withered, the autumn winds came,
> Snowflakes fell, the swallows once more have flown;
> Would that I were so brave
> As to approach your grave!
> But I fear the sound of my sorrowed weeping,
> Would disturb the soft rest of your shade! . . .
>
>   (121)

Here Gao again replays sound's absence as the narrator, moved by lingering paren-tal concern, denies himself even a visit to Sufei's graveside for fear of disturbing her with his audible grief.

The first three stanzas of "Sufei," even as they foreground the elements of sound and voice, represent the poet's voice with an ambivalence uncharacteristic of earlier recitation poetry. This ambivalence persists as the poem repeatedly shifts its allegiance between the registers of the heard and the seen. For example, in the fourth stanza, where we find the grieving poet sitting at his desk and disavowing the visual register of language by stressing the insufficiency of writing to express true, heartfelt emotion:

> Yet I am unable to lift my pen,
> To write, for you, my sorrowful emotion,
> That heart-rending anguish!
> When I think of you,
> Tears, soaking my paper!
> Tears, soaking my pen! . . .
>
> (121)

In the following stanza, however, the poem focuses on the intensely visual ex-perience of digging out from an old chest Sufei's personal effects: a *blue* bookbag, a *dark red* dress, a stack of cigarette-pack *picture* cards, and a treasured piece of *green* glass. Overcome by the sight of these items, the narrator wails in grief before collaps-ing into sleep. Yet the register of sound soon intervenes again, as late in the night he awakens to hear the night watchman sighing in the distance. This sudden interpola-tion of sound does stir the poet's emotions, but only to lead him into a stanza of bitter self-recrimination over his failure to prevent the death of his daughter:

> I have wronged you! Child!
> You were stricken simply with malaria,
> Yet in vain I let the doctors make off with my last penny.
> I am a worthless man!
> I sold my most valuable clothes,
> Only to buy you a white coffin
> And bury you deep in the yellow earth! . . .
>
> (122–123)

This stanza ends, we note, with an appeal to the visual imagination of color in im-ages of white coffins and yellow earth. The poet carries through on this emphasis on visual imagery in the next stanza. Here, deploying again the apostrophic mode typical of recitation poems, Gao again falls back on a set of images grounded in the register of vision:

> Tell me! Child!
> In that world,
> Do you still, a finger in your mouth,
> Stare at other people's children eating peanuts?
> Gazing at others' fancy clothes
> Do you sadly lower your head? . . .
>   (123–124)

Approaching its midpoint now, we realize that the poem has come to rely largely on visual imagery—the desolate, grassy-green grave, Sufei's multicolored belongings, and visions of wide-eyed Sufei herself in the next world—to carry its emotive thrust. As if sensing this preponderance of the visual aesthetic, Gao shifts back to the register of sound and voice. Prompted by the forlorn cry of a wild bird in the mountains, the I-narrator sets off into the dark night to search for the lost Sufei by the feeble, greenish glow of a dying lantern. It is here, just past the midpoint of the poem, that the poet's voice gathers strength by aligning itself with the present-time narrated action:

> Softly I don my coat and rise,
> Dim green lantern in hand, I move into the wind and rain,
> Into the dark night,
> Into the mountain peaks,
> Under the ink-black clouds,
> Crying out your pet name, Xiaoyu! Xiaoyu!
> Come here! Child! This is your home!
> Come to the green lantern!
> Don't be afraid!
> Your father is waiting for you in the wind and rain! . . .
>   (124–125)

Soon, however, the poet's voice fails him entirely, and he is enveloped by sounds of silence accentuating the impossibility of receiving any response from his intended hearer:

> But the candle turns to ash, the lantern goes out!
> So, too, my throat is bereft of sound,

I hear the frost come down,
Hear the worms turn in the ground,
And yet, Child! You do not reply! . . .

(125)

Stranded in the nighttime hush, the narrator turns his gaze toward a stock
symbol of silence and distance: a lone star shining above the mountain where Sufei
is buried. The sense of absolute separation inspired by the star leads the narrator
to resignation at the irreconcilable gap between him and the audience he is trying
to reach. Amid another bout of painful recollection and self-castigation, the poem
again evokes an emotive image suggesting the failure of communication:

Because you loved to write and draw,
When I laid you in the coffin,
Your mother, so stubbornly devoted!
In your right hand placed a pencil,
In your left hand placed a roll of white paper,
A year!
And I haven't received a letter from beyond the land's end,
Not a word written to your mother! . . .

(127)

The poem concludes in a mood of renunciation and annihilation. Done with
crying over his loss, the poet burns his poem of mourning and bids Sufei to rest in
tranquility before he makes a dramatic gesture of self-destruction, vowing to "walk
to the storm" raging in the wilderness (129). He closes with the lines:

Child!
If you hear knocking on your grave vault,
It is my last tear dropping into the Yellow Springs!
(129–130)

Here the poet-narrator raises the sound of his voice to address his lost audience,
the departed Sufei. But the next two lines, the couplet that leads the poem into the
silence of its own ending, consign the poem's last act of communication, the knock-
ing sound of the poet's last tear, ultimately and irreversibly to the underworld.

Despite the poem's air of finality, "Sufei" did not sound the death knell of war-
time recitation for either Gao Lan or other poets. As for Gao, he published a hand-
ful of poems between 1942 and 1945. One of these, "Song of Parting" (Songbie qu),
still contains the wartime recitation poem's characteristic high-volume apostrophic

address. But the other two, "Early Winter" (Chu dong) and "These Are Not Days for Shedding Tears" (Zhe bu shi liulei de rizi), are each dominated by a mood of death, sleep, and stillness (Gao 1987a, 106–111).

Recitation poems and their accompanying theoretical constructs, however, comprise only part of the story. Neither has much meaning if the poems are not actually given voice in the actual time-space of live recitation—a project that meant engaging with the complex and often intransigent everyday realities of the Chinese wartime situation. The next chapter moves on to the concrete specifics of where, when, and how poems were performed during the war. As one might expect, it was easier by far to write voice into poetry or to formulate theoretical ideals of poetic effect than to perform poems successfully in the unforgiving conditions of wartime. Attempts to control the slippage between the ideals of theory and the vagaries of reality, however, have much to tell us about the troubled, fragmented, but not unsuccessful project of establishing new poetry recitation as a modern genre of literature in performance.

CHAPTER 4

Wartime Recitals and the Consolidation of a Genre

As I HAVE ARGUED, the 1920s and 1930s saw the making of a strain of new poetry that foregrounded an imagined, sounding voice. Writing voice into a poem, however, is one matter, actually voicing a poem in performance quite another. Where the former creates a text easily available to traditional analysis, the latter launches the poem into the unreproducible, transient contingencies of sound, space, and social exchange. This chapter attempts to recover the unrecoverable: the performance texts of recited poetry during the War of Resistance period. The difficulties such a task poses are not few. Most fundamentally, the recited poem lives in the medium of sound, and like all sound phenomena "inhabits its own time and dissipates quickly" (Kahn 1999, 5). Yet even within such unavoidable ephemerality, the performed poem presents a significantly richer and more multidimensional experience than the poem in print. As Charles Bernstein has observed, acoustic performance, the creation of a poetic "audiotext," involves a multidimensional extension of the poem beyond a stable and familiar world of print. Performance enhances a poem's field of linguistic activity in ways that resist standard textual analysis, undermines the idea of a fixed and stable "version" of any one poem, and, through the physicality of sounded language, shifts poetry into a fluid, dialogic dynamic of social interaction (Bernstein 1998, 8–23). The orally performed poem, then, can only be understood as an irreducibly sociocorporeal phenomenon fully present only in the existential situation of its performance (Zumthor 1994, 224–225).

The sound of recited poems, then, is as fleeting as it is real. Nonetheless, however much of the auditory reality remains irretrievable from the many live performances of poetry during the eight years of the war, the very sociocorporeal occurrence of these events made an impact on literary history that continues to this day. Although we cannot hear, see, and feel what these poems sounded like in situ, we can through the historical record of recitation events try to understand how, where, when, and why they were delivered and listened to. This is because the absences of lost audiotext lying at the center of these performances are quite often surrounded by very concrete and detailed historical information: dates, times, addresses, names of performers and audience members, titles of poems, and sometimes even the weather. As it follows poems and poets through the war years, this chapter provides as thorough a recounting of context as possible by referring to the range of materials that record this lost poetry of performance. These materials includes diaries, memoirs, performance reviews, forewords, articles from contemporary journals and newspaper literary supplements, and, of course, printed versions of poems themselves. Always fragmentary and inevitably shot through with bias, evasions, and embellishments, these materials can nonetheless be woven into a narrative that traces the makings of poetry recitation's establishment as a new genre of performed literature.

I reconstruct this narrative chronologically by tracing poets and their poetic events from the early years of 1937–1938 in Guangzhou and the tricity (Hankou, Hanyang, Wuchang) complex of Wuhan, to the rural hinterland surrounding Wuhan, the Communist base of Yan'an, and finally into the middle and late years of recitation in Shanghai, Chongqing, Chengdu, and Guilin. Along the way we meet the major personalities of wartime recitation as they move from region to region and city to city, carrying with them the energy and agency without which there would have been no movement at all. We shall also observe how these personalities organized and institutionalized themselves and their projects in different places and at different times. If this narrative has its own particular emphasis, it is the vicissitudes faced when these individuals tried to elevate recitation to its imaginary ideal as an auditory mass art able to create a shared sense of emotive presence among all members of the nation. Although practitioners were reluctant to admit it, the exigencies of performance under wartime realities eroded faith in this ideal. But, as I hope to show, even as poetry recitation fell short of its original ambitions, the accumulated impact of staging new poetry in so many times, places, and circumstances not only established poetry recitation as a new performance genre but also initiated an aesthetics of the performed poetic voice.

Presence before Practice: Positing the Recitational Ideal

As discussed in Chapters 2 and 3, proponents of new poetry recitation tried to legitimate the public performance of new poetry by attributing to it the ability to transparently and directly communicate expressive and affective poetic content. This content was in turn believed to articulate the substance of a unified national being, grounded in what I refer to as national interiority. Writing in 1939, the poet Li Lei articulated the ideal of poetically mediated presence as follows: "The performer, with ringing metallic tone, recites aloud his poem before the crowd in a manner akin to song. The exceptional harmonious beauty of the poem flows into the deepest recesses of every listener's soul where it arouses great waves that slowly gather on the performer's every side, then forms a surge of hope for life's vitality that rushes off into freedom's distant wilderness" (Li 1987, 56). Li's recitational ideal, in fact quite similar to that constructed seventeen years before in Chen Nanshi's "Poet's Joy," describes a process of expanding emotive presence in which the sonorous, carefully modulated sound enters deeply and bodily into the receptive cores of the collective, listening subject, there generating an almost mystical sympathetic resonance that extends outwards into the nation-space.

As one might expect, few if any recitals excited such unequivocal and expansive response. The problem, amply identified by participants, seems to have been less a lack of emotional presence on the part of the performer than his or her perceived failure to discipline, modulate, and project this emotion. There is no lack of accounts that corroborate and expand Xu Chi's observation, noted in Chapter 3, of emotional outbursts during recitals. Gao Lan, as discussed previously, broke down and wept the first several times he attempted publicly to recite his "Weeping for Lost Sufei." Similarly, we are told that the poet Fang Yin brought a surplus of sentiment to the airwaves when, during a radio broadcast of his poem "Seeing Off the Child Refugees" (Songbie nantong), he became choked with emotion and had to stop and apologize to his listeners (Gao 1987b, 145). Public expression of sorrow was not the only symptom of such recitations. Other poets, overcome with paroxysms of poetic rage, pounded violently on the table in front of them (Gao 1987c, 15). Some, as one critic in Shanghai observed, would lose the sympathy of their listeners even before opening their mouths when they "swaggered on stage to recite with all the airs of a natural-born genius" (Shu 1941, 20). Still others—as Gao Lan relates about a publicly staged recitation by Mu Mutian and Jiang Xijin in the summer of 1937—might have felt a certain level of emotion themselves, but gave impassive deliveries that left their audience cold (Gao 1987c, 15). Perhaps most unfortunate were the inadvertently comic performances. Gao Lan, for example, writes of a comrade whose excessively animated reading of Lu Xun's famous short story "Diary of a Madman" was dubbed by one wag as "Madman Reciting a Diary" (Gao 1987c, 15). Other poets suffered humiliation over their failed efforts to recite in presentable Mandarin. For example, Shandongese poet Zang Yunyuan's sincere but linguistically substandard rendering of a poem celebrating the liberation of his hometown from the Japanese made him the laughingstock of his peers at a literary gathering in Chongqing (Zang 1979, 76–77). Finally, we hear of a painfully emaciated performer who, neck extended, veins in his head bulging, and one leg quivering uncontrollably, hoarsely shouted at the top of his lungs, "We are healthy!" (Gao 1987c, 16).

Judging from such reports, wartime poetry recitation was often an alienating rather than unifying or uplifting experience. Defects in performance were legion, but according to those present at such spectacles resulted mainly from a failure to find the oral and bodily conventions needed to adapt written text to a real-time performative moment. Looking back from the 1980s, the poet Gao Lan sums up wartime recitation's "most common problems" as "overly fervent and exaggerated intonation, facial expression, attitude, and voice. Some extremists would even go as far as ignoring the thought and feeling content of a poem, insisting on shouting everything at the top of their lungs with the intent of overwhelming the crowd and cowing them into submission. Others, confusing poetry with the script of a play, would imitate the voice, facial expressions, and movements of the characters in the poem" (Gao 1987c, 14–15). It was the search—bumpy and misguided, but persistent—for an ideal, poetically mediated, shared emotional presence that drove people to perform poetry during the war. But it was the performances themselves that, through error, accident, and accumulated experience, created a foundation for a mode of performance that would carry on into China's socialist and postsocialist future. The pages that follow reconstruct as carefully as reasonably possible the transformation of a transcendent recitational ideal into a historical legacy of new poetry recitation.

Guangzhou and Wuhan: Questioning the Aesthetics of Voice

After Japanese military advances through Beijing, Tianjin, Shanghai, and Nanjing in the fall of 1937, the flow of refugee writers and artists to Guangzhou and Wuhan turned these two locations into temporary centers of wartime cultural work. As the de facto national capital during this early stage of the war, Wuhan was the more active of the two sites. Both locations, however, hosted a significant amount of poetry recitation activity—the first of its kind during the war. In this section I contextualize and examine several recitation events that took place in these two cities, noting how during the initial stage of the war poets generated conflicted imaginations of their own and others' attempts to generate a sense of presence through the performance of new poetry.

By the end of 1937, the southern city of Guangzhou had become temporary home to a small but active enclave of poets affiliated with the China Poetry Forum Society (Zhongguo shitan she). Led by the indefatigable leftist poet Pu Feng, this group produced the journal *China Poetry Forum* (Zhongguo shitan) as well as a number of new poetry collections through the society's own press, Poetry Publishers (Shige chubanshe). In addition to introducing the genre of street poetry (*jietou shi*) later popularized in the Communist stronghold at Yan'an (Ke Fei 1937; Huang and Chen 1985, 2: 1410), Pu Feng and his cohort were among the first to practice and promote wartime new poetry recitation. Pu, a founding member of the leftist New Poetry Society in 1932, is remembered as one of the most outspoken proponents of poetry's massification, and his published writings from the early war period in Guangzhou do stress the potential mass appeal of poetry recitation. But he also kept a detailed and quite candid record of his activities of 1937 and early 1938 in

中國詩壇社歡送雷石榆同志赴戰留影

Members of the China
Poetry Forum Society
(Zhongguo shitan she) in
1938. From *China Poetry
Forum* (*Zhongguo shitan*) 2,
nos. 5/6 (September
1938): 5.

Cover illustration from the
20 April 1938 issue of *China
Poetry Forum* (*Zhongguo
shitan*).

diary form.[1] When read in tandem with his contemporaneous public statements in *China Poetry Forum*, Pu's diary offers rare insight into some of the war's earliest efforts at organizing, institutionalizing, and performing new poetry recitation.

Pu's diary reveals that the poetry performances he organized occurred almost exclusively in private rather than mass settings, such as organizational meetings of the China Poetry Forum Society or other special occasions of a literary nature. Attended by five, ten, or at most several dozen people and frequently held over dinner, these gatherings were routinely used as occasions for impromptu performances—"practica" (*shijian*) as Pu preferred to call them—of new poetry recitation and song (Pu 1938b, 26). By far the largest of these occasions was in fact not a symposium at all, but a welcome meeting for poet and wartime culture czar Guo Moruo held in Guangzhou's Changti Youth Hall on 8 December 1937 and attended by a crowd of one to two thousand (Huang and Chen 1985, 2: 1348). The large turnout was certainly due to Guo's celebrity status rather than the opportunity to hear new poetry recitation. For Pu, however, his recitation at the meeting was an affair of no small import, as we detect from his brief but telling discussion of the event in his diary.

Pu opened the meeting by delivering his poem "Welcome Address" (Huanying ci), while his colleague Lei Shiyu concluded the event with another, unnamed, poem. According to Pu, Lei's performance, overshadowed by Guo's speech just before it, "failed absolutely." As for his own recitation, Pu remarks:

> Naturally, I can't say for sure how successful it was. But it does, I believe, represent epoch-making progress in the new poetry recitation movement. I don't think anyone has ever raised his voice so loudly while reading a vernacular poem, and this time with such enthusiasm.
>
> Consequently, when I'd finished, quite a number of people applauded. This is clear proof that in the future the movement can develop with great strides. (Huang and Chen 1985, 2: 1349)

Pu's brief account provides little in the way of precise detail. How many people applauded? Just how loudly did he raise his voice? Was he able, or did he try, to correct his Hakka accent? The reader is left guessing. One does, however, sense quite clearly Pu's forced tone of poetic bravado, not only during his high-volume performance, but also afterwards, in the optimism stubbornly written into his self-review. It is a bravado that speaks less to any initial success of new poetry recitation than to the fragility of the human voice when asked to bear the grand, salvational ideals of the performed poem.

It was indeed this pressure to produce a poetic voice as heroic as the national wartime cause itself that led Pu to make such an evasive self-appraisal. For poets like

Pu Feng, Li Lei, and many others, poetry had to be "in harmony with the epoch, connected with the life of the masses, and in step with the War of Resistance" (Zang Kejia 1938a). The reciter's voice, as we saw in Gao Lan's early wartime poetry, was to resound with militant clarity and pyrotechnic intensity, or, as one of Pu Feng's associates described it, to resound like a "steel trumpet" that "arouses a sky-trembling roar" (Ma 1937, 8). At the same time, however, and as we saw in the performances of "Weeping for Lost Sufei," the emotions evoked during a recitation, especially among performers new to this fledgling art, could tip toward teary emotional collapse as easily as righteous fury, with neither necessarily exerting a desired effect on the audience. During wartime this issue of vocal sound and emotive quality figured most significantly during one common ceremonial occasion for poetry performance: the memorial service for deceased comrades. Records for two of these occasions, one in Guangzhou in January 1938 and the other in Hankou—one of the three cities comprising Wuhan—in October 1937, illustrate how recitational emotion was split between these two modes.

On the morning of 13 January 1938, about a month after Guo Moruo's visit to Guangzhou, Pu Feng and several poetic cohorts trekked up a hill studded with antiaircraft gun emplacements to commemorate the one-year anniversary of the loss of their friend and poet Wen Liu, who had died at the hands of an incompetent doctor after treatment for a fish bone caught in his throat (Zhongguo shitan 1938, 4). The hike to the gravesite was long—five miles each way—and very nearly aborted by plainclothes military personnel stationed along the route. The recital, however, was brief. At ten past ten o'clock a.m., with Pu Feng acting as master of ceremonies, the poets lined up facing the photograph of Wen Liu they had placed beside his grave, performed the customary three ceremonial bows, and began to read their work. After Pu read two of his poems, Huang Ningying then began to recite his "Wen Liu, the Motherland Cries out for You!" (Wen Liu, zuguo huzhao ni!). Midway through the poem, however, Huang and another poet became choked up with grief, leaving Huang barely able to continue his reading. Acting quickly, Pu—author of such poetry collections as Songs of Steel (Gangtie de gechang) and himself a declared practitioner of poetic Stakhanovism—cut short the recitation ceremony as soon as Huang brought his poem haltingly to a close. "Really," he remarks in his diary, "this is hardly a time to be shedding tears!" (Huang and Chen 1985, 2: 1377).

Pu's reaction to Huang's reading—or more accurately, the reaction he creates for himself in his diary writing—represents an attempt to control the emotional boundaries of wartime recitation. Feeling that Huang's display of personal emotion violated a militant aesthetics of wartime poetic performance, Pu ended the ceremony rather than let it devolve into maudlin expressions of individual grief. We get a fuller sense of his motivation for curtailing the graveside recitation when we look at the structure of Huang's poem, which in fact breaks these two registers of feeling into two stanzas. In the first stanza Huang details his own experience of losing a friend:

> I have pressed your photograph
> Close against my scorching hot body,
> Hoping to deliver to you a thread of warmth;
> I have violently slapped myself on the face,
> Hoping to shatter this illusory dream of life
> So that I might see you again when I wake.
> And yet, a year, oh, a year!
> I have found no way to shrink this distance between us.
> God saddens the past into clouds and mist,
> And lets them grow into cruel memories:
> Wen Liu—your dear name
> Shall forever swell in my heart!
>
> (Ningying 1938, 4)

In the second stanza the poem modulates to the grander sentiment of national crisis:

> But now, yet more cruel,
> The Motherland under heavy, heavy oppression
> Turns on its head, and with flesh and blood
> Creates a tremendous history.
> But, you, Wen Liu, Wen Liu!
> You, the pure son of new China,
> You, the beautiful flag of new China,
> You, the great pulse of new China,
> You, the courageous combatant of new China,
> When the Motherland needs you
> As it needs a leonine warrior,
> You sleep silently in the earth!
> Wen Liu—this sacred name of yours.
> We summon you,
> The Motherland summons you!
>
> (Ningying 1938, 4)

From the first to the second stanza, Huang's poem moves from the personal to the national, from attempts to overcome individual loss to the broad, collective project of resisting the loss of a national homeland. Coming halfway through the recitation, Huang's outburst of grief drew such a stern response from Pu because it represented interference of the personal, emotive voice of expression with the aesthetics of voice deemed suitable to the grand historical urgency of the poem's second stanza. Huang's performance crosses an invisible border of political sentiment, a transgression salvageable only by the imposition of silence.

* * *

At about same time as Pu Feng and the China Poetry Forum poets were promoting recitation in Guangzhou, farther north in Wuhan a much larger collectivity of poets and writers were pursuing poetry recitation on a larger scale. For a period of about a year, war and mass mobilization turned this prosperous center of trade and industry into what historian Stephen R. Mackinnon describes as "a laboratory for experiments in cultural change" (2008, 63). The relaxation of media control that marked this particular moment allowed a temporary blossoming of activity in the undertakings of music, drama, publishing, broadcasting, and, of course, poetry. It was in Wuhan that poetry recitation became a significant feature of wartime literary culture. New poetry specifically written for recitation was heard on radio broadcasts, seen in a number of journals and newspaper literary supplements, and experienced live at large literary gatherings.[2] Drama and film actors turned their talents to public poetry reading, and a set of recitation celebrities, including Gao Lan, started to gain recognition.

Wuhan also had the distinction of hosting the first large-scale public poetry recital of the war: the Lu Xun One-Year Memorial Meeting held in October 1937. Attended by several hundred people and chaired by Lu Xun's self-appointed successor, Hu Feng, the ceremonial gathering took place at Hankou's Wuzu Street YMCA. Those reciting included Ke Zhongping who, as we shall see later, brought the art of recitation to the Communist stronghold of Yan'an, as well as the actress Wang Ying.

A review of the ceremony's poetry recitals written by Mu Mutian, one of the founders of the leftist China Poetry Society five years before, further elaborates the sort of aesthetic regimentation of voice we saw in Pu Feng's diary entry. Mu compares Ke's and Wang's performances. The former he describes as a "resounding song" (yinhang gaoge), "a harmonious unity of bodily gesture, passion, and voice" which "arouses our heartfelt sorrow, thrills us, and irresistibly draws us along with Mr. Ke Zhongping to energize our march forward to destroy our national enemy, Japanese imperialism" (Mu 1987, 34–35).[3] The performance of the Gao Lan poem "Our Memorial" (Women de jili), however, receives a quite different appraisal: "Aside from hearing 'tears,' 'horizon' and suchlike words, I detected the plaintive warbling of orioles and swallows. Not at all did it arouse the mad thrill of poetry, nor from that performance did I experience the sorrow of mourning. What I did feel was tediousness as I waited impatiently for the performer to wrap things up" (34). Although he doesn't mention her by name in the article, Mu's criticism is clearly directed at Wang Ying, the only other person to recite at the meeting. We note, too, that Mu directs his critique at recitational style only, not the poem itself. In the same article, which in fact promotes Gao Lan's recitation poetry, Mu makes a point of praising "Our Memorial" as a text "free of pessimistic sentimentalism," and "mournful but not gloomy, making the very most of its positive effect" (36–37). His assessment, then, is leveled specifically at correcting not the content or form of a written poem but its live, vocal performance. Like Li Lei and Pu Feng, Mu insists upon a masculinist, high-volume, heroically expansive recitational style. By opposing these two modes of vocal expression, Mu regiments the sound aesthetics of new poetry recitation in much the same manner as Pu Feng did at Wen Liu's memorial. Both Pu and Mu attempt to institute a politics of significant sound by suppressing a "soft" aesthetics of the poetic voice in favor of a sound quality ostensibly more attuned to evoking the sort of shared presence required by the historical context of a nation at war.

Mu's was not the only reaction to this particular event, however. Writing several years later, the editor of the literary supplement *Battle Line* and patron of recitation, Chen Jiying, takes a more balanced view of the sound aesthetics of recitation. While granting that Ke Zhongping's performance was "quite moving," Chen also portrays Wang's reading in a very positive light as "sweetly agreeable [*wanzhuan*], expressing in full the author's original meaning, and receiving no small praise" (Chen 1941). By affirming Wang's performance, Chen takes a position quite different from Mu's: that recited poetry need not rely on a militant aesthetic of hardness to exercise emotional affect, but can just as viably create a more restrained evocation of feeling.

The divergent commentary on the performance of Gao's poem reflects not only the unsettled question of the vocal aesthetics of wartime recitation but a desire on the part of the movement's participants to mold poetry recitation into a viable art. Especially at this early stage of the war, poets were time and again made aware of the inconsistent results achieved in performances of new poetry. Several more large-scale recitations held in Hankou before the city fell to the Japanese illustrate this perceived deficiency. One was a combined music and recitation event at the Guangming Theater, whose participants included Mu Mutian, the female writer Xiao Hong, and poet Jiang Xijin. Recalling the poetry segments of the program, Chen Jiying rather evasively remarks that, "due to the mixed composition of the participants, the materials recited were not the sort that the average person would find acceptable, and the response was uneven" (Chen 1941). Also in Hankou, several poets took the floor during a lavish banquet held at a restaurant. The purpose of this particular gathering was for established poets and writers to judge poems written by students of the Fifth Military Region Youth Training Squad, one of many cultural work teams that ventured into the field to advance the wartime propaganda effort.[4] The proposed highlight of the meeting was a group recitation of Pushkin's narrative poem "The Gypsies," performed by the city's emerging celebrities of new poetry recitation, Gao Lan, Wang Ying, and Jiang Xijin. In Gao's recollection, the recitation program was added at the last minute and as a consequence suffered from a lack of preparation (Gao 1987d, 18–19).

Rural Recitation and Countryside Cosmopolitanism

Seated prominently among those attending this very same banquet was the established poet Zang Kejia. Zang was in fact leader of the Youth Training Squad, which owed its existence largely to his personal connections with the regional militarist General Li Zongren (Zang 1982, 136). While the Japanese closed in on Hankou in the summer of 1938, Zang was in the field leading a group of thirteen "soldiers of the arts and literature" (wenyi bing) on a cultural tour of duty near the front lines.

"One mouth,/two hands,/our weapons/the pens we hold." Written by Zang in the mountains near Shangcheng on 27 August 1938 to the accompaniment of "continuous machine-gun fire," these lines from the poem "We Fourteen" (Women zhe shisi ge) suggest the adverse conditions under which these poets worked, as well as the heroic aura with which they often illumined themselves for the public eye (Zang 1938b, 420–421). There can be no doubt that Zang and his thirteen comrades encountered considerable practical difficulties, personal trauma, and even life-threatening dangers while trekking through the hinterlands of Anhui, Henan, and Hubei. However, Zang's depictions of his field propaganda work, and in particular the idea that his group "recited poetry on a number of grand occasions," requires some qualification (Zang 1989, 334).

Just what the phrase "grand occasion" could mean in the wartime discourse on poetry recitation becomes clearer when we take a closer look at the record Zang has left of these field performances. While the squad did make sincere and inventive attempts to use spoken poetry as a means of introducing national consciousness into the countryside, we find that even deep in the rural hinterland, poetry recitation found its best audience within the more circumscribed intersubjective space of the poets themselves. This is not to say that Zang and his group did not rise to the challenge of adapting and deploying recited poetry to the forbidding cultural terrain of the Chinese backcountry. Rather, we find that where they truly excelled was in wholesale relocation of their own familiar, urban culture of poetry into the unfamiliar spaces of rural China.

Before looking at how these poets transferred their cosmopolitanism to the

countryside, it should be noted that new poetry recitation was one of many perfor-
mance forms the squad deployed during their tour of duty. Zang and his comrades
applied most of their creative energy not to reciting poetry but to performing street
plays, singing patriotic songs, and posting slogans. When they did recite, it was on
very specific occasions. For instance, in the city of Huangchuan in southern Henan,
the squad members performed several poems, but found their ragtag bunch hope-
lessly upstaged by the simultaneous presence in town of the star-studded Shanghai
Number Two Salvation Drama Troupe. Elsewhere, at a gathering of troops headed
for the front, squad member Zou Difan delivered an impassioned reading of his
poem "Tonight We Cross the Zhang River" (Jinye, women duguo Zhanghe) using
the local Hubei dialect. In the idyllic but desperately poor western Hubei town of
Junxian the squad encountered a group of refugee middle-school students from
Shandong, for whom Zang recited in his native Shandongese a poem written spe-
cifically for the occasion, "Hometown Accent" (Xiangyin; Zang 1982, 139-142).[5]

Such events suggest that poetry recitation, like most forms of rural cultural work
in the nonoccupied regions early in the war, was an improvisatory and unpredict-
able affair. As Zang Kejia put it, poets in the field penciled their poems in tattered
notebooks resting on one knee and vowed to perform them "at every opportunity"
(Zang 1938a). Such opportunities, however, were not naturally forthcoming. Before
performing in the countryside, Zang's squad typically had to bang gongs or hawk
candy to draw a crowd, and at times a good portion of the audience was composed
of local militia ordered to attend by their superior officers (Zang 1989, 334).[6] In
some cases, too, recitation poetry was conspicuous by its absence from the squad's
performance programs of street plays, songs, and lectures—a necessary concession
to Chinese villagers' utter lack of exposure to new poetry, not to mention its recita-
tion, which they referred to as "drama without costumes" (bu huazhuang de xi; Gao
1987c, 9). Despite these practical difficulties—or, perhaps more accurately, because
of them—even in the isolation of the mountainous backcountry poets created occa-
sions for recitation by holding impromptu literary symposia.

The most striking, though hardly surprising, feature of the squad's cultural
fieldwork is that they appeared to be much more at home organizing rural repro-
ductions of urban literary symposia than when attempting through poetry to instill
national awareness in rural dwellers. Zang's account of a recital held in Shangcheng
well illustrates this centripetal tendency. While stationed in this temporary cultural
base camp lying near the intersection of the Hubei, Anhui, and Henan borders,
the squad first convened a preparatory meeting in a tea pavilion on the riverbank
outside of town. After a round of speeches and debate, they drafted a conference
agenda, which was then printed in booklet form along with several poems. The rally
itself began the next day at seven o'clock in the evening in a small courtyard filled
to capacity with "youths, lovers of literature and the arts, both men and women,"

who gazed at the freshly printed booklets "as if at some mysterious object." The chairperson opened with a recited poem, to which the assembled educated youth listened as they cracked melon seeds in their teeth and sipped tea. The participants then joined into an at times heated point-by-point discussion of the items on the agenda: (1) "Poetry—Bugle of the War of Resistance"; (2) the form and content of recited poetry; (3) the difference between recitation poetry and the traditional forms of mountain songs (*shan'ge*), folk songs (*minyao*), drum songs (*guci*), and ditties (*xiaodiao*); (4) methods of poetry recitation; (5) how to promote the poetry recitation movement. The gathering concluded with several of the attending poets reciting with "varying tone, demeanor, and diction." This finale to the recital, according to Zang, "caused everyone's hearts to thump wildly as their souls became intoxicated by poetry" (Zang 1938a).

Such hyperbolic descriptions of audience reaction to recited poetry, while surely exaggerated to a degree, also contain the unavoidable grain of truth that such poetry was still very much by and for an intellectual audience. The collective effervescence Zang depicts is limited to a small, receptive, and self-selected audience of new poetry enthusiasts taking part in the carefully orchestrated, almost ritualistic form of the literary symposium. It is interesting to note, too, that among the resolutions reached during the several hours of debate and discussion were the conflicting positions that "the recitation of poetry is a bridge for approaching the masses" and "recitation poetry possesses its own special character" and thus should not be mixed with traditional forms of oral entertainment—precisely the sort of bridge the "masses" could appreciate. It would seem that, for these poets, the desire to communicate with the wartime populace ran up against their own unwillingness to compromise their proprietary claims to the genre of new poetry. Like Pu Feng, who hopefully looked to the future when appraising the dubious effect of his welcoming recitation for Guo Moruo, Zang and his comrades could in the end only agree on the necessity of waiting until this "new form" of poetry became "established" (*jianli*; Zang 1938a). Precisely what this form would be, however, none could say for sure. Elsewhere in China debate and often quite painful experimentation continued.

Poetry Recitation and Communist Culture at Yan'an

New poetry recitation came to the Chinese Communist stronghold of Yan'an in late 1937 with Ke Zhongping's arrival from Wuhan and his subsequent election as head of Yan'an's first formal literary association, the War Song Society (Zhan'ge she). Though better known for its later promotion of street poetry, the War Song Society directed its initial efforts toward poetry recitation. Evening meetings during the first month of the society's existence all included recitation, and a brief recitation program during a meeting to commemorate the 9 December 1935 student protest movement apparently met with some success (Sha et al. 1987, 68). However, a recitation some weeks later by Ke Zhongping at the Shaanxi Commune New Year's Eve Party fell decidedly flat. According to one commentator, Ke's intonation resembled less poetry than a speech by French Communist Party leader Marcel Cachin. In his own critique, Ke chastised himself for switching arbitrarily between singing and a dry lecture-like delivery, and for covering lapses in memory by "emitting odd sounds, awkward laughs, and notes drawn out for an unnecessarily long time" (Xue et al. 1938, 263). Notwithstanding these shaky foundations, by January 1938 Ke and his poetic cohort felt confident enough to stage Yan'an's first public recitation performance, the Evening of Poetry and Folk Song (Shige min'ge yanchang wanhui).

The January 26 Evening was the largest and most fully documented of the over twenty recitation performances subsequently held in Yan'an. It bears mention, however, that the record we have of this particular event comes to us in a genre destined for notoriety in Chinese Communist culture—that of self-criticism; for the January Evening, as its organizers publicly admitted in the Hankou journal *Battleground* (*Zhandi*), was "unanimously recognized as a failure," "the most dismal evening of entertainment in Yan'an during these past several months" (Sha et al. 1987, 68). When reviewing the account of this ill-fated poetic venture, we are reminded of just how precarious and immature recitation as a performance art was at the time, as well as how difficult—perhaps impossible—was the task of converting new poetry into a mass art form.

The Yan'an Evening may well have been doomed from the start by the elements. Because it was held in the middle of the north China winter in an auditorium with unpapered windows, the poets and vocalists who took the stage had to struggle to make themselves heard over the sound of audience members stamping their feet to keep warm. Exacerbating the audience's discomfort was the length of the performance. The program comprised too many acts, among which the least enjoyable were reportedly the folk songs. These were rendered with grinding monotony by amateur singers, many of whom appended verbose introductory statements that, in Ke Zhongping's words, "drove to exasperation those sitting on the cold benches" (Sha et al. 1987, 67). As for the featured portion of the performance, new poetry recitation, Ke blames its failure upon the "people's" (*renmin*) lack of interest in new poetry, a problem he links to a predicament of poetic diction. According to Ke, the language of the new poetry they performed suffered from being insufficiently "massified" (*dazhonghua*), and yet where this poetry did employ "mass" language, it failed to be "poetic" (*shi de*). The ability to incorporate the "melody of the masses," he adds, is something "we have yet to achieve" (65).

Leaving aside the question of how many bona fide members of the masses did in fact attend what was most likely an affair by and for the Yan'an intellectual cohort, the critique of the Evening illustrates well the desire to differentiate poetry recitation from other performance genres by framing it as an art of pure expressive sound untainted by the disruptive excess of visual "noise." We see this attempt at generic regimentation most clearly in criticism of the performers' tendency to blur the line between drama and recitation. According to Sha Kefu, himself an accomplished musician and singer, the reciters "placed too much emphasis on action and posturing, and too little on clear and lively recitation itself." To make his point, Sha singles out one performer who "rushed about the stage as if acting in a one-man play" (65–66). Recitation, both Sha and Ke insist, is primarily an "art of the voice" (*shengyin yishu*). Thus the performers are offered the following set of recommendations, with parenthetical commentary suggesting the nature of their excesses: "During performance the reciter can, according to the feeling communicated by the material recited, in a natural manner (don't exaggerate!) convey a full range of emotions using facial expressions. Hand gestures may be used as well (don't overdo it!). But this does not mean that recitation absolutely must involve action and posturing. When reciting we should avoid unnecessary, and in particular unnatural, expressions and movements" (67).

The War Song Society had distributed a total of three hundred tickets for the event. About two hundred people showed up for the performance, and by curtain's close more than half of these had drifted out the door. "It was a failure," writes Ke Zhongping, "but there were some bright spots: (1) Chairman Mao stayed until the very end. This left us feeling, even in our deep mortification, that we must in the future strive hard. (2) This was the first time that folk song and new poetry were performed together. . . . (3) By following the program through to completion we demonstrated our enthusiasm, sincerity, and perseverance" (Sha et al. 1987, 67).

Despite such hopeful declarations of future commitment, poetry recitation never developed into a major performance genre in Yan'an. And indeed, if Mao *had* left the Evening early, recitation might eventually have been excised altogether from the Chinese Communist cultural repertoire. In any event, poets continued to recite their own and others' works in the following years, and Guang Weiran, as we recall from Chapter 3, included recitation in the libretto to what was to become a classic of the official Chinese Communist repertoire, *Yellow River Cantata*. Through the next several years at Yan'an, recitation continued to be listed along with street poetry as a mass art form, but due perhaps to its inauspicious beginnings, the performance of new poetry seems never to have moved beyond the role of sideline entertainment at the Communist base's frequent weekend cultural soirees. More institutionalized performance genres, such as drama and music, both formally taught at Yan'an's Lu Xun Academy of Art and Literature, rapidly overtook recitation in popularity. Later, after Mao's political rectification campaign and the literary strictures imposed by his infamous "Talks on the Arts and Literature" of 1942, even these "westernized" genres of music and spoken drama had themselves to make room for the politically revamped peasant music, dance, and drama, known as "new rice sprout songs" (*xin yangge*), which dominated cultural policy in Yan'an from late 1942 onward (Ai Ke'en 1987; Holm 1991).

Shanghai's Solitary Island and the Rank and File Society

With the exception of Pu Feng, who rarely stayed long in one place after join-ing the military in 1938, the spread of poetry recitation during the war tended to follow the dispersal of its practitioners from their original point of concentration in Wuhan. Ke Zhongping's arrival in Yan'an in late 1937 was instrumental in the introduction of recitation to China's northwestern "liberated region" (*jiefang qu*). Gao Lan, as will be discussed, made his way from Wuhan, through Changsha and Guilin, to Chongqing, where for a time he became a well-known poet and per-former in the wartime provisional capital.

Jiang Xijin, who wrote poems and poetic commentary under the name Xi Jin, left Wuhan, first going to Guangzhou and then to Solitary Island (Gudao), the foreign-administered concessions of Shanghai that remained a neutral zone off-limits to the Japanese until the outbreak of the Pacific War in December 1941. Jiang began his literary career as editor for several journals while working in the Hubei Province Department of Finance in the mid-1930s. With the arrival of the War of Resistance, he became one of the most prolific proponents of poetry recitation, founding the journal *Tunes of the Times* (*Shidiao*) with colleague Mu Mutian, taking part in several early recitals in Wuhan, and writing frequently on the aims and activities of what was then called the "poetry recitation movement." His leftist bent was also typical of recitation activists; he joined the Chinese Communist Party in 1938. In the relatively safe haven of Shanghai, Jiang helped to organize the Shang-hai Poetry Symposium (Shanghai shige zuotanhui), later expanded into the Rank and File Society after the title of its twice-monthly journal, *Rank and File* (*Hanglie*), which published six issues from January to March 1940 (Shu 1941, 17).[7]

Like their forerunners in Guangzhou and Yan'an, the Rank and File Society poets first experimented with recitation at their regular meetings. The dozen or so members typically in attendance would read aloud their own poems as well as those submitted to the journal, comment on one another's work, and experiment with new methods of recitation (Shu 1941, 16; Hanglie 1940, 24). Unlike the War Song Society poets, and perhaps cautioned by the published reports of failed recitations at Yan'an and elsewhere, the Shanghai poets thoroughly prepared for their first major performance. After deciding to hold a public recitation in late 1939, the members spent four or five months selecting, adapting, and reading their poems aloud. During the final month "nearly everyone in the Rank and File immersed themselves in recitation" (Shu 1941, 20).

The Grand Poetry Recital (Shige langsong dahui), the first of its kind in Shanghai, began at two o'clock in the afternoon on 31 March 1940 in a YWCA assembly hall with a capacity of about 150 (Shu 1941, 20). To the organizers' delight, not only did the tickets sell out, but even more people, including two representatives of the Shanghai Municipal Police, demanded they be admitted to stand in the aisle. The Rank and File poets had not been optimistic about their event's reception by the public. During the planning stage they had seriously considered eliminating an intermission, fearing that the audience might take advantage of the recess to slip out early. One also detects a lack of self-assurance in the recital's "Opening Remarks," printed on the program and delivered to the crowd by female society member Guan Lu. These warned the audience that "this poetry recitation may perhaps disappoint you; although we have done our best to prepare through practice and revision, we are still exploring our way forward, and it will surely be some time before we can achieve perfection" (Shu 1941, 21–22).

Despite the poets' very real expectation of failure, the Grand Recital turned out to be an unqualified success. Intensive preparation no doubt contributed to the positive reception, as did the relative literary sophistication of a Shanghai audience whose tastes the performers could anticipate. But even in the cosmopolitan context of Shanghai, the Rank and File Society poets tailored their poems quite specifically to local circumstances both in the use of dialect and in the poems' narrative content. The weight given to dialect can be seen in the ordering and proportioning of the poetry selections. The poets opened the program with a series of four dialect poems: the first two in Shanghainese, and the next in Shaoxing and Shantou dialects. Of the fourteen poems recited during the event, only half were delivered in Mandarin. Four of these were original works by society members, another Ai Qing's well-known "My Wet Nurse, Da Yanhe." Two additional poems were translations: Armenian poet Siamanto's "Song of the Riders" and Qu Qiubai's translation of Pushkin's "The Gypsies," the latter performed by a group of five as the afternoon's culminating act. Four choral performances of patriotic songs were included as well, two each in the first and second halves of the program (Shu 1941, 21–22).

Local appeal figured most strongly in the stories some of these poems told. Typical in this respect was Zhu Weiji's "We Will Not Endure This" (Women bu yao rennai), a 250-line narrative poem, performed in Shanghainese, that details the drama, desperation, and hysteria of urbanites queued up to purchase a limited supply of discounted flour:

Faster and faster the queue-cutters
Charged to the front of the line:
. . . .
I saw the gendarmes rushing busily about,
Truncheons flailing harder and harder,

The most industrious among them the foreign cops, of course;
Those Chinese should have been spared such added agony.
They had to curl themselves into balls
Or cover their heads,
While struggling desperately to keep their places.
Someone near me said:
"They're here with cash in hand,
Not to rob the goods,
Yet now they're taking it in the neck,
Made to look like common criminals!"

(Zhu Weiji 1940, 35)

When read in Shanghainese, Zhu's eyewitness description of everyday life on the streets of wartime Shanghai certainly struck a chord with the local populace. Poet Han Bai's ninety-four-line "Death of Old Wang" (Lao Wang de si), also performed in Shanghainese, recounts the story of an office worker martyred during a labor protest. Mortally wounded by armed thugs and the factory boss' attack dogs, Old Wang collapses after coughing up blood in front of his family and coworkers, but not before silently and with shaking hand designating them the inheritors of the struggle. Han concludes:

This bloodstained truth, this bloodstained lesson
Cuts deeply into the tiny hearts of the children,
Their little eyeballs bulging, little fists clenched,
They know the road to take!

(Han 1940, 15)

According to Jiang Xijin, the recital engaged even the attention of these would-be youthful inheritors: several young children in the audience reportedly remained quiet throughout the entire performance. But even more gratifying was the reaction of a different listener. Jiang writes that the poets were "especially pleased to find a blind gentleman in the audience. When he came in on the arm of a child, the performers all agreed that no matter what, we had to make sure he understood us. As he listened his facial expressions changed along with the recitation . . ." (Shu 1941, 22). Jiang's special attention to this scene, a curious inversion of the classic trope of the sighted audience enthralled by the blind bard, suggests the pleasure that he and his comrades felt at mobilizing new poetry as the spoken word. To see—or even only to imagine seeing—their poems' emotional content registered on the face of a blind man represented the fulfillment, if only for an afternoon, of the desire to create a performance genre inspired by the emotive voice of national awareness.

The Rank and File Society held two more recitals in 1940—one to celebrate the late Lu Xun's sixtieth birthday, and another at a play in commemoration of Maxim Gorky. Neither measured up to their remarkable debut. Yet the very impact of the poems performed at the Grand Recital may have been responsible for a major set-back in their activities. Zhu Weiji and Han Bai's narrative poems in Shanghainese, as well as several others explicitly designed to encourage activism against corruption and injustice, seem to have brought their work to the attention of the British colonial authorities. Not long after the 31 March performance, the editors of *Rank and File* were escorted to the Special Branch of the Criminal Investigation Department, where Superintendent R. W. Yorke interrogated them about the content of their published poems (provided to Yorke in English translation). The journal's official registration was subsequently revoked, and the Rank and File Society, so to speak, lost its poetic license (Shu 1941, 17).

Recitation in Chongqing: Gao Lan and the Poetry Recitation Team

A third poet of recitation to depart from Hankou was Gao Lan. Born Guo Dehao in Manchuria in 1909 to a Han Chinese father and a Daur minority mother, Gao Lan attended middle school in Heilongjiang Province and Beijing before entering the Chinese department at Yanjing University in 1928. On the strength of recommendations from his mentor, the writer and scholar Guo Shaoyu, Gao found work in 1932 teaching middle school, first in Tianjin and several years later in Hankou, where the war overtook him in July 1937. Nineteen thirty-seven was also the year Gao devised his pen name. Having just completed a eulogistic poem to Tian Zhaoying, a war hero killed in Manchuria while fighting the Japanese, Gao reportedly looked up from his desk at a photo commemorating a meeting in Moscow of his two literary idols, Maxim Gorky and Romain Rolland. In a moment of inspiration, he borrowed the first syllable of the Russian author's sinified surname (*Gaoer-ji*) and the final syllable of the French author's (Luoman Luo*lan*) to create the nom de plume under which his subsequent poems appeared (Niu 1988, 154–156).

As a middle-school teacher in Hankou in 1936 and 1937, Gao had been actively involved in organizing student cultural resistance drama and poetry recitation even before that city became the first major wartime cultural center. Although he continued to be active in the wartime drama effort, Gao became best known for the writing and performance of recitation poetry. His poetic work appeared in print in the Wuhan literary supplements and journals, and, as mentioned above, in public performance at literary gatherings and on radio. His first poetry collection, *Gao Lan's Recitation Poems* (Gao Lan langsongshi ji) appeared in February 1938 in Hankou in response to letters from propaganda workers asking for an inexpensive volume of recitation poems they could carry with them on their tours of duty (Chen Jiying 1987, 33).

Following the evacuation of Wuhan in November 1938, Gao traveled overland for two months in the company of students and teachers through Hunan, Guizhou, and Guangxi to the wartime capital of Chongqing (Niu 1988, 157). Once again among China's displaced cultural elite, Gao regularly performed his poetry and eventually participated in the most significant attempt to institutionalize wartime poetry recitation, the creation of the Poetry Recitation Team. Before turning to the formation of that ambitious but short-lived organization, a review of Gao's involvement in literary activities provides some background to new poetry recitation as promoted in Chongqing. Following Gao's path through the city's poetry scene, we find among other things that recitation survived these middle years of the war largely through a process of institutionalization, specifically, the patronage of newspaper publishers and the support of ACRAWA.

Gao acquired his connection to journalism circles through the liberal-leaning *L'Impartial*'s wartime literary supplement *Battle Line*, which had been transferred from Wuhan and was still edited by the poet, journalist, and fellow refugee from Manchuria, Chen Jiying. The editorial relationship between Gao and Chen had in fact begun more than a year before the move to Chongqing. Impressed by Gao's poems and by the amount of positive feedback from *Battle Line* readers in Wuhan, Chen frequently published Gao's poetry and encouraged him to produce his first poetry collection (Chen 1987, 33). Shortly after Gao arrived in Chongqing from Hankou in January 1939, Chen invited Gao to provide the featured entertainment at a banquet *L'Impartial* was holding for *Battle Line*'s contributors and readers. Gao accepted the offer and, on the morning before the event, Chen advised him in a mentoring tone, "Today try not to go running about, don't talk too much, take an afternoon nap, and don't eat too much at dinner. Put all your energy into reciting" (Gao 1942).

Although rather intimidated by the prospect of appearing before a gathering of about forty cultural luminaries, Gao summoned his courage, took the floor, and delivered "My Home Is in Heilongjiang" (Wo de jia zai Heilongjiang), his over 300-line paean to the year-long cycle of robust folkways of his hometown on the banks of the Amur River and to the Manchurian resistance against Japanese invasion (Gao 1940, 23–33). Under the straitened conditions of wartime, electrical amplification was out of the question, making the public performance of this mini-epic a demanding task both mentally and physically. Recitations of the poem would frequently leave Gao breathless, hoarse, sweating at the brow, and hard-pressed to summon the reserves of strength needed for the final stanza's climactic, high-volume sloganeering (Gao 1987b, 144):

The Great War of Resistance!
The Sacred War of Resistance!

The blood of 450 million,
Redden the far-off snow and frost,
Redden my home—Heilongjiang!
(Gao 1940, 33)

To Gao's—and perhaps even more so, Chen's—dismay, the conclusion of the performance was met with a long, awkward silence, as if the crowd "had somehow been suffocated." The listeners did, however, eventually recover, and Gao left the banquet in a flurry of congratulatory handshakes, constructive criticism, and exchanges of address (Gao 1942).

A short five days later, Chen again contacted Gao, this time with the news that word of Gao's earlier performance had reached the celebrated editor of *L'Impartial*, Zhang Jiluan, and that Chen had already arranged another banquet recitation for Zhang and other *L'Impartial* employees. This time Gao recruited two friends for support: the Soviet-trained songwriter, poetess, and dramatist An E and the novelist, reportage writer, and fellow Manchurian Li Huiying. The trio performed three poems at this gathering, including an encore rendering of the grueling "Heilongjiang." The performance came off well enough, but most gratifying to Gao, who seems to have harbored genuine self-doubt concerning the actual appeal of recited new poetry to anyone besides other new poets, was the fact that Zhang Jiluan himself candidly admitted to reading aloud Gao's poems in private (Gao 1942).

While Gao's first appearances in Chongqing certainly helped consolidate his notoriety as a willing performer, in the following several years the security of his regular employment as a middle-school instructor began to crumble. Twice he was dismissed from work on suspicion of encouraging student activism, leaving him by the autumn of 1940 employed as a clerk in a dairy factory—a less than prestigious occupation for a Beijing-trained man of letters (Niu 1988, 158). Chongqing had in the meantime become an established center for a diverse community of poets, actors, and musicians, many of whom had until then been leading propaganda work in the countryside. Like the smaller enclaves of new poets in wartime Guangzhou, Yan'an, and Shanghai, these artists began integrating recitation into their regular symposia as interest in performed poetry experienced something of a revival in the spring of 1940. An evening literary symposium held in March of that year included recitations by the celebrated writer Lao She, poet Chang Renxia, Gao Lan, and Guang Weiran, who performed a portion of his *Yellow River Cantata*. In April 1940, the city also hosted a memorial meeting to mark the tenth anniversary of Mayakovsky's death, chaired by Hu Feng and featuring a number of recited poems (Chen Jiying 1941; Chen Mingshu 1994, 2, 356). Having perhaps heard of the success of the Rank and File Society recitation in February of that year, Gao and other poets in Chongqing met in the first half of 1940 to draw up plans for organizing a company of poets and other performing artists to stage regular public recitations in the city and surrounding countryside. A lack of funds stymied these ambitions until Gao and his cohort managed to obtain 300 yuan from *L'Impartial* through the offices of the patron of new poetry recitation, Chen Jiying (Gao 1942). Chen himself had broached the idea of setting up a recitation study society and performance squad as early as 1937 in Hankou (Chen 1987, 32). Three years later these plans came to fruition with the founding of the Poetry Recitation Team.[8]

The team's four meetings in November and December 1940 brought together poets, dramatists, and musicians from all over China. The inaugural session, a gala event complete with refreshments, was held at the ACRAWA Cultural Work Committee headquarters at Tianguanfu No. 7 on the afternoon of 24 November (Jiang Guipu 1940). The approximately sixty people in attendance were for the most part members of film and dramatic circles (Zhanxian 1940).[9] A handful of the senior celebrities of wartime culture—Guo Moruo, Tian Han, Lao She, Ai Qing, and Feng Naichao—lent the event the requisite imprimatur of authority. Chen Jiying delivered the inaugural speech. With obligatory rhetorical flourish, he described the recitation movement over the past few years as "fanatical" among intellectuals and the common folk, and the founding of the Poetry Recitation Team as "marking a new epoch in the history of Chinese culture." The purpose of the team, Chen stressed, was "not only to expand the domain of poetry to every level and bring to life dead Chinese poetry, but also to promote poetry writing through recitation, and by means of poetry written to be recited, to train countless recitation experts" (Chen Jiying 1940). After a series of reports from the attendees, the drawing up of organizational regulations, and the nomination of a seven-member executive council, the meeting closed with impromptu recitations of new and classical poetry (the latter performed by Guo Moruo, who had spent the ten years before 1937 in Japan), as well as Beijing opera and Russian folk tunes (Jiang Guipu 1940).

The team set to work in earnest over the course of three smaller meetings held in December. At the first of these, a fellowship meeting attended by about forty people, the newly selected committee members presented three-month plans for the team while other participants reported on regional recitation activities, including recitation in the Soviet Union. A "recitation practicum" a week later comprised a series of in-house recitations and critiques covering solo recitation (*dusong*) as well as the more experimental forms of dialogue recitation (*duisong*), recitation by turn (*lunsong*), and group recitation (*hesong*). On the evening of 20 December the team held a three-hour symposium during which various poets and musicians aired their views on poetry recitation's function, technique, stage presentation, relationship to music, difference from the practice of old-style poetry chanting, and history in England (Langsong tongxun 1941, 147–149).

Headquarters for the operation were located in the third-floor meeting room of the ACRAWA offices at Tianguanfu. There team members collected and edited poems, held informal discussions, and mimeographed their periodical *Recitation Dispatch* (Langsong tongxun; Zang Yunyuan 1979, 75). By the end of 1940 the team was prepared to recruit and organize new members willing to work toward its chief goal: freeing recitation poetry from the intellectual circles in which it had been circumscribed and "reciting among the worker and peasant masses" (Gao 1987c, 9). At the time, according to Ren Jun writing some years later, some team members did "set out into the streets and the outlying areas of the city to carry out recitation" (Ren 1948, 161). The effort to bring poetry to the street, however, never had a chance to develop. Almost immediately after its founding, the team's attempts at public recitation were squelched by Guomindang authorities, who feared the arousal of mass dissent against their anti-Communist position (Gao 1987c, 9).[10]

Chengdu and Guilin: Cosmopolitanism, Communism, and Combativeness

The suppression of Chongqing's Poetry Recitation Team did not mean the end of poetry recitation during the war, but it did mark the period's last attempt to bring poetry to the masses in the interests of a wartime resistance movement. From 1941 onward, the pattern and motivation of poetry recitation in the cities of the non-Communist, unoccupied regions changed subtly but significantly. Instead of claiming to seek out a new audience among the masses, new poetry recitation developed in the context of annual festivals, commemorative meetings, and gala events organized by and for intellectual circles. At an ACRAWA symposium held in Chongqing in March 1940, for instance, the early summer Dragonboat Festival (Duanwu jie) celebrating the legendary Chinese poet Qu Yuan was declared Poet's Day (Shiren jie; Chen Mingshu 1994, 2, 382).[11] Similarly, in the years after 1940, the mid-April anniversary of Mayakovsky's death became an occasion for literary gatherings and poetry readings. An interesting though isolated exception to the practice of recitation at small literary gatherings was a public recitation of Gao Lan's 217-line poem "Decade" (Shinian) at a September 1941 Citizen's Rally held to commemorate the tenth anniversary of the Japanese invasion of Manchuria. The poem was read over loudspeakers to accompanying orchestral music and concluded with a blast of battle sounds and war drums (Gao 1987c, 14). Also, as in Wuhan several years before, new poetry recitation could be heard on radio broadcasts (Ren 1948, 161). For example, in December 1941, a trio recital of Fang Yin's "Ordinary Night Talk" (Pingfan de yehua) was transmitted by Chongqing's Central Broadcasting Station (Xinhua ribao 1941).[12]

But rallies and radio aside, by the later years of the war, poetry recitation was relegated to literary soirees catering to the cosmopolitan tastes of the modern literati. Poets trimmed their ambitions in part due to political suppression by agents of the Guomindang, but also because weariness of the extended war meant that they and their audience had even less patience for the histrionics of the early war years. As one critic wrote in a review of one of Gao Lan's poetry collections, "the instruments able to express the emotions of the War of Resistance are not limited to the monotonous bugle. . . . The poet should play stringed instruments, the violin, or woodwinds to express the full variety of feelings of the people during wartime" (Shi 1943). Recitals of these later war years consequently turned toward more purely literary performances. For instance, the modestly scaled Literature and Art Recital sponsored by the Chengdu branch of ACRAWA in May 1943 featured a program of decidedly highbrow material. Performers chose an eclectic range of texts, from scholarly essays on Chinese painting and German Romanticism to Zhang Tianyi's controversial short story "Mr. Hua Wei," a portion of a play by Sophocles, and of course poetry, including original verse recited by the authors, several poems by Lermontov, Shelley's "Ode to the West Wind," and excerpts from both Pushkin's *Eugene Onegin* and Housman's *A Shropshire Lad* (Kong 1943).

The demand for more variety, however, did not as a rule exclude politics from the agenda. Even as the poetic battle cries grew muted among poets in the Guomindang controlled regions of China, certain groups of intellectuals were lobbying for a political edge to their public poetry. One of these groups was the Guilin branch of ACRAWA, which began to sponsor a program of regular Saturday night recitations not quite a year after the Chengdu recitation. The in-depth review of the first two of these performances, published in the literary supplement to the Chongqing *New China Daily* (*Xinhua ribao*), suggests how certain of China's poets, guided by senior literati, were now steering recited poetry to the left and into the fold of Chinese Communist culture.

As for the city itself, wartime Guilin was no stranger to literary activity. During the six years between the fall of Wuhan and Guilin's evacuation during Japan's last-gasp offensive into Hunan and Guangxi in September 1944, the city earned the nickname Cultureville (*wenhua cheng*) both for the large number of refugee writers who had fled there and for the estimated 179 bookstores and publishing houses lining its streets (Cai 1994, 3; Laughlin 2008, 399–400). It was in this bibliophilic setting that poets initiated the city's first carefully planned and regularly scheduled recital, the Evening of Poetry Recitation (Shige langsong yehui). The inaugural performance, held on a Saturday night in April 1944, generated a festive atmosphere of "lively music, hot steaming tea, and friendly faces." No more than half an hour after the doors opened the hall was filled to capacity, and by the time the program began the entranceway was blocked by those who had arrived too late to get tickets. ACRAWA branch secretary Shao Quanlin delivered the customary introductory remarks, after which the performers took the floor to recite a total of seven poems. Under the watchful eyes of elder critics and Communist Party members Shao, Tian

Han, Zhou Gangming, and Meng Chao, a pair of actors from the New China Drama Society (Xin Zhongguo jushe) opened with a series of poems by the well-known poets and Yan'an veterans Ai Qing and He Qifang. An E then recited Pushkin's early romantic lyric "The Cossack," and several more poets recited works of their own, not named in the report. The program also included two folk songs. Tian, Zhou, and Meng then offered lengthy critiques of the performance as a whole. Tian in particular noted that, although the poems selected were all "healthy" (jiankang), there ought to have been more emphasis on "combativeness" (zhandouxing; Hai 1944).

The word "combativeness" should be read as a political code word in this context, and one whose meaning we can infer by comparing the second evening's program with the first. Three of the poems performed the first night—Ai Qing's "The Call of Dawn" (Liming de tongzhi) along with He Qifang's "The Calm Sea Conceals Waves" (Pingjing de hai maicangzhe bolang) and "I Sing for the Young Men and Women" (Wo wei shaonan shaonümen gechang)—had been written within the last two or three years at the Communist base at Yan'an. In accord with the dominant, sanctioned mood in Yan'an at the time, all are unmistakably positive in tone. But when read more closely for their construction of voice, they differ notably from the poems performed at the subsequent, corrected, recital. For instance, Ai Qing's "The Call at Dawn," like most of the poems performed either night, fits comfortably into the recitational aesthetic. It opens with a call for poets to "arise" and tell the populace to prepare to welcome a long-awaited salvational presence, a "harbinger" and "messenger" from the dawning in the east (Ai Qing 1991, 574–578). The poem, however, speaks through the first-person voice of the "messenger" himself, an aesthetic choice that, in the Communist program, would be viewed as arrogating the salvational mission to an individual "I" rather than to a collective force under party guidance. He's "I Sing" similarly casts a first-person voice in the familiar recitational mode. The first stanza repeats four times the anaphoric "I sing . . .", while in the second the poet asks that his song "fly into the hearts of youth/to find your place of rest." He Qifang then depicts the poet projecting his voice outwards into space:

All the gladness and fine thoughts
That have ever made me quiver like the grass,
All turn to sound that sails out to every quarter,
Like a soft breeze
Or a ray of sunlight.
(He 1995, 130)

Again we note that, however brightly optimistic the tone, the poet's voice originates within the subjectivity of the individual poet himself, and not from a larger collective political entity. An even greater violation of this rule occurs in the other He Qifang poem recited that night, "The Calm Sea Conceals Waves." In the form of a conversation between two sides of a conflicted, split subject, "Waves" constructs an interiorized double voicing contained within the unfolding dialogue of the poetic text. Alternating from one stanza to the next, one voice, gloomy and melancholic, wishes to restrain its inner impulses, to "build myself a dike,/So that in days to come I may calmly go/Until I cease to flow"; in response to this attitude of retreat, the second voice gently but firmly reasons that such self-confinement will be in vain, because "that which must explode will in the end explode,/A rock when struck will make sparks" (He 1995, 138–139).

Read as a group, it becomes clear how these three poems align themselves with a recitational aesthetic by foregrounding the speaking voice, a feature that surely prompted their selection for a program of live recitation. Each, however, also locates the source of the sounded poetic voice within an individual subject, and in the case of "Waves," a subject divided against itself. Such constructions of the poetic voice, then, represent precisely what "combativeness" is *not*, making them the defining Other of a new requirement for voiced poetry. The apparent corrections in the program of the second recitation, held just one week later, begin to suggest the nature of this change.

The first poem on the program was He Qifang's "Shout" (Hanjiao), a poem dated to late 1940, which begins:

Shout, yell!

You on the riverbank
Hauling wooden barges loaded with wares
Along the treacherous shore,
Shout, yell!

You carrying stones
Climbing the mountain
To build a house,
Shout, yell!

You coolies on the docks,
Shout, yell!

You, soldiers on the battlefield,
Attacking the enemy,

Beside fallen corpses,
Shout, yell!
(He 1995, 113-114)

Once again we hear the first-person voice of the poet inscribed with an emphasis on volume, sonic projection, and direct address conforming closely to the recitational aesthetic formed during the war. But if "Shout" belongs to the same general category as the poems of the first Guilin recitation program, it differs fundamentally in its construction of the poet's voice. Here the poet addresses, not the broad spectrum of the population or a generalized notion of "youth," and certainly not an internally split subject, but a specific segment of the people: the masses of workers, soldiers, and other oppressed peoples comprising the motive force of revolution. Moreover, the poet's voice exhorts this imagined audience not simply to open its ears and awaken but to raise its own voice, an incitement that transfers vocal agency from the poet to the revolutionary masses, making the former an integral part of the latter, not its vanguard. The poem achieves this by reversing the speaker–auditor relation and merging the poet's voice with a collective "we." The poet becomes the audience when he announces, "I've heard the shouts from people of all kinds./I've heard the shouts from places everywhere, I've even heard the shouts from every epoch" (He 1995, 114). No longer does the poet's voice expand over the soundscape; instead, the vocal soundscape of people, space, and historical time is heard by the poet. When the poet does raise his voice, he does so en masse and within the auditory milieu of a wide, collective movement:

We shout
"Comrades, forward!"
I hear the pace of our ordered ranks,
I hear the sound of our bugle.
(He 1995, 114; italics added)

The advance is, implicitly, toward a communist utopia, a place where,

No one goes hungry,
No one is cold,
Women don't sell sex,
And men don't toil like beasts.
(He 1995, 115)

Returning to the term "combativeness," we can see how Tian Han's use of the word can at one level be construed as encouraging aggression against the Japanese invaders, but in fact points to the active advancement of a revolutionary agenda. This political subtext runs throughout the remaining program, not so much in poems that manipulate voicing, but in works that appropriate the voice of the international revolutionary vanguard state, the Soviet Union, and the voice of opposition to the Guomindang's wartime program of white terror.

Following "Shout" came the twelve staccato lines of Tian Jian's quasi-Mayakovskyan lyric "Freedom Approaches" (Ziyou xiang women lai le). Tian's quick verbal drumbeat of "freedom" approaching "like a storm,/like a petrel" "over the wilderness/of Asia" served as fitting introduction to the evening's imported centerpiece: a speech on Vladimir Mayakovsky's poetry and life, followed by three of the Soviet author's poems. In his prefatory speech, the performer elaborated on the mental effort he had expended, "not only to uncover this great poet's character and feeling from his poetic works, but to disclose the poet's passion for the new life and new world in his life of battling and in the social realities that produced the poet." He then recited "Very Good!" "In Re Conferences," and "Decree to the Army of Art," the last delivered in both Chinese and Russian (Hai 1944). Further reaffirming the Soviet connection was a performance of the young poet Yuan Shuipo's 1941 paean to the Russian defense against the Nazis, "Sent to a Sunflower on the River Don" (Jigei Dunhe shang de xiangrikui): "Under fascist oppression,/The suffocating people in China's Occupied Regions—/Ah, you, the sunflower upon the Don,/You have brought them ever more hope and confidence" (Cai 1994, 546–547). Rounding out the evening was the poet, literary theorist, and fellow party member Feng Xuefeng's "Ode to Snow" (Xue de ge), a long and contemplative piece, but one with a covert political message of its own (Feng 1948, 4–15). Feng, as those in the audience were surely aware, had written this and other poems under conditions of great deprivation while he was incarcerated in the Guomindang's Shangrao concentration camp on suspicion of having leftist sympathies.[13]

Conclusion

As the performers at the second Guilin Evening of Poetry Recitation one after the other took the stage, members of the audience, seated by ticket number in a colorfully decorated hall, held in their hands sheets of pale-yellow paper neatly printed with the following: "Leave us your criticism of the Evening along with your thoughts on how we might in the future improve it (in terms of content, technique, arrangements, stage setting, etc.). What portion of this performance did you enjoy most? Which part was the least successful? What would you like to have performed next time? Is there anything you would like to perform yourself? What is your address? Name?" (Hai 1944).

This questionnaire, brainchild of the Evening's master of ceremonies, shows how much poetry recitation had changed since the beginning of the war. No longer are poets asking themselves how they might tailor their poetry to appeal to the masses; instead, through the closed circuit of aesthetic feedback mediated by a questionnaire, they are asking how best to adjust recitation to suit their own tastes. By the standards applied at the outset of the war, such insularity could only be viewed as a failure, or even a betrayal, of the oft-repeated ideal of using orally performed poetry to awaken urgent and emotional presence in the nation-at-large.

Nonetheless, at the same time, the Guilin recitals speak as much to the retreat of unworkable recitational ideals as to the advance of recitation as literary practice and, with it, the construction of the sounding poetic voice. Between Guangzhou and Guilin, from 1937 to 1944, poetry recitals had gone from impromptu, unpredictable affairs unsure of their audience, style, and subject matter, to carefully programmed events by and for educated, and usually literary, circles. New poetry may have failed to break away from the literary salon, but the gradual institutionalization of the poetic recital enlarged the salon to accommodate, not only a greatly increased number of poetry reciters, but an expanded audience aware of recitation as a performance art in its own right. Moreover, as the Guilin recitals attest, recitation may have failed to reach the actual masses, but it had begun to charge poets with the duty of speaking in an imagined, revolutionary, mass voice.

CHAPTER 5

Zhu Ziqing and Situational Poetics

Sounding Out an Alternative

THE "POET'S JOY," to return to the title of Chen Nanshi's early imagination of the recitational aesthetic, had been for the sound of poetry to resonate widely and deeply among the national populace. Through the 1930s and 1940s, this ideal was reformulated by Ren Jun, Li Lei, and Hong Shen until it emerged as the ideological undercurrent persistently invoked to lend larger meaning to the poetry recitation activities of the War of Resistance. Though the project as such was challenged first by poets of less populist sympathies and later by the unforgiving exigencies of real-world performance, throughout these several decades those who were committed to poetry recitation imagined the medium of sound rendering poetry transparent to one and all. On the strength of its sheer invisibility and immateriality, poets tended to fetishize this pure penetrating sound as the erasure of form in all its inhibitive manifestations. This was in its way a solution—though a deceptively simplistic one—to the problematic of content versus form so strongly posed during the May Fourth-era invention of new literature, and in particular poetry. For the poem made vocal promised instantly to transcend textual opacity to allow the stifled interiority of pure content expand unencumbered into the grand collective sense of a shared subjectivity.

As I hope the foregoing chapters have shown, the belief that the sounded poem could directly impact audience subjectivity figured deeply in this antiformalist bias. In this chapter, I examine an alternative conception of poetry recitation, one that modified the problematic of recitational expression by removing its defining moment from the essentialized inner world of subjective content and relocating it in the shifting configurations of performance time and space. This view of poetry recitation emerged from the turbulent eve of revolution in the years 1947–1948. Its originator, Zhu Ziqing, was at the time the chairman of the Chinese Department at Beiping's Tsinghua University. While living in the midst of the atmosphere of student unrest on Beiping campuses during the late 1940s, Zhu found his interest being drawn to poetry recitation as a form of agitational practice that might hasten social change during a time of intense political activism. Before his untimely death in August 1948, he began to develop what I describe as a "situational" understanding of poetry recitation, the idea that the "text" of a recited poem is coextensive with the existential moment of its performance and, by entering that moment, changes it.[1]

Although innovative in its particular context, to call Zhu's reevaluation of recited poetry something wholly new would be inaccurate. In a general sense, his attention to recitation not only grows out of its popularization as a genre during the War of Resistance, but also builds upon that period's intensely instrumental attitude toward performed poetry. Zhu also works within the ideological mainstream of wartime poetry recitation by giving priority to sound over sight, the heard over the seen. But Zhu takes the sound-sight distinction in a new direction. Earlier proponents of recited poetry tended to disparage form in favor of content understood as a virtually unmediated transmission of impassioned fellow-feeling otherwise obscured by the tyranny of writing and print. Though sympathetic to the power of sound and attuned to the motive force of the masses in history, Zhu turned his attention not to the domination of content but toward an idea of the recited poem as a larger manifestation of form—form not limited to the printed poetic text, but encompassing the total situational dynamics of live performance. The recited poem, Zhu argues, is formally unrealized and thus aesthetically unsatisfying when simply seen on the page or read to oneself or a small group. Only at the moment it enters the ears, and thus the bodies, of an emotionally receptive mass audience and encourages them to undertake concrete action does it achieve "completion" (*wanzheng*). In redefining the aesthetics of the performed poem to include the entire recitation event, Zhu revises accepted notions of what constitutes the recited poem by obviating the issue of poetic content. For if the "poem" only functions as poetry during the unique time-space configuration of its public performance, the search for abiding meaning or feeling anterior to the text becomes quite irrelevant. No longer is the moment of recitation imagined as an anchoring of subjectivity in a reified idea of essential and shared emotion; instead, it works on the fluidity and contingency of its moment to construct a temporary intersubjective communality.

Beyond the discourse of recitation in China during the postwar period, Zhu's attention to the poem-as-event rather than the imagined projection of poetic emotion as a reified "thing" also anticipates, or at least echoes, some much later theorizations of oral performance, the experience of sound, and the contemporary poetry reading. Like scholar of oral literature Paul Zumthor, Zhu would agree that recitation is fully sociocorporeal, in that the spoken word "necessarily belongs in the course of an existential situation that changes it in some way and whose totality is brought into play by the bodies of the participants" (Zumthor 1994, 224–225). Also, the production of such a situation depends upon the medium of sound, which, according to Douglas Kahn, "is not only experienced as occurring *in between* but as surrounding the listener, and the source of the sound is itself surrounded by its own sound." What this makes for, Kahn continues, is a "mutual envelopment of aurality" that "predisposes an exchange among presences" (Kahn 1999, 27). Finally, as Peter Middleton observes, the intersubjective network among the audience and reader produced by sound, staging, and the presence of the performer can constitute "a virtual public space which is, if not utopian, certainly proleptic of possible social change" (Middleton 1998, 295).

The social potential of bodies, sound, and space all bear a special relevance to Zhu Ziqing's writing on recitation, for on Beiping's campuses in 1947–1948 recited poetry had become part of a vision of utopian social change. Indeed, just as Zhu envisioned the recited poem as inseparable from its moment of performance, so was his thought on poetry recitation embedded in its own moment of revolutionary history. With this milieu in mind, I examine Zhu's rethinking of recited poetry within the context of the student protests that surrounded and inspired him. Also, to demonstrate more precisely the type of poem and performance Zhu's theory responded to, I offer a "situational" reading of a recitation poem written at the height of the protests by one of Zhu's students in 1947: He Da's "Don't Fear Death—Fear Discussion" (Bu pa si—pa taolun). It is this close interarticulation of theory, history, and poetry that marked the moment of recitation on the eve of revolution. This moment was, however, not without a certain irony. For even as Zhu's theory articulated the poem to history in a bid to hasten the coming of revolution, the artistic discourse created by the revolution, as we shall see in the next chapter, worked to foreclose the spontaneous motive potential Zhu had heard in the recited poem.

Recitation as Situation

In the late 1940s, Zhu Ziqing may have seen himself a belated convert to new poetry recitation as an art of social change, but he was no newcomer to either new poetry or the practice of poetry recitation. Since the late 1910s he had been a keen observer of the Chinese modern poetry scene, first as a poet and prose stylist, and later as a critic, anthologist, and educator. His 1927 article "Singing New Poetry, etc." offered the first substantial consideration of the problem of reciting Chinese new poetry (Zhu Ziqing 1996a). Throughout the 1920s and 1930s he attended salon readings among Beiping's academic circles, and during a trip to England in the early 1930s he made a point of attending the public recitations at Harold Monro's Poetry Bookshop and other venues (Zhu Ziqing 1994b, 237, 240, 247). He claims not to have participated in wartime recitation events, however, until 1945, and his contributions to the discourse on the subject only began to appear late in the War of Resistance, well after the early wartime peak in recitation activities. In all, Zhu published seven essays on the pedagogical and artistic aspects of oral performance of poetry and other genres between 1944 and his death from stomach cancer in August 1948. The first of these he wrote in 1943 and 1944 while teaching in Kunming, the isolated southwestern city where China's major universities had relocated and consolidated as Southwest Associated University in the face of Japanese invasion. The last he produced in 1947, a year or more after he had returned to Tsinghua University. It was around that same year that Zhu's attitude toward recitation changed abruptly. From bookish approbation and historical analysis of recitation as an aid to national language education and a means of advancing new poetry's contributions to national literature, he shifted to a strong enthusiasm for the direct social effect that poetry recitation could play in revolutionary action.

We can trace Zhu's intellectual shift toward a revised aesthetics of new poetry to his geographical move in late 1946 from the relative political backwater of Kunming to the hotbed of student agitation in Beiping. Recalling his own intellectual trajectory, Zhu writes that during the war years the self-styled recitation poems he had come across seemed only dubiously worthy of the name "poetry." Such poems struck him initially as little more than "abstract principles" combined with weak and undeveloped imagery, as instruments of propaganda rather than "fully realized works of art in and of themselves" (Zhu Ziqing 1948b, 34). Though he did not go so far as to condemn such poetry outright, he did urge that, for the sake of balanced literary development, the loosely structured and highly colloquial wartime recitation poem not be permitted to overwhelm new poetry that stressed quiet and careful formal technique.

Zhu never relinquished his conviction that these two streams of new poetry should peacefully coexist, but his guardedly dismissive—and not entirely unfounded—negative attitude toward recitation as a tool of agitation had in fact already begun to change in Kunming in 1945. There he had heard fellow professor Wen Yiduo perform Ai Qing's "Dayanhe, My Wet Nurse" and a member of the New China Drama Society recite a satirical poem by the young poet Zhuang Yong. The substantially greater impact these poems achieved when recited to a crowd rather than read to oneself or to a few individuals intrigued Zhu or, as he puts it, led him to consider how "sometimes the same poem, though it may not look at all good, can sound very good" (Zhu Ziqing 1948b, 34–35).

It was also in 1945 that Zhu published the essay "American Recitation Poetry," which included a partial translation of the American recitation poem by Russell W. Davenport, *My Country* (1944). The several observations Zhu offers here are, strictly speaking, not of his own making; at this stage he was still borrowing and assimilating, edging cautiously toward the idea of recitation poetry as an independent genre grounded in the sense of the sounding voice. Such poetry, Zhu records, "has to appeal to the everyman (*dazhong*), and thus must be specially written—subject matter, vocabulary, and intonation all must be specifically selected" (1948c, 44). Then, citing an American critic of radio verse drama, he notes how the simplicity and accessibility of poetry designed to be heard is certain to have a positive influence on poetry of print, whose imagery has become much too "complex" and "individual" (Zhu Ziqing 1948c, 44).[2] These several criteria, reinforced by Zhu's perception of the reported success of Davenport's *My Country* among the American audience for poetry, indicates Zhu's further inclination toward the idea that recited poetry could be taken seriously and on its own merits as a literary subgenre with a character and purpose all its own.

But it was only after returning to the turbulent milieu of Beiping that Zhu's thought on the form of recited poetry assumed an added and original theoretical dimension. Back at Tsinghua after a nearly ten-year absence, Zhu found himself in the midst of emotionally charged and at times violently suppressed student-led demonstrations often involving thousands of participants.[3] These protest actions deployed a varied repertoire of cultural agitprop activities—chanting, slogan shouting, leaflet distribution, street theater, song, lecturing, and cartoons—that drew heavily from forms of protest action developed and refined in the many patriotic protest movements since the 1919 May Fourth movement (Wasserstom 1991, 206–214). A new addition to the students' cultural arsenal in the late 1940s, and one suited to the relatively sophisticated environment of urban and academic Beiping, was poetry recitation. Taking their cue from the War of Resistance recitation work, student poets both male and female recited at campus rallies, on street corners, and in city parks. The performers for the most part came from student poetry organizations, such as the New Poetry Society (Xinshi she) active at Tsinghua and Peking universities (Beijing Dang'anguan 1991, 188).

As a witness to the frequently galvanizing effect of this politically committed public poetry, Zhu attempted to work out the aesthetic principles of why and how these poems achieved the effect they did. His two most substantial essays on the topic are "On Recited Poetry" (Lun langsong shi)—which I have already cited—and his introduction to poet He Da's poetry collection *We're in Session* (*Women kai hui*; He 1949; Zhu Ziqing 1996b, 501–509). Both pieces were written in 1947 amidst the tension and clamor of almost incessant demonstrations, and in both Zhu unequivocally asserts that recitation be viewed as the "mainstream of today's poetry" (1948b, 35). In these two essays, Zhu's affirmation of recited poetry implied its tie to the student demonstrations, and it is there, at the nexus of poetry and political protest, that the idea of situational form was born.

According to Zhu, the artistic text of the recitation has to be reimagined in a manner analogous to the social text of the demonstration, that is, as situation rather than object, as fluid event rather than static print. The dimension of sound is crucial to achieving this situational form, because sound extends the boundaries of the poem into a living, breathing, collective human situation. "I gradually came to see," Zhu writes, "that most poetry suited to recitation or meant for recitation is fully realized only when recited. Most recited poetry of this sort lives only in the sense of hearing, the sense of hearing of the crowd; when reading it to oneself or at a salon one feels it to be, if not immoderate, then unorganized, insipid, or bland. Yes, by the look of it, it's not poetry, or, at any rate, doesn't resemble poetry. But recited before a large crowd it is poetry indeed. This is a kind of heard poetry, a new poetry within new poetry" (1948b, 35).

Here Zhu extends the identity of poetry beyond the borders of the printed text and into the consciousness and activity of the crowd. Recitation poetry, this sounded poetry, takes on substance as a meaningful poetic subgenre only as it unfolds as an auditory text experienced simultaneously by a collective. No longer do the usual standards used to judge a poem hold, for the recited poem attains aesthetic fullness only in the moment of the poet's and the audience's auditive immersion in sound. "One has to go listen," Zhu elaborates, "to participate in gatherings, to enter the crowd and listen before you can be receptive to it, or at least understand it. Merely read the poem in written form and it will seem overbearing, unruly, hotheaded, didactic; but when you enter the crowd to listen, you will after a short while no longer experience it that way" (1948b, 37).

Zhu understands recitation poetry more as experience than text, as an intense, dramatic address directed outward and into the audience, eliminating the gap between the poem and its auditors, thereby creating an open-ended, real-world space of immediacy and involvement. This fusion of aesthetic object and mass audience response Zhu describes as the "atmosphere" or "mood" (fenwei) essential to the full realization of the recitation poem. Such poetry—and here we must think of poetry in a larger sense as active, externalized, shared experience rather than written text— "must be able to express everyone's hate, joy, needs, and hopes; it expresses these feelings, not in calm recollection, but in tense, focused, live performance" (1948b, 36).

In his introduction to We're in Session, Zhu illustrates this externalized aesthetic by citing "Our Talk" (Women de hua) by He Da, a student of his at Tsinghua in 1947 and an activist in poetry recitation since the early years of the War of Resistance:[4]

We need the kind of talk that's
clear-cut
like a machine gun trained on a target
word upon word
is shot after shot
    of fiery red tracers
dead on the mark
        (Zhu Ziqing 1996b, 505)

Zhu describes this brief poem as an example of the "concise and clear-cut" (*jianduan er gancui*) diction that recitation poems require (505). One can also read it as a reflexive poem about poetry, and more specifically, as the sort of poetic event Zhu theorizes. Certainly, the idea of poetry as a weapon was one of the great clichés among Chinese poets from the late 1930s well into the Cultural Revolution era. The gun metaphor He deploys, however, suggests at once the recited poem's direct address to its audience, and a situation where the spoken words of the poem, like tracer bullets radiating outward from the flashing and clattering mouth of a machine gun, connect poet and audience in an intensely experienced field of dynamic action. The word-bullets here are aimed, not to kill, but literally to impact the poem's auditors en masse, and thus move them to collective response in an atmosphere of compelling urgency.[5]

A Poem in Its Moment: He Da's "Don't Fear Death"

One as theorist and the other as poet, both Zhu and He espouse a vision of poetry as real-world intervention, a mode of literary discourse fully realized only at its moment of extension outward and into a collective and politically active human subject. Zhu states this point in the clearest possible terms: "Recitation poetry comes into direct contact with actual life; it is a device for propaganda, a weapon for struggle. And propaganda and battle are either action or work" (Zhu Ziqing 1948b, 36). To understand more concretely how the poems Zhu encountered at the time dissolved the dichotomy between the "work" of art and the "work" of social action, we can turn to He Da's poem "Don't Fear Death—Fear Discussion," first as a text that fits Zhu's imagination of the situational recitation poem, and then as a poem written and performed for a unique juncture of time, place, and circumstance.

After noting the exact day on which it was written—3 June 1947—Zhu includes the entire text of "Don't Fear Death" in his essay "On Recitation Poetry":

We don't fear death
but we do fear discussion

Our emotions are running high
and if anyone tells us to stop and think
we'll shout him down, punch him out
we'll bellow at the top of our voices
    Get the hell out
    you shameless conspirator

Don't you get it?
we are nothing but emotion

we rely entirely on emotion
and absolutely won't use reason
    to rein in our emotion

But friends
we can't carry on this way
    we don't fear death
    nor should we fear discussion
    for democracy—we must discuss
    and to fight—we must discuss
    we don't fear death
    nor do we fear discussion
            (Zhu Ziqing 1948b, 39–40)

"Don't Fear Death" is clearly an occasional, even disposable, poem easily dis-
counted as a didactic, tendentious harangue. Indeed, after he had read the poem
to one of his classes, half of Zhu's students in fact described it as "flat and straight-
forward." Zhu, however, suggests that in an actual performance situation outside
the sterile confines of the classroom, the poem would take on an energy unavail-
able to more "roundabout" poetry of the "eye" (40). This is because, he continues,
recitation poetry is "a form of dialogue or report whose directness, intimacy, and
naturalness can only come from its appeal to the crowd." The wording of such
poems must be "strictly tailored," but with latitude left for the reciter "to complete
the written poetic manuscript by deploying his intonation and expression in accord
with the mood of the crowd," a process dependent on the time-based activity of
listening rather than the space-based work of reading (41). Zhu does not elaborate
further on the structure or performance of "Don't Fear Death," but by knowing the
precise day on which it was written, we can attempt a speculative reconstruction of
how these features of the recitation poem could have functioned within the living,
active context of June 1947; in other words, we can reread "Don't Fear Death" off
the page and into the unfolding of a singular, situational moment of performance.

For several weeks before "Don't Fear Death" was written, university students in
Beiping had been mobilizing both on and off campus for a one-day, multicity pro-
test against the civil war planned for 2 June 1947 (Wasserstom 1991, 267). Under
pressure from the authorities, the National Student Union on 30 May cancelled
the protests. Nonetheless, on the morning of that second day of June, students in
Beiping were dismayed to discover a blockade of sandbags, barbed wire, and armed
police surrounding their campuses (Beijing Dang'anguan 1991, 184). Should we,
the students asked themselves, storm the barricades and go on with the march,
or remain on campus and wait things out? Opinion was divided, with the more

impetuous protestors held reluctantly in check only by orders from their respective campuses' branches of the Student Union (184).

He Da's poem must be read within this sociocorporeal moment of crisis, as a time-based text in dramatic dialogue with the fluid *fenwei* of a particular performance situation. Such a reading requires our attention to how the poem uses grammatical and formal elements to involve its listeners in a dialogic, dramatic progression. This progression turns on the use of the first-person plural pronoun *women* (in English "we," "us," and "our"), repeated in nearly every line. The poem, then, is clearly dominated by pronominal invocation of collective identity, including the reciter, in which "we" acts as a deictic hinge linking the verbal text of the recitation poem to the human text of the recitation event. In the performance situation, this auditory engagement drives a series of dramatic gestures and vocal effects designed to open up the poem to the human space of the event, and thereby to alter the situational reality.

The poem as a whole is structured to enact a shift in the mood of its audience from volatile emotionalism to measured reason by modulating the emotional atmosphere of its auditors. It does so by heightening the audience's self-awareness of its collective emotional identity, with the reciter alternately stepping in and out of his or her participation in the collective *women* in order to produce an effect of distancing or alienation. The process begins with the first couplet. The slogan-like first line, "We don't fear death," arrests the audience's attention by appealing to the mood of self-sacrificing righteousness and martyr's bravado animating the charged situation for which the poem was written. Then, however, the paired line, "But we do fear discussion," deflates this initial, agitational effect by leading the listeners to reflect critically on their emotional state.

The second and third stanzas repeat this alternation between agitation and distancing. Stanza two enlarges the first line's engagement of mass emotion by seeming almost to endorse the confrontational mood of the audience. These six lines in fact skirt the border between critical description of the emotional atmosphere and approbation of the violent tactics toward which the student protest was tipping on 3 June. That is, the performer of the poem, who in effect enters the identity of crowd through repetition of the inclusive "we," is positioned on an exhortational footing that would appear to encourage shouting, punching, and violent, high-volume denunciation.

Such dramatic scripting fed into a very real desire for punitive mass violence against those who would thwart the students' collective will. During the previous several weeks of buildup to the proposed anti–civil war protest, students suspected of radicalism in Beiping and other cities were frequently arrested by police or assaulted by members of the Guomindang-sponsored Youth Army (Qingnian jun) and unidentified thugs (Wasserstrom 1991, 266–268; Beijing Dang'anguan 1991,

169–181). As a result, writes one student chronicler, the mood on 2 June was "impetuous" (*jizao*), with the students feeling powerfully indignant at being "treated like prisoners and criminals," and some seriously considering a reaction against the "crass measures" of the blockade by "charging through the barricades and carrying on with the demonstration" (Beijing Dang'anguan 1991, 184).

Returning to the poem, we find that, hard on the heels of the poem's affirmation of violence, the text begins to turn on itself and, with the same rhetorical motion, leads the audience to reflect on its dangerously impulsive emotional condition. To do this, the poem temporarily shifts its stance vis-à-vis its listeners by introducing the second-person-plural address "you" (*nimen*) in the phrase, "Don't you get it?" The "you" here does not refer to the student audience, but functions as the students' own address, through the voice of the reciter, to the imagined presence of their adversaries. This deictic shift is a key point in the poem's construction of situation, for it in fact repositions the poem's auditors "outside" their own collective identity, leading them to stand outside and scrutinize their selves in the time of the poetic reading. It is into this moment of self-aware oscillation that the next several lines fall: "we are nothing but emotion/we rely entirely on emotion/and absolutely won't use reason/to rein in our emotion." The repetitive declaration of emotionality in these four lines generates a tone of self-parody wherein the audience, hearing words put into its mouths by the reciter, is forced to reconsider its own emotional excess. By maneuvering the audience into this ironic self-awareness, the poem attempts to disarm the impulsive reaction it had just elicited and affirmed through the performance of stanzas one and two. Finally, in the concluding stanza, the poem lays out its actual intent: to caution the student protestors against a precipitous, ill-considered, and almost certainly self-destructive response to the campus blockade.

To be sure, He Da's poem falls far short of standards typically used to judge a poem's literary quality. "Don't Fear Death," however, was never intended to describe a poetic situation with layers of beauty and complexity designed to give pleasure during many rereadings; rather, it aims to engage and construct a unique, unrepeatable historical situation. It is thus a poem whose full formal features are unrecoverable, because its form is realized only in the performative dimension as a flesh-and-blood reciter articulates the poem's textual structure to an ongoing, real-time situational text. It demands, therefore, to be read as a poetic text-in-context, a poem inseparable from the collectively created moment of performance that, according to Zhu Ziqing, renders a recitation poem complete.

Conclusion

Precisely because the full situational text of "Don't Fear Death" belongs to its moment, we can never know what precise effect the poem might have had on its gathered listeners, if indeed it was recited at all. And even if an account of its live recitation were available, any rereading of the text more than sixty years later would be far removed from the dramatic physicality of mood and atmosphere in the explosive days of early June 1947. Given these inherent limitations, this discussion of "Don't Fear Death" can only demonstrate how, when set in its immediate historical context, understanding a poem designed for recitation becomes, not a question of what the poem "means" or "expresses," but a question of what it does, that is, how its tropic structure reaches into the audience at a specific historical moment and reconfigures the intersubjective network constituted by reciter and audience. Such a poem, Zhu would observe, attains full aesthetic realization only when recitation actively integrates poem and situation—in other word, when the formal structure of the poem opens up into an unstable, contingent, and highly specific set of what would normally be regarded as extrapoetic circumstances.

It was perhaps the excitement of seeing poetry assert its role in the flux of historical becoming that led Zhu so strongly to champion recitation in the years before he died. No doubt, Zhu was not immune to the poetic modern's perpetual yet rarely satisfied desire that poetry *do* something in the world. But even as Zhu formulates the means by which poetry partakes of history, his eagerness to unify the two threatens to dissolve the former into the latter. "Recitation poetry," Zhu writes, "is poetry of the masses, a poetry of the collective. Although the writer is an individual, his point of departure is the masses, he is but the mouthpiece of the masses" (1948b, 35–36). And even more definitively: "There is no 'I' in recitation poetry, only a 'We'; there is no center, only a group." "This," Zhu concludes, "is a revolution in poetry and, one could say, a poetry of revolution" (1996b, 502).

Zhu did not live to see the consummation of China's mass revolution in 1949 and thus could not observe the fate of recitation under Chinese Communist cultural policy. He did, however, speculate on what would become of poetry recitation, and his vision of the future, when considered through more than a half-century of historical hindsight, appears quite prescient. While returning home after a poetry and song rally at Peking University in 1947, a friend conceded to Zhu the powerful agitational effect of recited poetry, but added that "this is likely just the poetry required by the present era, not the sort of poetry that can last forever" (1948b, 42). To this registration of doubt Zhu rebuts that the "private world" and the "public world" "have gradually come together as political life has become a part of private life; this is to say that the private life cannot divorce itself from the political. Collectivization [jitihua] will not, it seems, be limited to these turbulent times. The trend will persist and develop, although its methods will likely differ by time and place. And thus recitation poetry will persist, develop, and live on in its wake . . ." (1948b, 43).[6]

In a sense, Zhu's prediction was on the mark. Recitation poetry in China did live on in the decades following the student protests, and these were indeed years in which a state-sponsored ideology of public, collective life increasingly penetrated the sphere of private life. Also as Zhu had foreseen, recited poetry did become "revolutionary poetry," though not perhaps along the lines he had imagined. For where Zhu's aesthetics of recitation extended poetic form into a spontaneous and fluid revolutionary moment, after 1949 poetry recitation tended to reduce the poem to a reified revolutionary consciousness. Under the Maoist cultural apparatus, as we shall see in the next chapter, poetry recitation was concerned less with constructing a living intersubjective moment than with demonstrating the presence of a deep subjectivity in touch with the springs of absolute belief and commitment. The highest expression of this commitment and the index of absolute value toward which the staged performance of this poetry referred was a pure and heartfelt "revolutionary passion." From a mode of open-ended situational practice where Zhu Ziqing and He Da had left it in 1948, poetry recitation was converted into a carefully regimented, yet precariously balanced, system of devotional performance.

CHAPTER 6

Calculated Passions

The Lyric and the Theatric in Mao-era Poetry Recitation

AS WE RECALL from Chapter 4, poetry recitation's first major debut in Yan'an was hardly an auspicious event. If on that cold January evening in 1938 Mao Zedong had not sat through the entire spectacle of The Evening of Poetry and Folk Song, this new and fragile art might have been condemned to lasting banishment beyond the realm of the Chinese Communist cultural practice. Even so, recitation in the immediately ensuing years gained only a modest foothold among the primarily peasant-oriented performing arts of the rustic Communist base area. But as Mao's regime consolidated itself over the next several decades, the recited revolutionary lyric would evolve far beyond its awkward first act to play a role both vital and deeply problematic in the psychic economy of Maoist cultural production.

This chapter explores a flourishing culture of official Mao-era poetry recitation that peaked in popularity during the early 1960s. These were years when modern Chinese poetry advanced onto the public stage through a widespread, primarily urban enthusiasm for revolutionary poetry recitation. As never before, poetry expanded into a mass-performance art, a state-sanctioned cultural form aimed at engaging and placing on public display the revolutionary passions of China's urban populace.

But even though this period was marked by an unprecedented lyric enthusiasm, it was also driven by an inherent antagonism in the realm of aesthetics and ideology. Recited poetry entailed a fundamental contradiction. Was it the spontaneous expression of authentic, lyrical "revolutionary passion" (geming de jiqing), or simply a consciously cultivated art of dramatic performance? Was poetry recitation what it aspired to become—a sincere performance of deep revolutionary being—or was the show truly no more than a show, an effect of carefully crafted revolutionary bearing? In this chapter I attempt to make sense of the mechanisms that drove and perpetuated this tension. In the process, I hope to question, or at least complicate, a tendency to portray this era as one dominated by a seamlessly monolithic political aesthetic of cultural production and reception. I hope as well to offer a clearer, more dynamic picture of what has too often been dismissed as barren and static years of official poetry production and performance through the 1960s and up to the post-Mao emergence of the "Misty" (*menglong*) poets who contravened state-sanctioned poetic production. This was, after all, the tradition against which the Misty poets rebelled, and to understand the latter, it is necessary to look critically at the former.

My investigation of this troubled poetics of performance begins with a narrative of poetry recitation's nationwide expansion in popularity among China's educated urban masses. From there it moves on to a close analysis of the problems that poets and professional actors found themselves grappling with when they tried to locate the elusive wellsprings of revolutionary passion in their poetic performances. The final section presents an example of late Cultural Revolution–era poetic pedagogy— taken from a 1975 primer of poetry recitation—in which we may see in graphic format how the era's imperative to produce a voice of abstract ideological purity became weighed down by its own mechanisms of pedagogical support.

Poetry on the Public Stage

By 1962, the year this analysis of Mao-era poetry recitation begins, the public performance of poetry had already acquired an approved position in post-1949 official cultural practice. During the late 1950s and early 1960s, poetry recitation had typically taken the form of *saishi hui* or "poetry competitions" held on the agricultural "front lines" of the people's communes, or as an element of grand official cultural events held in Beijing and other large cities. The primarily rural *saishi hui* grew out of the late 1950s' literary policy of bringing folk poetry into the mainstream of poetic discourse (Fokkema 1965, 202–208; Zhou Yang [1958] 1995, 457–467). Much like the period's farm and factory production, poems were created by quota and reported statistically in the millions; and not unlike the massive agricultural communes that typically sponsored such events, *saishi hui* were often scaled large. Such mass literary rallies were intended to demonstrate how the productive forces supposedly unleashed by the Great Leap Forward could drive, and in turn be driven by, an equally grand florescence of mass-produced, socialist-inspired poetic production.[1] In 1959, for example, a poetry competition between two Hebei counties, reportedly broadcast province-wide, brought entire families to the microphone to celebrate "the bumper harvest, the drive for steel, the building of dams and reservoirs," and other such accomplishments (China Reconstructs 1959, 29). At the Celebrate a Bumper Harvest Poetry Competition held by a production brigade in Hebei's Huayuan Commune in 1960, fifty or so party secretaries, model field-workers, repairmen, schoolteachers, cooks, health workers, and grain station overseers took the stage alone, in groups, as entire families, or paired in married couples "to sing of the Three Red Banners, the wonderful hometown, and the joy of a plentiful harvest" (Wan 1960, 46).[2] Meanwhile, official spectacles in the cities filled China's new performance halls with thousands of onlookers for poets' and actors' recitation of made-to-order poems denouncing American imperialism and praising Third World unity. If, for instance, you were one among the three thousand who attended the Beijing Zhongshan Park Concert Hall's verbosely titled Support the Asian, African, and Latin American Peoples' National Democracy Movement Anti-Imperialism Poetry and Song Rally, you would have heard Guo Moruo's "The Confession of Eisenhower," Yuan Shuipo's anti-American lampoon "Portraits of Clowns," and an impassioned declamation of another anti-Eisenhower verse-Philippic, "Open Fire on the God of Plague" (Wan 1960, 73).

By 1962, however, cultural institutions began moving poetry recitation into spaces of urban, educated mass culture lying between the grassroots level of the countryside and the exclusive echelons of Beijing's cultural galas. Supported first in Beijing by the official poetry magazine *Shikan* (Poetry journal), Central People's Broadcasting, and Beijing's multipurpose centers of sparetime enrichment—the culture palaces—poetry recitation became a topic of training, research, mass activism, and, not least, entertainment. This upsurge in poetry recitation for urbanites opened somewhat modestly in January 1962 in the Beijing City Working People's Culture Palace with the formation of a sparetime recitation study group headed by poet and erstwhile schoolmate of Mao Zedong, Xiao San. Along with other veteran

A broadcast poetry competition (*saishi hui*) during the Great Leap Forward. From *China Reconstructs* 8, no. 3 (March 1959): 29.

An actor from the Beijing
People's Arts Theater recites
on stage. From *China Re-
constructs* 12, no. 8 (August
1963): 29.

poets, Xiao opened the two-month session with the goal of "spurring the unifica-
tion of poetry with the masses and cultivating more poetry recitation talent" (Yin
1962, 74). Already by the end of the month, participants from the study group
along with local actors were set to appear at a Spring Festival poetry recital in the
Museum of the Chinese Revolution, where they would "meet with the masses" to
recite recent and yet-to-be-published poems (Shikan 1962a, 74). During April 1962,
"in order to more systematically acquaint listeners with poets and their works,"
Central People's Broadcasting mobilized professional actors to read the work of
poets Zang Kejia and He Jingzhi for the first in a series of radio broadcast poetry
recitation programs (Shikan 1962d, 74). To celebrate Poets' Day the following June,
nearly a hundred professional and amateur poets recited poetry both old and new at
another rally in Beijing (Shikan 1962b, 64).[3] By that autumn, poetry recitation was
firmly enough established to serve as a headline topic at professional conferences,
such as the Poetry Recitation Symposium sponsored by *Poetry Journal* and Central
People's Broadcasting in September (Benkan jizhe 1963), and as the featured mode
of performance at high-profile cultural events, like the Aid Cuba Poetry Recital
held in Beijing's Capital Theater and attended by over a thousand of the city's

poets, writers, musicians, actors, literary and cultural cadres, workers and students (Shikan 1962e, 74).

Barely one year after that first, modest training session in January 1962, "many in the capital's literary circles were swept up in a passion" for poetry recitation. Tickets for a series of three recitation events sold out rapidly, performers complied with repeated curtain calls, and avid fans wrote letters to the sponsors requesting ever more performances (Ge 1963, 15). To satisfy the demand, more official literary institutions joined in the wave of recitation. Supported by the China Writers Association and the Beijing branch of the Federation of Literary and Art Circles, stage and movie actors in the capital organized the Beijing Drama and Movie Actors' Sparetime Recitation Research Team, a group committed to studying the recitation of all forms of literary works and to organizing recitation rallies in coordination with propaganda duties (Shikan 1963a, 74). Due perhaps to the celebrity of its members, events including actors from the team invariably played to packed halls, with even more people outside listening at the doors and windows (Xiao 1963, 57). Later in the year, Beijing's premier dramatic venue, the People's Arts Theater, began to

The audience at a poetry recital. From *China Reconstructs* 12, no. 8 (August 1963): 28.

A professional actor provides instruction in poetry recitation to a commune member (*center*) in the Beijing suburbs. From *China Reconstructs* 12, no. 8 (August 1963): 27.

devote Sundays to programs of poetry recitation (Shikan 1963c, 74). Educational institutions, too, promoted the art of the performed poem. At upper-middle schools in Beijing, teachers selected star student reciters to take part in special study under the tutelage of Recitation Research Team actors (Shikan 1963b, 70).

Although the fever for poetry recitation had begun in Beijing, it was by no means limited to the capital. In June 1962, Shanghai as well as the second-tier cities of Tianjin, Wuhan, Hefei, Nanning, Suzhou, Changchun, and Yinchang joined Beijing in hosting nationwide children's recitation activities involving rallies, competitions, and, in the larger cities, training courses (Shikan 1962c, 64). The Spring Festival season in 1963 witnessed recitation events from Xi'an to Guangzhou, and, in honor of China's selfless model soldier, more than a dozen cities held "Learn from Lei Feng" poetry recitals that included solo recitation, group recitation, and recitation to musical accompaniment, as well as costume recitation and poetry recitation plays (Yin 1963a, 74; 1963b, 70). More sparetime training courses began to appear as well. Deep in Harbin's Manchurian winter, and then again in the summer, branches of the Communist Youth League dispatched hand-picked youth to spend Sundays learning the art of recitation from stage actors, directors, and language instructors (Luo 1963, 74).

Farther south, in the warm June of Nanjing, tickets sold out three days in advance for the Hundred Flowers Poetry Recitation Rally at that city's book market, where the audience listened to local poets praise the sterling character of socialist heroes and describe the progress of class struggle both domestic and international (Zeng 1963, 74). Not to be outdone, Shanghai in that same month featured a poetry and song recital featuring actors from the city's People's Arts Theater, two "Devote Youth to the Motherland" recitation recitals, a tour of factories and workers' clubs by a workers' sparetime poetry recitation troupe, and a recitation training course designed "to assist basic-level work units initiate poetry recitation activities" (Yin 1963c, 74). Soon afterwards, in Nanjing, Xi'an, and Hefei, poets both professional and amateur from "factories, farms, and the army" recited "flaming poetic phrases" in recitals offering sympathy and support to their "black brothers' struggle for rights" in America (Shikan 1963d, 56). As the summer progressed, the new thirst for recitation arrived at the coal-mining city of Taiyuan. There, according to reports, elderly workers camped out at the door, train engineers skipped dinner, and laborers showed up still clad in work clothes in order to secure a seat at the local culture palace's Workers' Poetry Recitation Team performance (Zhi 1963, 8). In 1964, perhaps the largest poetry gala of all took place at the Shanghai Workers' Culture Palace. At a conference attended by over five thousand, more than five hundred amateur poets divided themselves into teams corresponding to their factories' output—steel, machinery, textiles, and so on—for a poetry "duel" on the theme of "wind and thunder rock the five continents" (Lü and Chen 1964, 68).

By 1964 reports appearing in *Poetry Journal* spoke of a new peak of enthusiasm for poetry recitation across the country and a new depth of integration between recitation and the era's mass political campaigns. At urban mass marches and rallies in support of Third World independence movements in Latin America, Africa, and Southeast Asia, poets raised their voices in militantly impassioned chorus against the "monstrous crimes of colonialism" (Shikan 1964, 39; Mei 1964, 44; Yin 1964, 58). Out in the countryside, troupes of performing artists mixed poetry recitation with renovated versions of traditional performing arts to spread the word of the official campaigns to emulate the People's Liberation Army and the Chinese Communist equivalent of Stalin's Potemkin Village, the Daqing oil fields (Jiang 1964a, 29).[4] In the heavy industries, too, workers recited poems like "Onward, We Masters of the Oil Fields!" "I Love Our Chemical Testing Station," and He Jingzhi's "Song of Lei Feng" to halls so crowded that once again people reportedly posted themselves outside open windows to hear the otherwise sold-out performances (Cao 1964a, 27; Jiang Tian 1964, 39).

Calculated Passions: The Lyric and the Theatric

These accounts of audience enthusiasm may sound almost too exuberant to be true. And perhaps they should. Mao-era media functioned less to produce independent, objective-style reporting than to propagate an optimistic vision of a socialist utopia in the making. Nor should one forget that the writers of these articles and reports themselves had an interest in boosting the profile of their chosen genre.[5] But even though these stage-managed descriptions of poetry recitation should be read advisedly, they cannot be totally discounted. In fact, it is the very aura of staginess pervading the period's discourse that offers an avenue of critique into an otherwise impenetrably sanguine representation of the practice of recitation.

The stage, observes Xiaobing Tang in a study of Mao-era Chinese spoken drama, was central to a "logic of the popular imagination" dominated by "a culture of lyrical exuberance and transcendence" (Tang Xiaobing 2000, 165–166). This logic of the stage functioned at several levels: the dramatic staging of plays carefully engineered to mold the revolutionary political identity of a young audience; the bureaucratically managed, manipulative "staging" of lyrical culture by central authorities anxious to mobilize youth in line with the practical desires of the state; and, as a consequence of these two, the transformation of "life itself" into "a grand stage for purposeful action" (Tang Xiaobing 2000, 194). The burgeoning of poetry recitation—the staging of the poem—certainly corroborates the idea of such a lyric age. What I emphasize, however, is how attention to the stage production of poetry, the original lyric genre, foregrounds contradictions and tensions of High Maoist cultural production toward which a focus on the period's drama can only gesture.

In seeking out these contradictions, my analysis of Mao-era poetry recitation impels cultural critique of this period in a direction different from a prevailing view of that period's cultural production. To be sure, as Elizabeth Perry has noted, techniques of "emotion work" or "emotion-raising" (*tigao qingxu*) in the form of staged public performances have figured centrally in Chinese Communist propaganda operations, from the Jiangxi period (1928–1934) to the recent campaigns against Falun Gong. Communist mass mobilization, Perry observes, made the most of the "ambivalence and malleability" of human feelings, so that the emotions generated by politicized performances, like speaking bitterness, denunciations, and self-criticism, could be perfectly genuine (Perry 2002). All the same, there has been a tendency when reading the literature and art of Chinese Communist orthodoxy to assert and then explain the relentless efficacy of literature, film, drama, and poetry as aestheticized politics shaping human subjectivity to the will of the state. For example, in his study of film from this period, Ban Wang uses a psychoanalytic approach to show how the aesthetic dimension of Chinese revolutionary cinema "reproduces ideology in the collective unconscious, at the level of sensibility, affect, desire, and pleasure" (Wang 1997, 154). Even more grim and uncompromising is

Wang's view of the Cultural Revolution era, which he describes as a time when the permeation of everyday life by ritualistic theatricalization became a process, comparable to hypnosis, through which "one's aesthetic taste and unconscious cravings can be trained, altered, and then pushed in the service of the authoritarian order" (217). Michael Dutton offers a similarly bleak vision when he explains this same power of inwardly experienced political devotion during the Cultural Revolution as a product of Foucauldian discipline designed to both modulate and stimulate a political devotion grounded in Bataillean symbolic excess. By such logic, writes Dutton, the Cultural Revolution's mandatory daily rituals, such as performing the loyalty dance or the wearing of the Mao badge "were transformed into disciplinary mechanisms that actually helped create the very sense of devotion being celebrated" (Dutton 2004, 20).

There can be no doubt that the ideological programming of mass culture in China during these years penetrated people's psyches to an unprecedented degree. Even so, it behooves us to look for the fissures that insinuate themselves into what might otherwise appear to be a totalized structure of cultural production and reception. I shall argue that the practice of poetry recitation, when considered within the cultural logic of the stage, can reveal points of potential rupture in what might seem to be an unyielding Maoist cultural monolith. To disclose these sites of immanent tension, I turn to an aesthetic antagonism embedded in poetry recitation—that between the lyric and the theatric.

As Tang asserts and the period's upsurge in poetry recitation events suggests, the cultural milieu of the early 1960s was grounded in a logic of theater that propagated and sustained a culture in which "poetic diction and imagery offered the master medium of expression and communication" (Tang Xiaobing 2000, 165–166). Theatricalized lyricism is precisely what recitation had become by the early 1960s. Combining the drama with the lyric in this way, however, creates a certain quandary. Theatricality by its very nature involves a certain intentional and accepted duplicity. Actors do not become the characters they play; they merely create such an illusion during the fixed time and space of a dramatic performance. Lyricism, especially in the Chinese tradition, eschews such doubling. As discussed in Chapter 1, the notion of poetry as genuine, heartfelt expression has persistently informed orthodox poetic discourse since Chinese antiquity. Indeed, the modern bisyllabic compound for "lyric" (shuqing), retains the idea of poetry as the expression (shu) of heartfelt and genuine sentiment or affections (qing). As to what precisely constitutes qing, as well as its counterpart zhi (will or intent), opinions have varied over time and from commentator to commentator.[6] During the Maoist "lyrical age," however, the fundamental content of thought and feeling resident in poet and poem could not have been more clear. By ideological fiat, poetry was driven by the psychic engine of "revolutionary passion."

In line with the traditional inclination toward the lyric logic of expressiveness, to recite a revolutionary poem required that the reciter allow him- or herself to become the perfect conduit for voicing the political passion presumed to inhabit a properly revolutionary poem. Ideally, the projection of this passion came unbidden, or more precisely, in the form of a lyrical emission that, in line with a long-standing current in Chinese poetic tradition, was "psychologically and physiologically 'natural'" (Owen 1992, 43). A 1975 poetry recitation primer, entitled simply *Shige langsong* (Poetry recitation), describes well the experience of giving voice to the revolutionary poem: "Those who like to recite share this experience: when you come across a good poem you are moved by its revolutionary passion, feel a powerful desire to recite, and can't help but read it aloud" (Gan 1975, 1–2). The affinity with the "Great Preface's" dictum on poetry is unmistakable here, except that generic intent or affections are replaced by politically up-to-date "revolutionary passion." Moreover, the primer adds that without this passion the performance of the poem amounts to nothing or, worse than nothing, empty theatricality: "As the conveyer of the thought and feeling of a revolutionary poem, the reciter has to fuse his own thought and feeling with the poem as it expresses the revolutionary passion of the proletariat; otherwise there is but mechanical recitation or rote reading . . ." (Gan 1975, 3).

When we take a closer look at how those who recited—and in particular actors—approached the task of staging such poetry during this age of politicized lyricism, it becomes apparent that the heartfelt expression of revolutionary lyric feeling and the calculated mechanics of revolutionary theater were not so easily detached one from the other. In fact, we begin to perceive how the period's talk about poetry recitation was animated by a tension between the natural and theatrical so freighted with the danger of deception that the difference between real feeling and deliberate dramatics had to be elided or denied for fear that revelation of self-doubt and self-awareness would break the spell of ideological certainty. To compensate for this immanent instability, many professional reciters represented the performance of poetry as the magnification of emotive poetic content rather than as a codified dramatics of giving voice to revolutionary verse. And yet, due to the deeply stage-scripted nature of public discourse during this age of ideological extremes, the very act of asserting the primacy of spontaneous poetic content entailed a deliberate and mechanical application of decidedly nonspontaneous, prefabricated formulae. In other words, the performance of poetry became a task in which the demands of lyric sincerity and theatric affectation met head on, with the result that revolutionary recitation became an oxymoronic project consumed by the need to efface its own built-in contradictions.

One might conclude that the persistent and deeply fraught denial of difference between the heartfelt and the calculated equipped all "to deceive, to act a role" (Fliegelman 1993, 80). Such may have been the case, but I would venture that deception and role-playing are terms too one-dimensional to capture the psychic mechanisms at work here. Better, perhaps, is to observe how the dual imperatives of the lyric and the theatric—the expression of revolutionary passion and the disavowal of the normative "stage directions" guiding that expression—divided the human subject between two incommensurable extremes. The two were incommensurable because asserting the presence of revolutionary being required constant attention to the manipulative promptings that scripted revolutionary bearing. In its strongest form, this is a scheme in which the desired fullness of revolutionary presence receded even as it was approached, and thus trapped the subject on a psychic roundabout supporting and empowering the same ideology that constructed it. On the other hand, to assume such a closed system of ideological control would be a simplification that easily ends up occluding as much as it might reveal. The alternative I propose is to underscore the precarious balance of contradiction that, even as it perpetuates faith in the Maoist monument to revolution, constitutes as well that monumental structure's most vulnerable point.

Acting the Lyric, Staging a Narrative

That stage and film actors led the field in poetry recitation during the early 1960s contributed in no small way to the anxious slippage between the lyric and the dramatic. Years before, during the War of Resistance against Japan, stars of the stage and screen—such as Bai Yang, Zhang Ruifang, and Shu Xiuwen—had actively recited poetry, especially in the wartime Guomindang capital, Chongqing (Ren 1948, 161). Two decades later, actors again stepped into the limelight, leading to a proliferation of "professional" (*zhuanyexing*) poetry recitations (Lu Mang 1964). Thespian reciters from professional groups like Beijing's Sparetime Recitation Research Team performed in both the city and the countryside, but enjoyed greatest success among educated young people in urban areas (Zang Kejia 1963, 54). In Beijing in the early 1960s, some actors specializing in poetry recitation developed their own coterie of fans. These celebrity reciters would be greeted with applause the moment they stepped onstage. Many even armed themselves with a repertoire of short poems in order to satisfy the inevitable demands for encores (Yuan 1963, 49).

However, beyond the ovations and curtain calls, we also find these reciting poets and actors speaking as critics and observers of their own or others' poetry recitation efforts. Dominating these critiques was a very careful self-policing effort aimed at determining the presence or absence of a natural revolutionary authenticity in the staged poem. What these poets and actors began to notice when listening to themselves and one another is the fact that, when pressed into the service of political theater, the voice of poetry somehow failed to ring true. As early as 1962, poet and aesthetic theorist Zhu Guangqian remarks on a "dominant style" (*zhan youshi de fengge*) heard at recent poetry recitation event. Poets, actors, and amateur poetry fans, Zhu says, nearly all read in "an impassioned tone using the intonation and posture of an actor reading lines" (Zhu 1962, 59). Not long afterwards, veteran poet Zang Kejia registers a similar complaint, and again points the finger specifically at actors. While granting that actors generally recite better than the poets themselves thanks to actors' greater mastery of enunciation, pacing, and stage manner, Zang notes that "some actor comrades' recitation fails to make the grade." He attributes this shortcoming to the habit of applying the "heightened voicing, vigor and passion, hand gestures, and facial expression" suited to strongly political poetry when reciting "relatively short, highly metrical, and more temperate works" (Zang Kejia 1963, 54).

When actors themselves met to carry out autocritique of their own performance styles, as they did at the Symposium on the Art of Recitation in Beijing in October 1963, they identified the vocal component of this "false feeling and formalism" by name as the "recitational intonation" (*langsong qiang*; Benkan jizhe 1963, 56). As one might expect, all the actors at this symposium criticized recitational intonation and agreed that "the feelings in poetry recitation should be natural and true" (57). But on the question of how this vocal formalism arose, and what precisely constituted the "natural," opinions were less than unanimous. "Unnatural" intonation could, on the one hand, arise spontaneously from the emotive experience of reading a poem. Actor Sun Daolin, for instance, reflects that when reciting Guang Weiran's "Ode to the Yellow River" (Huanghe song), "in order to express the impassioned yet somber emotion and grand breadth of spirit, the recitation naturally assumes a chant-like flavor." Sun's colleague Li Keng, on the other hand, explains the problem in terms of conscious, if misapplied, technique: "Sometimes, in order to enunciate clearly or for stress, an actor will prolong words, or pause and separate words from each other, which when done poorly sounds unnatural. Over time, this can become a habit and form an 'intonation'" (*qiang*; 57). Compounding the problem was the realization that breaking these habits and returning to the "natural" presentation of poetry required an equally conscious effort. To achieve the "natural and true," Li says, "it is necessary to strive incessantly," and adds that he himself had struggled for years before overcoming his own tendency toward stilted enunciation, "What we are pursuing," he concludes, "is not theatrical effect, but accurate expression of the thought and feeling of the work" (57).

Sun and Li's comments on poetry recitation begin to intimate the difficult dialectic of matching the content of revolutionary poetic being to the form of revolutionary poetic bearing. Content was the favored term in the dyad, as Li indicates when he asks for a mode of poetry recitation that is natural for its rejection of vocal histrionics in favor of an understated expression of a poem's "thought and feeling."

By this he meant that the reciter need only tap into poetic content in order to give a "natural and true" performance of a poem, because once properly in touch with the work's thought and feeling, the reciter would reexperience its originary revolutionary sensibility. An authentically executed performance would then follow.

Further complicating this deceptively simple—but as we have seen in previous chapters, firmly established—schematic of content over form was the era's unusually narrow approved bandwidth of poetic sensibility. According to a 1958 recitation primer, preferred materials for recitation included "teachings of revolutionary leaders, exploits of heroes and exemplary persons, praises of the Party or the government, accusations and exposés of enemy crimes" (Yan 1958, 2). Along the spectrum of poetic feeling, a later primer mentions just six basic types of emotive intonation that a poem might arouse: high passion, excitement, joy, deep thought, anger, and recollection (Gan 1975, 34). Sun Daolin's lapse into a chant-like reading of "Ode to the Yellow River" stands as one example of how this expressionist logic could go awry, for to presume the presence of sublime emotion and spirit in a poem immediately cues its performer to ascend to a higher plane of vocalization. But, as the comments of these poets and actors tell us, the supercoded voice of revolutionary sublimity could easily fall prey to imputations of falsity.

As if reacting in denial against this slipping of the lyrical into the theatrical, advice on poetry recitation from the period firmly insists on the primacy of authentic feeling over matters of oratorical or dramatic technique, at times to a point where poetry recitation resembles spirit possession by the poem's original author. Actor Cao Borong writes, "In order to represent [zaixian] the poet's character, feeling, and hopes . . . as much as possible one has to unify and merge one's own thought and feeling with the poet's thought and feeling, and thus make the poet's language one's own living language . . ." (Cao 1964b, 113). Zhu Lin, veteran wartime actress and author of her own recitation primer (Zhu 1960), reminds the would-be reciter that, not only is poetry recitation "powerful" and "the most simple art form for carrying out revolutionary propaganda and education," but "any good poem is the most emotionally moving embodiment of the poet's revolutionary thought and feeling." Successful recitation is not assisted even by the "finest technique," Zhu continues, but depends instead on "undergoing education with a conscientious attitude so that your own thought and feeling resonate with the thought and feeling of the poem. Only then can you sincerely and with perfect assurance disseminate the thought of the poem to millions in the masses and recite with the most authentic, most pure feeling" (Zhu 1964, 55, 56, 57).

Gan Yuze's 1975 primer Poetry Recitation (Shige langsong) states the case even more emphatically. Listing the "basic skills" of poetry recitation, Gan gives absolute priority to authentic feeling by asserting that "the reciter has to fully merge mind and body with the thought and feeling of the poem, to recite with a powerful wish coming from inside. . . ." Meanwhile, the other three basic skills—clear enunciation, natural intonation, and strongly accented rhythm—all are matters of "technique" (*jiqiao*), and thus merely secondary to expressing the poem's content (Gan 1975, 58).

Following such principles could lead to tremendous anxiety over whether one was indeed able to recite a poem in public with the proper degree of inner belief. This was because failure to transmit the proper political passion expressively in fact implied the reciter's own ideological deficiency. As Zhu Lin writes in her 1960 primer: "If the reciter him- or herself totally lacks political enthusiasm and a clearly defined class position, comprehension of the work will be extremely shallow and, we can say with surety, he or she will not be able to express accurately the ideological content of the work. Nor will the broad masses receive any inspiration or power from this kind of 'recitation'" (Zhu 1960, 1–2). According to this logic, faulty performance points to flawed political identity, and problematic political identity, as is well known, was at the time grounds for public criticism, if not ostracism and persecution.

The degree of anxiety that performers expressed, however, differed widely between poets and actors. Due perhaps to their proximity as original authors to the presumed source of revolutionary creation, but more likely to their closer involvement with the actual work of writing poetry, poets were concerned less with reliving the inner authenticity of a poem than with drawing attention to the technical specifics of poetry *as* poetry. We have already seen how Zang Kejia took actors to task for letting their impassioned style run roughshod over the formal intricacies of certain poems. Echoing Zang, Zhu Guangqian asked reciters to "detect the musicalization of speech" essential to poetry, recommending that they "fully address the error of undue expressionism and the importance in poetry of formal rhythms of prosody" (Zhu 1962, 59). Poet Xiao San likewise described recitation as working primarily on the material of language rather than on one's political consciousness. For Xiao, successful recitation, first, required well-formed poetic phrasing that possessed well-conceived imagery, rhythm, and rhyme, and second, that such poems be performed in "a variety of speech that has been polished and made artistic, that possesses the beauties of prosody and rhythm" (Xiao 1963, 62).

Actors, on the other hand, and especially those whose star status and stage savvy generated much of the excitement over poetry recitation during the early 1960s, tried to demonstrate a deep empathy with the revolutionary poetic content of their performance poems. The way they did so, however, only further confirms the staged, or perhaps more accurately, scripted quality of the deep lyric utterance. When asked to speak or write about their experience of reciting poetry, these actors structured their personal poetic relationship with lyrical revolutionary authenticity in the set form of the confessional narrative of enlightenment. This use of the

confessional mode was hardly fortuitous. The official confession—or more accu-
rately, self-criticism—had been a fundamental mechanism of Chinese Communist
political discourse from the Yan'an rectification movement of 1942 on through the
mass campaigns of the post-1949 years.[7] The reciting actors' confessional narratives
clearly and consistently invoke this standardized disciplinary practice and, more
specifically, do so in a way that subordinates conscious application of technique to
a renewed understanding of a poem's authentic revolutionary content.

For example, in one of a series of articles published in *Poetry Journal* in late
1964 and collectively entitled "Poets and Actors Discuss Recitation," the profes-
sional stage actor Jiang Xiangchen portrays the path to revolutionary enlightenment
as the resolution of a "riddle" posed by the performance of two different poems:

> I had prepared one poem well in advance, and thought it meticulously pol-
> ished for performance. The other I had only come across three days before
> the show, but because of the thrill it gave me and the resonance it generated,
> I made a crash effort at the last minute to work it up. My comrades, however,
> all said that I had read the second poem better. I found this truly perplexing.
> Only after attending by chance a revolutionary martyrs' commemorative po-
> etry recital sponsored by the Children's Club did I come up with an answer
> to this "riddle."
>
> The reciters were all Young Pioneers. I was enthralled by the way many
> of the children recited works commemorating the martyrs in clear, melodi-
> ous voices expressing sincere and unaffected feeling. Just as one boy walked
> on stage, an instructor who was sitting next to me said, "This student is our
> best reader. He just loves to recite." Listening carefully, I found that the child
> performed quite well indeed. He was relaxed and did not give the impression
> of reciting lessons. I noticed, however, that he had shed his childlike naïveté
> and sincerity, leaving behind only meticulously crafted body language and
> vocal delivery. It was all a bit contrived and artificial. This, of course, was not
> the child's fault—he had learned his manner from others. At that moment I
> suddenly realized why I had failed when reading that first poem.
>
> Before anything else, the reciter has to be emotionally moved by the text
> he recites, to enter deeply into the world that the poet creates by experienc-
> ing it with the entire soul. You have to transform the poetic phrases into
> your own authentic feeling and actual sensations so that you yourself become
> an incarnation of the poet. Then the poem can flow naturally from the inner
> heart instead of being forced out. The inner heart feels what it feels, and in
> a way that cannot be faked. In other words, if you don't feel a thrill that you
> absolutely must communicate to others, if you haven't carried out detailed
> analysis and understanding of the entire poem, then you cannot recite well.

This requires above all that the reciter understand life, be clear about what to love and what to hate, and not be a bystander in life. Otherwise, no matter how proficient your technique, you won't move the listeners or arouse a powerful resonance. (Jiang Xiangchen 1964b, 117–118)

As confession and cautionary tale, Jiang's anecdote reveals the actor-reciter's anxiety over backsliding into a mechanical imitation and becoming, in effect, a performing automaton unconnected to the sources of revolutionary passion. Merely acting out a poem, no matter how skillfully, cannot substitute for centering one's subjectivity in the locus of revolutionary authenticity as embodied in the originary experience of the poet. The problem for the reciter, then, is to submit to the natural aesthetic guidance of revolutionary passion. But as Jiang's carefully crafted, self-critical anecdote reveals, to attain this natural, lyrical delivery itself requires a highly prescriptive and self-conscious narrative process describing just how one arrives at "artless" access to a poem's inner meaning.

Jiang's account in the same article of performing another poem—Li Ji's "Petroleum Song" (Shiyou ge)—illustrates how the production of this seemingly natural expressiveness requires constant and conscious vigilance. According to Jiang, despite hasty preparation, his first performance of "Petroleum Song" came off well. In due form, he attributes this initial success to an inner sense of pride and excitement inspired by the declarations of national self-sufficiency in energy production publicized by the ongoing campaign to emulate the successes of China's Daqing oil fields. During repeat performances of the same poem, however, he admits to having concentrated only on technique, with the result that the original passion faded and his delivery fell consistently flat. But ideological rejuvenation was not far off. Following a visit to Daqing and meetings with the model workers "Iron Man" Wang Jinxi and "Living Lei Feng" Zhang Hongchi, the poem was "injected with new life." "No longer," effuses Jiang, "was it necessary to think about which words to stress, where to pause, where to speed up, or where to slow down; instead I used the language of the poet to express all that I had experienced in my heart . . ." (Jiang Xiangchen 1964b, 118).

For Jiang, formal perfection in the performance of poetry can only proceed from the inside out, as amplification of heartfelt passion. But producing a naturally expressive performance depends on following a carefully scripted process of recognizing and internalizing revolutionary consciousness. Moreover, the process of recognition and internalization occurs as a micronarrative of poetic revelation that is itself a deeply formalized and readily reproducible performance. Now whether Jiang in point of fact truly experienced what he claims to have experienced is an open and unanswerable question. One might argue that the confessional narrative template structuring his story possesses its own performative power to create belief.

Or one could say that the ready-made quality of the narrative structure—which Jiang applies twice in fluent succession—vitiates his claims of deeply sincere performance, because these narratives resemble nothing more than performance pieces in and of themselves. But one thing is certain: Jiang's carefully patterned denial displaces the location of agency, and thereby mystifies the use of consciously manipulative theatrics—the theatric skill at which he is a professional practitioner. Thus, instead of the actor performing the poem, Jiang would have us believe that the poem—and behind that the poet, and behind *that* the presence of revolutionary passion—performs the actor.

Jiang's attestations to the nearly magical guiding power of authentic inner conviction could be ignored if they were not duplicated so consistently by other actor-reciters of the time. Writing in the same issue of *Poetry Journal*, actor Cao Borong recounts a moment of crisis in preparing Ge Yuan's "Think of Girón Beach" (Xiangxiang jilong tan) for a 1962 poetry recitation rally in support of Cuba. Like Jiang, Cao insists that the reciter "does not speak for himself, but speaks for the poet" by "unifying to the greatest extent possible one's own thought and feeling with that of the poet" (Cao Borong 1964b, 113). Unlike Jiang, Cao demonstrates this recitational ventriloquism through a curiously reflexive variation on the standard confessional narrative. For Cao, the linchpin in the narrative of sudden illumination is none other than the recited lyricism of revolutionary passion itself.

Compelled at the last minute to perform the Ge Yuan poem, to which he had previously given only a cursory glance, Cao describes himself as having been at a total loss as to how to properly modulate between the voicings of the poem's several sections.

> Because I had not resolved the problem of my ideological comprehension, I couldn't settle my thoughts during my crash preparation of the poem. The more I read it through, the less fluent it became; the more I committed it to memory, the more halting grew the delivery; the more I analyzed, the more flaws cropped up. I thought to myself: The first three stanzas imitate the speech of American imperialism, but how can I do a self-parody? How modulate between the first three stanzas and the stern warning in the fourth? How make the quick emotional transition from the stern warning into the last stanza's humorous satire? There were problems all over that simply could not be resolved, so I steeled myself with the thought: "Never mind. I'll just listen to the others' recitations and see what happens!" (Cao 1964b, 114)

Fortunately for Cao, comprehension arrived in a flash as he "received enlightenment and encouragement from the revolutionary passion" of his comrades' performances. A quick reanalysis of the poem then brings the revolutionary intent of poet Ge Yuan into instant focus, and this sudden command of original intent generates an effortless performance: "I saw the problems that had bedeviled me cut through as with a sharp blade. I understood the phrases that had escaped me, and the method of artistic treatment quite naturally took care of itself" (Cao 1964b, 114). "Artistic treatment," Cao concludes, "is born of comprehension, and without the grounding of comprehension, artistic treatment is absolutely out of the question. Dynamics, stress, speed, and use of pauses cannot be willfully arranged when reciting, but must instead express a certain comprehension, a definite thought and feeling" (115). Comprehension for Cao, however, is not the product of consciously willed close reading and research. Instead, it is the affective thrust of revolutionary passion derived from others' performances that enables him to avoid the pitfalls of conscious interpretation and enter directly into a state where the revolutionary passion of the original poet takes over as his own subjectivity. But that is not all. Cao's shortcut is worth noting because, in attributing the discovery of lyric passion to the selfsame experience of lyric passion, he obscures the theatricalized contrivance of the structured narration. In the interest of putting content first, passion feeds passion in a parable that would, if it could, consign *itself* to oblivion.

How to Read a Revolutionary Poem

Actors who made a practice of reciting poetry provide some of the most prominent examples of the problems involved when trying to rationalize calculated performance as natural presence, but their pronouncements on poetry recitation are by no means the only place to find this psycho-poetic sleight of hand. The recitation primer, because of its status as a pedagogical text specifically designed to regiment public performance, spells out with particular clarity the tension between poetry recitation as deliberately mechanical stagecraft or spontaneous revolutionary expressionism. Like the actor-reciters I have discussed, the primers insist on the absolute necessity of political passion to successful recitation. At the same time, these textbooks give intensely technical and detailed instructions for disciplining the reciter's vocal apparatus during performance, and in the process unveil the constructedness of "deep" revolutionary subjectivity.

From among the three recitation primers I have cited—Yan Renyi's 1958 *Recitation Basics* (*Langsong jichu zhishi*), Zhu Lin's 1960 *First Steps toward Recitation* (*Langsong chubu*), and Gan Yuze's 1975 *Poetry Recitation*—I offer here a discussion of Gan's text. My reason for choosing Gan's primer over the others is that, first, *Poetry Recitation* deals exclusively with the recitation of poetry, and second, Gan's text stands as a summation, not only of the earlier primers (both of which it borrows from and builds upon), but of the early 1960s' practice and discussion of poetry recitation. Also, Gan's primer culminates in a heavily annotated "reading" of a section from what was perhaps the most popular recitation poem of the early 1960s, "Song of

Lei Feng" (Lei Feng zhi ge). This closely guided reading, when juxtaposed with Gan's avowal of the poem's deep revolutionary content, offers an extreme and even graphic illustration of the oxymoronic project of staged lyricism.

"Song of Lei Feng" is itself a sixty-seven-page "lyric long poem" (*shuqing chang-shi*) extolling the sterling socialist character and tireless self-sacrifice of the People's Liberation Army's most heavily popularized revolutionary paragon. The poem was repeatedly staged for performance during and after the "Learn from Lei Feng" campaign of 1963. It could be heard in the nationwide recitation rallies glorifying Lei, at touring shows in the countryside, at oil refineries in Xinjiang, and over the airwaves, where it was reportedly one of the poems most requested by the radio audience (Wen 1963, 65–66; Jiang Tian 1964, 39; Yu Huilao 1963, 73; Hui 1964, 67). An excerpt from "Song of Lei Feng" also appears in *Poetry Journal's* own 1965 anthology of recitation poetry, and a young Bei Dao, later to achieve prominence as a Misty poet in the early post-Mao years, recalls reciting the poem from the rooftops during his youth. The poem in fact remains a standard in the poetry recitation repertoire to this day (Shikan she 1965, 35–54; Bei 2000, 250).[8]

Due perhaps to its prominence as a standard in the recitation repertoire, or quite possibly to the attraction of associating the model hero with a model reading, Gan Yuze touches on "Song of Lei Feng" several times in *Poetry Recitation*. In addition to including a section from the poem in the primer's appendix as an "example for analysis" (to which I shall return later), Gan also makes a point of mentioning it in the book's first chapter, "The Reciter's Revolutionary Passion." There, like Jiang Xiangchen, Cao Borong, and many others before him, Gan inserts a version of the reciter's confessional narrative.

Soon after "Song of Lei Feng" was published, Gan tells us, a recitation enthusiast was overcome by excitement and rushed out to perform the poem. Some workers who heard this spontaneous performance suggested that the poem had been recited with more volume than emotional substance. Chastened by this criticism from the revolutionary vanguard class, the reciter applied himself to a thorough reading of *Lei Feng's Diary* and commemorative essays on the model soldier. He subsequently found himself "profoundly moved by the great communist fighter Lei Feng's sublime thought and vivid exploits, and became determined to take Lei Feng as a model by devoting his youth to the Party and the People." That is to say, by realigning his own subjectivity with that of the revolutionary model's purported authentic experience, the reciter was able to stage a much-improved performance. Or, as Gan explains, "only a revolutionary can with full-voiced revolutionary passion recite the overflowing enthusiasm of revolutionary poetry" (Gan 1975, 3–4).

Despite such testimony to the importance of inner passion for the success of a recited poem, the greatest portion of Gan's primer is given over, not to affirmations of the primacy of emotive revolutionary subjectivity, though these are interpolated throughout, but to a highly technical discussion directed at refining and regimenting recited speech. To read the annotated excerpt from "Song of Lei Feng" in the mode Gan intends, it is necessary first to detail his pedagogic apparatus—an elaborate diacritical scheme whose exacting thoroughness reveals the constructed quality of revolutionary passion's spontaneous voice.

Gan's first step is to spell out the basic phonology of the Beijing standard dialect, from the "five categories of initial consonants" (*wuyin chuzi*) and the "four vowel forms" (*sihu dingxing*) to the accurate production of tones (*shengdiao*; Gan 1975, 12–29). The rationale for this linguistic discipline, Gan explains, is to ensure absolute transparency of the poet's "meticulously polished and carefully selected" words and phrases, "each of which expresses the author's thought and feeling as well as comprehension and personal experience of the world" (12). The unstated assumption here, one might add, is that a poem's revolutionary content is best voiced according to an ideologically centered and wholly homogenized national standard rather than a cacophony of mutually unintelligible dialects. Performing the purity of revolutionary passion, it would seem, demands an equally pure voicing of the officially standardized Mandarin.

Above this most basic layer of regimentation, Gan describes a painstakingly complex and almost obsessively thorough taxonomy of vocal effects, including pauses, stress, and intonation. Pauses, for example, are of three relative lengths and four basic types. The length of a pause is denoted in the poetic text by the symbols /, //, and //. These symbols can in turn refer to pauses that are grammatical, logical, psychological, or based on division of the poetic line into grammatically or logically discrete words or phrases, which Gan refers to as "sense-groups" (*yiqun*). Stress, indicated by dots (•) below the text, Gan subdivides into three categories based on grammatical structure, logical sense of the phrase, and the rise and fall of emotion. In any of these three instances, stress is used "to highlight the central import of the thought expressed by a poetic phrase, or to emphasize the special inner meaning of a word," and can be enunciated by "pausing, changing the length of sounds, modifying volume and pitch, and the weight and urgency of spoken tone" (Gan 1975, 39, 43). How the reciter would enact these stresses—through volume? pitch? length? some combination thereof?—is left to the imagination. A properly inspired recitation of the poem, however, would presumably find these stresses and make the most of them, though at this point one might begin to wonder how revolutionary inspiration could survive under the steadily increasing weight of instructional overlay.

Above the category of stress, Gan imposes yet another level of voicing: intonation. Like pause and stress, intonation subdivides into several varieties, each with its own diacritical mark: rising ↗, indicating surprise, anger, complaint, venting grievance, a call to attention, an order, doubt, uncertainty, and inconclusiveness;

falling ⬊, denoting self-confidence, affirmation, lack of doubt, assuredness, sighing, sorrow, request, and the close of a statement; inflected ~, expressing implied meaning, suggestiveness, irony, and humorous satire; and finally level →, registering narration, explanation, solemnity, seriousness, mysteriousness, humility, and indifference (Gan 1975, 43–46).

Finally, after a brief explication of rhythm, speed, terminal rhyme (indicated by the symbol Δ), and proper breathing, we are ready for the poem: part three of "Song of Lei Feng." The poem's overall tone, Gan advises, should be "solemn and composed," so as to lead the audience and one's self to consider the central questions posed by this section of the poem: "How shall one live?" and "How shall the road be traveled?" The recitation otherwise should be executed "in a semi-elevated voicing, with rhythm alternating between slow and fast, but mostly at a slow and unhurried pace. Tones should be full and the rhymes enunciated loudly and clearly" (60). The effect of Gan's recitational method is, however, best observed firsthand by viewing a portion of his annotated version of poem, here provided in an English translation:[9]

. . . Look / to the base / of Mount Kunlun:
The Red Flag / waves in the breeze,
    ●   ●
The Great River / eastward flows. . . .
    ●   ●
    Observe / so high / in the heavens:
          ●
    Clouds and mist / gathering,
    ●
    Wind and rain / sweeping. . . . ⬊ //   (take breath)
    ●   Δ
A hundred-thousand words ——
Together form
A cloud-parting / mist-piercing
Soaring / rainbow!. . . . /
    ●   ●   Δ
    Two words ——
    For China's
    New generation
    A glorious / name!. . . . //   (read "O" immediately after inhaling)
    ●   ●Δ
O, / To remember you
        ●

———Lei Feng! ↗
    • Δ
O, to think
    •
of you
———and make Revolution! ↗ //   (take breath; tone gradually shifts)
       • Δ
The springtime   (slowly)
Of 1963
    Made us
    Oh so   (with elation, boldly)
    • •

    Impassioned! ——— /
     • Δ
History gives the answer to   (slow down)
 •   •   •
How   (with solemnity)
 •
One
Shall/live! →
 •   •
   How
    •
   The road
    •
Shall be traveled!. . . . ↗ //   (take deep breath) (pause)
 •   • Δ

                          (Gan 1975, 62–63)

Gan advises the performer upon reaching the end of the poem to "slowly gather your-self, all the while gazing intently at the audience in order to maintain a connection with them, and step away only after the audience's mood has gradually settled" (58).

In graphic detail, Gan's Cultural Revolution–era primer begs the question this chapter has done its best to explore: the dilemma of poetry recitation's existence in the contradictory space between subjective immersion and dramatic calculation. At this late stage of high revolutionary culture, it becomes ever more apparent how the practice and pedagogy of poetry recitation forces the performing subject into a self-conscious and potentially unsustainable shuttling between an abstracted imagi-nation of revolutionary being and a concretely scripted method of theatricalized revolutionary bearing. As a new generation of young Chinese poets hoped to prove, the time had come to reclaim the sources of poetic sincerity from the seemingly outworn ideological mechanism of Mao-era recitation.

Recitation after Mao

It has become a commonplace that the poets labeled as "Obscure" or "Misty," whose work began to surface around the time of the Democracy Movement of 1978-1979, produced poems that broke with the style and content, if not always the heroic or even hieratic attitude, of the Mao-era political lyric (Yeh 1998; Li and Hung 1992, 94-95). But given the popularity of officially sanctioned poetry recitation during these poets' formative years—most were urban schoolchildren during the peak of the recitation movement—it seems unavoidable that these young poets, and their poetry, would have been shaped by that period's performance aesthetics. Moreover, at the height of their popularity in the 1980s, these same young poets often recited before crowds of hundreds or even thousands of enthusiastic listeners (Bei 2000, 252-253; Link 2000, 6), leaving one to wonder about the continuity of the public voice of revolutionary lyricism into the post-Mao years even among this young poetic alternative. Here we might note that the preeminent instrument for making poetry public in the immediate post-Mao years was the wall poster, a medium of public expression closely identified with Cultural Revolution-era cultural practice. Given the similar prominence of poetry recitation as an established cultural form for staging political outcry, to what degree and in what aspects did post-Mao poetry extend the poetic practices of the past? Was this poetry informed, either negatively or positively, by a revolutionary recitational aesthetic?

There are assuredly no simple answers to these questions. Just as the publication and performance of poetry at the time flourished in a gray zone somewhere between officially sponsored and underground samizdat literature (Goodman 1981, 16-17; Link 2000, 138-142; McDougall 1979), so the poems themselves resist any single defining category in terms of either form or subject matter. Nonetheless, in concluding this chapter, I will point out how several early poems by one of the leaders of the Misty group of poets, Bei Dao, adopt the form of a recitational aesthetic even while shifting away from the Mao era's officially sanctioned politico-literary rhetoric.

Two of Bei Dao's earlier poems, "The Answer" (Huida) and "All" (Yiqie), lend themselves to such a comparison. As for the former poem, it is interesting to note that the film academy student Chen Kaige, later to become a famous director, performed "The Answer" at an underground recital in 1979, using, much to Bei Dao's dismay, "the revolutionary style of recitation" (Bei 2000, 252). Possibly more dismaying to Bei Dao, "The Answer" is now frequently included in poetry recitation anthologies alongside poems by Tian Jian, Zang Kejia, Mao Zedong, and even "Song of Lei Feng" (Huang Zhipeng 2007; Lan and Liu 2006; Li Xiaoyu 2004).[10]

Such affiliation with literary orthodoxy is very likely due to its reproduction of the recitational aesthetic. The climactic third through fifth stanzas of "The Answer," for example, unambiguously shift into a stance of oratorical defiance that hearkens back, not just to Mao-era political lyric, but to the recitational effusions of the War of Resistance, and before that, of Jiang Guangci's political lyricism:

> I came into this world
> Bringing only paper, rope, a shadow,
> To proclaim before the judgment
> The voice that had been judged:
>
> Let me tell you, world,
> I—do—not—believe!
> If a thousand challengers lie beneath your feet,
> Count me as number one thousand and one.
>
> I don't believe the sky is blue;
> I don't believe in thunder's echoes;
> I don't believe that dreams are false;
> I don't believe that death has no revenge.
>   (Bei 1990, 33)

One might say, then, that in terms of its formal qualities "The Answer" replicates or even reaffirms the official revolutionary ideology it would otherwise oppose. This is not to diminish the antiauthoritarian thrust of the poem. "Fighting poison with poison," as the Chinese proverb goes, certainly has merits as a means of political subversion. Not to be overlooked, either, is how the poem's notoriously "obscure" content defamiliarizes the established, officially sanctioned regime of poetic diction. For instance, the images of "paper, rope, a shadow" offer little or no immediately decodable meaning within the semantic realm of Maoist revolutionary symbolism. We note, too, that the poet at the outset of the poem lists these inscrutable items as his, the speaker's, God-given tools, a move that foregrounds this opaque imagery as a "weapon of the weak." If we read the imagery of paper, rope, and shadow in this manner as synecdoche for the deliberately obscure, "The Answer" comes across as a case of poetic content destabilizing from within the quite recognizable form of the recited revolutionary poem.

Such internal deformation is even more distinct in another of Bei Dao's best-known, and eminently recitable, poems, "All" (Yiqie). Here the poet voices an insistent series of declarative anaphora that in form echoes the absolutist slogans of revolution, but in content delivers a string of conundrums:

All is fate
all is cloud
all is a beginning without an end
all is a search that dies at birth
all joy lacks smiles
all sorrow lacks tears
all language is repetition
all contact a first encounter
all love is in the heart
all past is in a dream
all hope comes with footnotes
all faith comes with groans
all explosions have a momentary lull
all deaths have a lingering echo
                              (Bei 1990, 35)

To reiterate: only a minority of poems that have been placed under the Misty rubric can be read in this manner; more often the poems express an idiosyncratic and highly personalized lyricism that differentiates them from formalized Maoist political lyric. But as Gregory B. Lee observes, such an aesthetics of disengagement by China's unofficial lyricists of the 1970s and 1980s reflects a "rejection of 'politics'" that itself unavoidably engages in a "reaction to the ideology that had become dominant and institutionalized in the structures and organs of the state and party since the founding of the People's Republic of China" (Lee 1996, 115). Looking at "The Answer" and "All" against the historical background of recitation, we can see how this antiofficial reaction functions in unexpected and perhaps unacknowledged dimensions.

Conclusion
In ending this chapter, I would remind the reader that officially sanctioned Mao-era poetry recitation, while unique in terms of the pressures placed on performers to measure up to extreme ideological standards of the times, represents just one episode in a continuing history of poetry recitation as a cultural practice. Even as the theorists and practitioners of recitation invoked a quite modern idea of pure revolutionary passion, the concept of expression informing that invocation derived from China's earliest poetic theory. Moreover, examining official poetry recitation also gives the lie to the myth of a uniquely monolithic revolutionary culture, especially when one considers reciters' own reception of these poems. Instead of the transparency and assured purity of intent that one generally experiences when reading the era's officially sanctioned poems in written form, reciters' accounts of giving

concrete voice to the poetry intimate a sense of self-doubt spurred by formidable ideological dilemmas—dilemmas that eventually even appear in print on the pages of poetry recitation primers. Finally, as I suggested in my brief discussion of Bei Dao's poetry, the influence of official recitation reemerges even among poets seeking to repudiate the excesses of Cultural Revolution–era culture. Taken together, these several aspects of poetry recitation in the 1960s and 1970s recommend that we think of Mao-era poetry and performance culture less as victims of extremist aberration and artistic stagnation than as cultural forms possessing their own continuities, complexities, and dynamic contradictions.

CHAPTER 7

From *Yundong* to *Huodong*

The Value of Poetry Recitation in Postsocialist China

CLAD HEAD TO TOE in olive drab, the woman poet Fangzi steps to the front of a small audience of reporters, poets, and prospective home buyers gathered in the front hall of a newly opened sales reception center in southwest Beijing. A scale model of a high-rise apartment building to her right and a cobblestone pool of lazy goldfish behind her, she grips a wireless microphone and reads:

> What is home?
> None other than a sturdy and attractive house,
> Where your house is,
> There your love resides,
> Where your love is,
> There is your career,
> . . . .
> Sing praise to one's house. Sing praise to one's family. Sing praise to our true
> paradise.
>
> (Li Hongjie 2005)

It is 8 March, Woman's Day 2005, and the seven woman poets of the Hay Tribe (Gancao buluo) are holding a recital of their work to initiate the First Genre Don Women's Art Exhibition and to mark the opening of the second year of sales at the Genre Don (Gediao) luxury housing estate, a project run by the general manager of the Beijing Yilianxuan Real Estate Development Company and Hay Tribe founding member Liu Bo.

About two months later and far to the west, on a stage erected below the out-stretched arm of a towering Mao Zedong statue in Kashgar's People's Square, professional recitation artist Yue Bin wears a close-fitting dark-brown suit with matching tie as he gazes into the distance, past the assembled ranks of Party VIPs, bouquet-wielding middle-school students, and uniformed soldiers, to recite poet Luo Ying's "I Am the Eagle of Tashkurgan":

Sleepless I lie through the night in Tashkurgan
The dazzling sunlight warm as ever in my breast
I see Mount Mutzagata glistening under a moonlit sky
Ah, Lake Kara Kul holds a bright rounded moon
Like a poem, the breeze through the Stone City calls forth my hot tears
Ah, my dream, how is it you and the Tajik maidens unnerve me?
I cannot remain silent and desolate as an ancient courier post
For this beautiful earth makes me sing aloud
Ah, I am the brave eagle of Tashkurgan, and I shall soar through the long
    night . . .

                                      (Zhang Tongwu 2005)

It is "Southern Xinjiang Reverie–Kashgar Spring Poetry and Song Recital," an out-door gala of poetry and patriotic song celebrating the start of the 2005 Southern Xinjiang International Travel Festival and the fiftieth anniversary of the founding of the Xinjiang Uighur Autonomous Region. The master of ceremonies introduces the author of "Eagle," Luo Ying, as "a man of broad-ranging talent." What he says is true, for Luo is in fact better known as Huang Nubo, Beijing-based real-estate mag-nate and board chairman of the Beijing Zhongkun Investment Group, a sponsor of the recital and mastermind investor behind the development of five tourism zones stretching from the border with Pakistan eastward over the length of Xinjiang's southern tier.

On the surface, these two recitations could hardly appear more different. The cozy, informal air of the first, with the women poets in casually fashionable bo-hemian attire, reading their own works from books or printouts in a sometimes stumbling, linguistically not quite standard, generally unrehearsed, and minimally theatrical style, evokes the subdued, highbrow air of the independent poetic avant-garde. Similarly, most of the poems recited by the Hay Tribe members–like Liu Bo's "Witch" (Nüwu), Xiaoxiao's "Broken-hearted Butterfly" (Shangxin de hudie), or Du Dongyan's "Hurt" (Tengtong)–speak of the intense yet obliquely expressed pri-vate experience that often characterizes China's contemporary poetry, and women's poetry in particular (SouFun.com 2005). As for the Hay Tribe poets themselves, they comprise a small and loose literary club unaffiliated with China's semioffi-cial national literary organizations. Even the venue of the reading–small, privately funded, intimate–suggests the exclusive marginality so often invoked as a feature of China's contemporary poetic avant-garde.

In contrast, the official features of the Kashgar recital could hardly be more evident. After speeches by local party worthies, a line-up of professionally trained, golden-voiced recitation artists take the stage to declaim. With flawless enuncia-tion, dramatic modulation, and expansive, operatic, gestures, they present a carefully programmed set of poems, mostly contemporary panegyrics to Xinjiang's scenery and ethnicities authored by older-generation members of China's literary establishment. Between the recitations, professional singers from local branches of armed forces cultural performance troupes belt out patriotic numbers like "Why Are the Flowers So Red?" or "Hurrah for Public Servants." A register of the event's sponsors, printed on the stage's backdrop over a panoramic image of southern Xinjiang's pristine mountains, puts to rest any doubts as to the event's debt to state bureaucracy. Above the Zhongkun Investment Group are listed the Xinjiang Uighur Autonomous Region Propaganda Department, China Central Television, five separate regional administrative offices, and the poetic branch of the China Federation of Literary and Art Circles, the China Poetry Association.

While the differences between the two performances—from setting to sponsorship, clothing, texts, audience, voicing, and so on—lead the observer to label the one "independent" and the other "official," to draw such a distinct ideological line would be misguided. For, as I hope to demonstrate, a larger frame of reference encompasses both poetic events. In a certain respect, this larger context relates to both performances' connections to the real-estate industry and to China's burgeoning diversity of poetic activity in recent years. But these two factors—one economic, one literary—make up only part of the picture. Performances like these, I argue, are symptomatic of an ongoing reorganization of public life in urban China of the twenty-first century, a reorganization embodied by the amorphous, omnipresent, and thoroughly naturalized practice of the cultural event, or *huodong*.

To comprehend the significance of *huodong*, which I will henceforth refer to as "event," this chapter first compares the clusters of linguistic and historical meanings attached to that term with meanings linked to the related term *yundong*, or mass campaign. From there I argue that during the 1990s, in tandem with the Chinese state's deliberate promotion of the culture-economy as a strategy for stimulating economic growth, a decentralized and highly autonomous practice of staging events has in many ways replaced the centrally initiated, politically coercive form of the mass movement as a way of mobilizing the population to meet larger development goals. The practice of poetry recitation is, one must admit, only a very small facet of contemporary event making. However, contemporary Chinese poetry's history of complicity with and distance from the dominant forces of state and market make it a particularly intriguing object of study, especially when trying to work out the links between culture and economy as transformed by the shift from state socialism to the current period of postsocialist economic reform.

As will be discussed shortly, events comprise an almost endlessly fluid category of social organization. Indeed, the Genre Don and Southern Xinjiang Tourism Festival described above already suggest how, within the very small subcategory of the poetry recitation event, one finds a striking range of variation in terms of scale, motivation, participation, and sponsorship. To meaningfully survey all varieties of poetry recitals would far exceed the space limitations of any analysis. Instead, this chapter seeks only to introduce the idea of the event as a category of social and cultural practice through which poetry is mobilized in support of the culture-economy. Here I draw attention to the deployment of cultural events in the form of poetry recitals to enhance the economic value of land. To illustrate this trend, I analyze in some depth a particularly striking, but by no means unique, case of poetry's relation with property development: the events comprising Yilianxuan Real Estate Development Company's 2004–2005 publicity campaign for the Genre Don luxury housing estate in Beijing. The chapter concludes with some thoughts on possible implications of the culture-economy's appropriation, through recitation, of contemporary poetry.

Discovering *Huodong:* One Researcher's Experience

Because this study is based largely on a semiethnographic approach—that is, obtaining data through physical observation, personal participation, and dialogue with informants—a few words of background revelation are in order. My interest in cultural events comes out of ten months, spent mostly in Beijing during 2005–2006, trying to locate, observe, record, and analyze instances of contemporary poetry recitals. Such recitals, I soon found, are alive and well in urban China. Before the first few months of research had passed, I had managed to see, hear, and obtain recordings of contemporary poetry recitation, referred to in nearly every case as *langsong,* performed in a remarkable variety of modes and contexts. For instance, in an amateur recitation club I joined soon after arriving, members gather on Sunday afternoons in a restaurant dining room to share performances in a spirit of fellowship and mutual critique. In contrast to the stylized, dramatic presentation of "red classics" favored by many at that club, I also saw and took part in a loose-jointed, anything-goes avant-garde event in Beijing's Dashanzi Art District, where *langsong* was printed on the program to refer to unscripted, interactive verbal performance art. I have accompanied poets and recitation enthusiasts as they recited poems for one another at small soirees in private homes, but have also witnessed recitals replete with dance, song, and elaborate stage effects that were cosponsored by businesses and local governments and attracted crowds of hundreds to large auditoriums.

School recitals are another feature of this immensely variable performance art. At one end of the spectrum I attended, not only the annual recitals run by student poetry clubs at Peking, Peoples, and Nankai universities, but at the other was also invited to a year-end gala recital by students of the Pinggu Primary School in Beijing's outlying suburbs. Contemporary *langsong* can replay the Mao-era drama of cultural guerilla warfare, as with a retired factory worker I know who recited a poem called "Cry of Rage" in Beijing's Jingshan Park to excoriate corrupt government officials for tolerating coal-mining disasters. But it may just as well be featured in a highbrow book release, as when the consummately intellectual poet Xi Chuan read aloud from his latest book of poems in the courtyard of a small bookshop near Peking University. And, as one would expect, Chinese fans of recitation make enthusiastic use of the audiovisual capabilities of the Internet.

In short, if one cares to look, poetry recitation can be found almost anywhere in China today. Given the geographic dispersion, size variation, and often impromptu nature of such recitals, the actual frequency of performed poetry is impossible to gauge. But the many people I spoke with on the topic—editors, poets, actors, enthusiasts—all attested to an increase in poetry recitals over the past ten years or so. As several put it, China is experiencing a recitation "renaissance." My own observations, gained firsthand or through media reports, certainly confirmed that China suffered no lack of *langsong*.

Yet, despite the myriad of recitals this apparent renaissance made available to me, I still felt that I had somehow failed to grasp exactly what was going on. In fact, the more closely I bent my attention to the style and staging of the performances—whether viewing them live, reviewing them on my own video recordings, or watching prepared recordings in DVD format—the more I felt I was missing something. Certainly there was much to be said about the performances themselves, but it seemed that the real significance of poetry recitation lay, somehow, elsewhere.

Looking back, I suspect that the problem arose from something linguistic anthropologists identify as a defining feature of verbal art forms in performance. On the one hand, writes Richard Bauman, "All performance, like all communication, is situated, enacted, and rendered meaningful within socially defined situational contexts" (1992, 46). But at the very same time, performance by its very nature decontextualizes itself. Much like the formal features and artistry of a written poem set it apart from everyday language, performance "puts the act of speaking on display—objectifies it, lifts it up to a degree from its interactional setting and opens it to scrutiny by an audience. Performance heightens awareness of the act of speaking and licenses the audience to evaluate the skill and effectiveness of the performer's accomplishment. By its very nature, then, performance potentiates decontextualization" (Bauman and Briggs 1990, 73). It was, I believe, my close scrutiny of *how* recitation elevated language above the everyday—from voicing to text selection, gesture, costume, music or sound effects, mise-en-scène, and even advertising—that distracted me from the surrounding social and historical forces that animated the performance genre I had chosen to examine.

In the end, coming to understand poetry recitation in a meaningful context—or put more colloquially, being able to see the forest for the trees—was a practical rather than an intellectual process. After attending dozens of recitation events over the course of eight or nine months, I found myself able to reflect upon my acquired competence as a participant in poetry recitals. This is not to say that I recited well, though I was from time to time invited publicly to read a poem or two. Instead, what I mean by participatory competence refers to something more like local knowledge, which in my case meant developing the network of contacts I needed to find out about recitation events, presenting the identity of someone worth inviting to such events, and learning how to anticipate and in some cases incorporate myself into the ritualized flow of recitation-related gatherings. Initially, I performed all these tasks unreflexively, as a matter of gathering the information I thought I needed for my research. In time, however, as I grew to feel more at home as an active participant, I found myself able to recognize, and thus consider from a certain intellectual distance, the conventionalized patterns of behavior in others, and myself. The greatest realization, and the one that prompted me to write this chapter, was how my research work, and even my identity in the "field," had come to be dominated less by an attempted analysis of poetry recitation itself than by personal participation in a flourishing social practice of the cultural event, the rich and vibrant matrix without which poetry recitation could hardly sustain itself.

Another reason I had overlooked the category of event for so long was simply because, as a form of everyday social practice, events are so closely and variously woven into the familiar fabric of contemporary life as to appear unexceptional. They seem to happen everywhere and all the time. This was driven home to me while still in Beijing, not long after I had begun thinking about "event" as a frame of reference. One afternoon I brought up the subject of *huodong* at a small party (another form of event) attended by Beijing poets, artists, and musicians. Before I could finish my thought, a woman sitting nearby suddenly interrupted to invite me as a "special guest" to an art-related event she was organizing in the northern suburbs. A few days later, while visiting a city in southwest China, I rang up a local poet. I was hoping to meet with him to ask for some in-depth information on his experience and opinion of literary *huodong*. No luck. He was attending a poetry event in faraway Xiamen, and wasn't it a pity I couldn't make it to the recitation program?

From *Yundong* to *Huodong*

Events are as pervasive as they are hard to define. The term can be used to refer to something as small as a kindergarten class planting a tree on Arbor Day or as large as National Day festivities on Tiananmen Square. An event may be organized by nearly anyone, from several members of a literary club to the executives of a private corporation, a local government committee, or simply a group of friends looking for a few hours of fun. Events can be set to occur nearly anywhere: in a city square, a park, an art district, shopping mall, a school or company auditorium, a restaurant or bar, even the living room of a private home. Because of this amorphous quality, in urban China today, events are taken almost entirely for granted. But being unremarked is not the same as being unremarkable. To the contrary, a closer examination of the word itself gives insight into some of the most important economic, social, and cultural transformations in the People's Republic of China over the past several decades.

One way to draw out the rich linguistic and historical connotations of *huodong* is to compare that term with the related term *yundong*. Both terms are readily translatable: the former as "event" or "activity"; the latter as "mass campaign" or "movement." Much is lost, however, in either rendering. Simply translating the two terms occludes root meanings and semantic accretions essential to understanding the function of the event, and by extension poetry recitation, in China today.

First, it is immediately apparent that these two bisyllabic compounds share their second ideograph—*dong*, or "motion." But from there the two terms begin to part ways. As any standard Chinese dictionary will tell you, the *yun* in *yundong* implies motion that is systematic, guided, and purposeful, from the mechanical movement of a watch or machine, to the bodily motions of organized sport and exercise, the purposeful transportation of goods and people, the crafty manipulation of the masses, and even the ineluctable workings of destiny (*mingyun*). In contrast, the initial ideograph of *huodong*, *huo*, which includes the semantic element for "water" on the left, suggests the spontaneous, undirected, and endlessly flexible actions of life and nature. *Huo* spreads its connotative web to capture the free and unpredictable, the mobile and modifiable, the undirected and leisurely—a loose tooth, a mobile home, an adjustable clothes rack, an after-dinner stroll, or even the multipurpose pleasure of a rec room.

Dictionary definitions may suggest the span of meanings for these two words, but the full semantic orientation of any lexical item depends on its sociohistorical accretion of meaning. Such is emphatically the case with *yundong* and *huodong*, for both these two forms of social "motion" have played critical roles in defining public life under the Chinese Communist regime. The term *yundong* is deeply colored by the history of a state apparatus intent on orchestrating a collectively coordinated forward drive of economy, society, and ideology. The Chinese *yundong*, according to Gordon Bennett, refers to a "government-sponsored effort to storm and eventually overwhelm strong but vulnerable barriers to the progress of socialism through intensive mass mobilization of active personal commitment" (1976, 18). The classic *yundong* as practiced from the early 1940s in the wartime Communist base Yan'an up through the 1970s comprised "a series of organized, planned actions for a particular purpose" devised by the highest levels of party leadership, transmitted down through an ad hoc command organization to the lowest levels of the party apparatus, and then applied directly to the "masses" (A. P. L. Liu 1971, 87). The *yundong* was the Mao era's dominant political and administrative form of leadership, the key institution of political participation, and the major organizing force of public life.

Yundong-related activities included, not just strictly political work such as discussions, rallies, lectures, and the infamous criticism and self-criticism sessions, but also multiple forms of cultural propaganda (A. P. L. Liu 1971, 87). Carried out by the hierarchy of semiofficial professional organizations under the China Federation of Literary and Art Circles, this cultural work of *yundong* demanded the intense publicization of a single topic for a short period of time with the goal of creating a quick response. Since speed was of the essence in such campaigns, genres favored for *yundong* were those that could be rapidly made to order, easily comprehended, and quickly consumed, such as exhibitions, storytelling, big-character posters, cartoons, songs, films, slide shows, and stage productions of drama, opera, or dance (King 1966). As we saw in Chapter 6, poetry recitation, too, became an important genre for such topical social mobilization.

Despite their many shared organizational features, as well as the overarching nation-building purpose, *yundong* varied in important ways. For instance, the emphases of *yundong*—in terms of geographic scale, participative demands, and penetrative intensity—fluctuated with the political winds of the time (A. P. L. Liu 1971, 87–117). And, of course, the specific messages articulated through *yundong*-related cultural work varied with the policy directives of the moment. As a technique of statecraft, however, Mao-era *yundong* were designed to advance the construction of state socialism by propagating the values of self-sacrifice, voluntarism, patriotism, submission to party authority and, during the most turbulent movement of all, the Great Proletarian Cultural Revolution, absolute devotion to Mao Zedong. As a sweeping strategy of state-building that often relied upon brutal physical and psychological coercion, the historical importance of *yundong* cannot be underestimated. In their more extreme application, socialist-era *yundong* evinced a "passionate desire to politicize the *weltanschauung* of every man and woman" and in their time "laid the necessary psychological and physical foundation for new patterns of national integration" by displacing family and clan-based communication with state-guided, nationwide "mass experience" (A. P. L. Liu 1971, 115, 117).

Yundong by no means ended with the initiation of post-Mao economic reforms, however. The 1980s and early 1990s, for instance, witnessed high-profile though short-lived campaigns against "spiritual pollution," "bourgeois liberalization," "allout Westernization," and "peaceful evolution" (Goldman 2002, 499–538). More recently, the Ministry of Propaganda has issued directives to wipe out "evil sects," exhortations to live by the "eight glories and eight shames," guidelines for constructing the New Socialist Village, and periodic warnings against official corruption. Nor has the cultural work of *yundong* become a thing of the past. Messages still descend through the hierarchy of party cultural organizations to be transformed at the grassroots level into print and television advertisements, stage plays, films, bill-boards, posters, and even outdoor chalkboard cartoons. Yet while the forms persist, the reliance upon and impact of *yundong* have receded vastly since Deng Xiaoping came to power in 1978.[1] In terms of scale, duration, and demand for popular par-ticipation, the mass campaigns of the post-Mao era are mere shadows of the *yundong* of the past, much to the relief of writers and artists as well as the general populace.

Where *yundong* have mostly faded from public life, *huodong*-style events have risen in their place. To be sure, events in the form of work-unit–sponsored parties, meetings, film screenings, athletic meets, and the like were present throughout the era of state socialism. In fact, *yundong* often comprised a series of events organized by party-recruited "activists" (*huodongjia*). Present-day events, though inheriting some features from the socialist era, have taken on a much more far-reaching, subtle, and complex role in the organization of everyday life, one that extends beyond the past economic structures of state socialism, of which the work unit represented the primary building block. As mentioned above, given their dizzying combinations of structure and function, to define such a multiform thing like the contemporary event is no easy task. A working description, however, might read as follows: a col-lective pursuit of leisure, entertainment, socializing, networking, self-improvement, and/or publicity that frames a certain time, space, and participatory sphere outside the flow of everyday life and labor. Most important, the cultural event as I examine it here is ultimately organized by the culture-economy and its emphasis on demo-cratic consumerism. To flesh out and lend specificity to this necessarily open-ended definition, I now offer an elaboration of several key terms: time, space, and the two closely related expressions culture-economy and democratic consumerism.

In terms of time, events as practiced today differ quite significantly from the political campaigns of the past. As successive nationwide mobilizations, *yundong* in their era were a means of spurring a centrally orchestrated collective march through a teleological history toward a communist utopia. From 1949 on into the 1970s, the coming and going of *yundong* dominated the flow of time for Chinese citizens and other residents.[2] Even now, long after their political prominence has passed, refer-ence to major *yundong* of the past has become a commonplace means of segmenting the historical narrative of the People's Republic of China up through the 1980s. Thus, whether looking forward or backward, *yundong* determine the imagination of time on a scale of grand narratives of national destiny and history.

Contemporary *huodong*, on the other hand, operate on a smaller, more quo-tidian time scale. Rather than being linked directly to the timescale of a grand, modernist narrative of collective progress, they are more often tied to the pluralistic calendrical time of the five-day work week, official holidays, official and unofficial annual commemorations, academic scheduling, business cycles, and even the rota-tion of the seasons. Events in the form of poetry recitals, for instance, might take place at a recitation club on a Sunday afternoon, at a work-unit-sponsored party on May 1 International Labor Day, at the memorial service for a dead literary figure, upon the anniversary of a historical event (such as the end of the War of Resistance against Japan or the founding of the Chinese Communist Party), at a primary or middle school toward the end of the academic year, at a promotional "show" (*xiu*) designed to publicize a book release, or during the traditional season of poetry in China—spring. Just as often, however, the scheduling of events corresponds to only the most local time frame, especially when linked in a series or nested one within the other. For instance, a week-long tourism festival—a common form of event today—may be internally scheduled to include a press conference, an opening ceremony, a poetry recital, a song-and-dance show, rally races, raffles, an academic conference, a food fair, and a closing ceremony—all of which can be individually referred to as discrete events. In terms of temporality, then, events are, once again, both decentralized and highly fluid.

In terms of space, too, contemporary events differ from the state-sponsored political campaigns. Whereas the latter represented the top-down, coercive infiltration of private, everyday life by the political goals of state socialism, the former arise and proliferate spontaneously in the public spaces of leisure-time use. Events by their very nature require a place in which people can more or less freely gather to see and be seen, exchange information, play, spectate, and/or perform. Venues for the small-scale literary events that I have attended, for example, have very often been precisely the hotspots of consumerist recreation: bars, restaurants, bookstores, and coffee shops. Larger literary events—such as conferences, poetry festivals, large-scale poetry recitals, and the like—of necessity use sites provided by private, semiofficial, or official institutions. These can range from auditoriums at universities, libraries, and museums to the performance spaces offered by municipal district culture halls, city squares, and even trade-show exhibition buildings. Thus, much like their temporal organization, the spaces for events are decentralized, flexible, and often tied, directly or indirectly, to commercial interests.

It is the commercial aspect of events that offers a key to understanding their larger significance. As suggested by their frequently market-oriented temporal and spatial nature, the time and space of events cannot be considered apart from the evolution of China's overarching economic policy of "reform and opening-up." In fact, the recent proliferation of events, and in particular the category of cultural event to which poetry recitals belong, ought to be understood as an epiphenomenon facilitated by a specific sea change in the Chinese Communist mode of governance—what Jing Wang refers to as the postsocialist regime's deliberate policy of expanding and exploiting the culture-economy as a means of generating economic growth. Such growth is driven by the conversion of culture to capital. Put simply, the symbolic value of culture, used as a form of "value added" for

A member of a Beijing recitation club performing in a restaurant during a New Year's Eve party. Photo by author.

An open-air poetry reading in the courtyard of a bookstore in Beijing. Photo by author.

A contestant at a recitation
competition held in a Beijing
city culture hall. Photo by
author.

various commodities, enhances the economic value of capital, which in turn spurs consumption. Increased consumption then contributes to economic development, and economic development favors the state by inducing political obedience and displacing calls for political reform (J. Wang 2001, 69–104). In terms of methods of statecraft, Wang argues that the emphasis on the culture-economy has also meant the regime's self-transformation from a coercive to a regulatory state apparatus. Put differently, the state has changed itself from an entity accustomed to launching periodic political campaigns to stamp out "poisonous weeds," to one that allows a diversity of cultural flora to grow, especially the varieties of popular culture embedded in market-driven, leisure-time "democratic consumerism." Democratic consumerism, according to Wang, refers to the regime's promotion and reconstruction of the "public" as a space of consumer goods and leisure culture "open and accessible to all" (2001, 73). Thus China's "weekend culture," Wang stresses, is "first and foremost an official discourse born from a well-calculated state policy" (2001, 73).[3]

The influence of the shift to culture-economy, it is safe to say, has left no aspect of contemporary Chinese social and cultural life untouched. Given poetry recitation's affiliation with the Mao-era socialist political culture of the past, and considering poetry's stubborn lack of market value in comparison with more readily commodified artistic forms (such as fiction, film, and art), one would expect recitation to have sunk into cultural oblivion. On the contrary, as already mentioned, recitation continues to flourish, especially in China's major urban centers. This is so because recitation has been mobilized as an element in the endlessly flexible repertoire of the cultural event. Instead of falling victim to the mass-culture market economy, poetry recitation has become a minor but vital form of literary practice, and one whose smallness in terms of popular recognition belies its significance as an index to the conditions of cultural and social life in the People's Republic of China at the onset of the twenty-first century.

Poetry, Purity, Property

While poetry and the land have deep roots in many poetic traditions, the relationship between poetry and land development seems to be a unique feature of postsocialist literary activity with Chinese characteristics. One cannot help but be struck by the sheer number and variety of poetry-related activities, and poetry recitals in particular, that to some degree involve the promotion of real-estate and local tourism interests. During the past five years or so, poetry events have been deployed in this manner from Inner Mongolia in the north to Guangzhou in the south, from Ningbo in the flourishing coastal east to the cities of Xinjiang in the poor and land-locked west.[4]

The partnership may at first seem strange: how does one create a relationship between land, one of the most heavily commodified items in China's reform era, and what is perhaps the era's least commodifiable cultural product, poetry? It is, in fact, precisely the apparent mismatch between poetry and the market that opens the former to utilization by the latter. An explanation for this strange union can be found in the connections between recitation events and the culture-economy.

To take a step back, poetry is by no means the only artistic genre impacted by the forces of commodification during the past fifteen years or so. Countless fiction writers, painters, and filmmakers have to varying degrees cashed in on the opportunities presented by a growing domestic and international market for their products. For example, Chinese filmmakers from a range of cinematic styles have contributed to the culture-economy by linking the cultural work of film directing to the entrepreneurial work of advertising and promotion, and nowhere more actively than in affiliation with land developers. Thus, in recent years film directors from avant-garde and commercial circles have collaborated with wealthy developers to tout commodities from cell phones to the Beijing Olympics to luxury housing estates. Such mergers are attributed to the coincidence between cinematic concern with space in recent Chinese film and commercial forces pressing to imbue space with cultural–and thereby economic–value (Braester 2005).

But film, given its potential for mass-market audiences and high production costs, represents a natural ally of commercial promotion and advertising. The marriage of poetry and property, while similar in terms of an economic appeal to cultural value, entails a very different set of practical issues. For one, Chinese new poetry does not enjoy, and indeed never has enjoyed, anything comparable to the mass audience of cinema, even during the peak of poetry's popularity from the 1960s through the 1980s. Further, given the distribution of poetry in low-budget, unregistered, and sometimes handmade "popular publications" (*minban kanwu*), not to mention the flourishing practice of publishing on the Internet, the production and distribution costs of poetry can be low to the point of irrelevance. Thus marketers would seem to have little to gain from linking products to poems, while poets have little artistic need for high levels of capital investment. Not surprisingly, then, China's contemporary poetry has maintained a significant distance from the pressures of cultural commodification.

The price of this distance has, of course, been poetry's marginalization by the array of mass-market cultural forms that have burgeoned throughout the 1990s (Yeh 1998; Wei and Larson 1995). This marginalization has been a double-edged sword for poetry, especially the sort identified as independent or avant-garde. One the one hand, the upsurge in popular culture has deeply eroded the audience poetry enjoyed in years past, especially during the "culture fever" of the 1980s. On the other hand, poetry's separation from the dominant and culturally leveling forces of the market enhances the aura of cultural distinction that surrounds poets and their work, for not only can poets exert independence from the market, but many also deliberately distance themselves from a semiofficial literary bureaucracy that–like almost any organization in postsocialist China–depends more and more for its financial survival on a symbiotic relationship with private business enterprise. Deliberately or not, then, independent poetry has remained relatively untainted by the two most powerful and mutually collusive forces in China's postsocialist society: money, as accumulated and controlled by a new capitalist class; and power, monopolized by the government bureaucracy (Xia 1999; Wank 1995). However true this may or may not be in actual practice, independent poetry is easily identified with traits in direct opposition to those purportedly held by the unholy alliance between capitalists and bureaucrats. In short, where the cash nexus tends to be regarded as dirty, calculating, lowbrow, and crude, poetry is perceived as elegant, pure, disinterested, and culturally prestigious.

Poetry, and independent poetry in particular, has thus acquired a latent symbolic value born of its economic marginalization. Generated by poetry's apparent antimarket nature, this symbolic value has quite ironically been appropriated by the market itself as a means of enhancing the value of its capital investment. Further, it is perhaps not surprising that the one sector of the economy where this unlikely merger has been most apparent is the real-estate market, which is not only one of the hottest zones of economic activity but also the area that, in the public eye, is most deeply tainted by morally questionable collusion between private enterprise and the state bureaucracy.

As for poetry events, these enter the picture as a convenient means of putting poetic culture on display, of framing poetry for a public that might otherwise have little or no contact with "high" literature. Such events, and most notably poetry recitals, thus serve as ideal vehicles not just for promoting a poetic and therefore "clean" corporate image, but also for appealing to a rising consumer middle class concerned with defining its own distinctive elite identity and lifestyle. To some extent, most real-estate-related poetry recitals take advantage of poetry's, and especially independent poetry's, identity as an "art of distinction." The Genre Don recitals, including the 2005 event mentioned at the beginning of this chapter, present a particularly interesting case, and one worth examining in some detail.

Genre Don and the Time-Space of Recitation

The Genre Don Woman's Day recital of 2005 was in fact only one in a series of poetry-related events. These included a press conference, a poetry contest, a proposed book release, and an earlier 2004 recital. Each invoked culture, and poetic culture in particular, in order to boost the economic value of Yilianxuan Real Estate Development Company's upscale Genre Don residential quarter.[5] A look at exactly how this was done offers one concrete example of how poetry *huodong* function within the culture-economy of the real-estate industry.

Although drawing upon intellectualist, high-culture concepts, the promotional message of the Genre Don marketing campaign was anything but subtle. Its first public event, a press conference held in late February 2004, trumpeted the cultural basis of the company's product, the Genre Don residences, by introducing the project's corporate slogan: "The Awakening of Humanist Property" (*renwen dichan de juexing*). On their own, the words "humanist" and "awakening" both evoke the history of China's intellectual elite: "humanist" (*renwen*) recalls the last gasp of reform-era intellectual culture, the 1990s debates on the "spirit of belles lettres" (*renwen jingshen*), while "awakening" (*juexing*) connotes Chinese intellectuals' efforts over the past century to forward a national enlightenment project. But, in the words of the company's general manager, poet-entrepreneur Liu Bo, the slogan encapsulates a somewhat different vision:

poetry and land, land and architecture, architecture and life itself are all
intimately connected. As the first in the real-estate world to raise the slogan

The Awakening of Humanist Property, we hope to use poetry to express the concept of humanist real estate; similarly, holding a poetry competition to support the publication of China's first book of poetry-architecture represents an innovation in the real-estate world, an organic union of real estate and culture. . . . (house.sohu.com 2004)

Whereas Liu's statement presents the basic outline of the culture-poetry-property connection, the cosponsor of the competition, editor of the journal *New Poetry World* (*Xinshijie*) Li Qingsong, used her public statement at the press conference to elaborate on the connection between poetry, the literary representative of high culture, and luxury residence, the market representative of high-end consumption:

A building that a real-estate company develops and constructs is a three-dimensional poem, and poetry is architecture written on paper. Poetry has been called the tip of the literary pyramid. Buildings need poetry to improve their quality, to elucidate the conceptual bases of their design and structure. The general manager of Genre Don is herself a poet. Her proposal for humanist real estate is in accord with people's needs for elegant art and high-quality lifestyle. . . . (house.sohu.com 2004)

Together, Liu's and Li's statements construct a linkage between poetic culture and the lifestyle culture of its target market, a class of prospective homeowners who, as rather baldly stated on a government-run real-estate information website, are "bourgeoisie possessing taste and cultural aspirations" (Invest Beijing 2005). While one may take issue with the premises of their logic, the goal of their statements could not be more clear: to convert the exclusive image of poetry into cultural capital for the Genre Don properties.

It is important to note, too, that in stressing Liu's dual role as poet and company general manager, the press conference statements also transfer the idea of poetic "purity" into the domain of real estate. By foregrounding her identity as poet-entrepreneur, Liu Bo places herself, and by implication her business operations, outside the morally ambiguous, profit-driven motives of property development. In fact, an article in a popular business magazine on "entrepreneurs with artistic dreams" does precisely this when it describes Liu Bo and other poetically inclined business tycoons as "acting according to conscience." The article then cites Liu as saying, "With regard to managing people and affairs, I rarely make judgments based on the numbers, but depend entirely on my conscience. The more complex a problem, the less I use business logic to handle it" (Liu Jianqiang 2004). Here again we see the conversion of poetry's antimarket, cultural capital into economic capital. For Liu Bo, a poetic identity implies access to an alternative moral vision apart from that of the economic realm, but at the same time plays into the creation of economic value by raising the mundane operations of commerce to a presumably higher moral plane, a place where the disinterested motives of pure art trump commercial calculation.

The core of the Genre Don publicity campaign, however, resided in its two poetry events: the Genre Don recitals of March 2004 and 2005; it is the former of the two on which I focus here. Once again, the appearance of actual poets at the Genre Don sales office helps substantiate Liu Bo's claim to be a patron of poetry.[6] Yet the larger significance of the recitals lies not in what the poets actually recited on those two days but in how they are framed as cultural events. The framing comprises two elements: the thematic message of the Genre Don publicity campaign itself and the disposition of the recital in time and space.

With regard to the first of these elements, the two recitals were, of course, embedded within the carefully developed rhetoric of the Genre Don marketing strategy. This rhetoric, which includes the "humanist real estate" slogan elaborated upon through the press conference statements and other publicity writings, determines the context of the recited poems, and thus influences their interpretation. But another important speech genre for contextualizing the performance is the oral introduction, a ritual component of all but the most informal poetry event. Liu Bo's introduction to the 21 March 2004 World Poetry Day Genre Don/ *New Poetry World* Poetry Recital, for example, presents the following interpretive frame for the subsequent poetry readings: "The reason that Genre Don has chosen World Poetry Day to stage its opening of sales is to propose the concept of 'humanist China, humanist real estate,' to promote elegant lifestyle and pursue 'poetic life,' which just happen to be coincident with the ideal realm of poetry" (Beijing Yilianxuan . . . n.d., 40).

This introduction in effect preempts the meanings of the recited poems, not by changing the poems themselves, but by associating the literary exclusivity of independent poetry with the lifestyle exclusivity of the Genre Don project. In addition to framing the poems, Liu's introduction also indicates how an event can invoke pluralistic calendar time to index both culture and economy. More specifically, the 2004 Genre Don recital coordinates business time—the Genre Don sales opening— with several other culture-related calendrical cycles. These include not only the global timing of the annual March 21 World Poetry Day sponsored by UNESCO, but more locally, the opening of a month-long series of events comprising the Peking University Poetry Festival, which began a little over a week later.[7] Not least, the recital was held on a Sunday, which confirms its participation in the culture-economy's ever-expanding leisure-time "weekend culture."

The multiple temporal orientations of this particular cultural *huodong* converged in a very carefully constructed space: the Genre Don sales office, located in

Street view of the Genre Don sales office in Beijing. Note the slogan atop the building, as well as the neon beer mug, wineglass, and coffee cup on the face of the building. Photo by author.

Interior of the Genre Don sales office. Photo by author.

Beijing's Xuanwu District. The 2004 recital was in fact held on the same day as the opening of this structure, whose naked metal panels and winding, bamboo-lined walkways might be described as an organometallic hybrid of Bauhaus modernism and Chinese culturalism. According to Genre Don publicity materials, the theme of the sales office is "spatial experience" (*kongjian tiyan*). This is an experience constructed both physically and discursively. Physically it is imparted by the building's threefold function: real-estate sales office on the ground floor, coffee shop and art gallery upstairs—in short, a combination of property development, leisure-time consumption, and symbolic display of high culture. Discursively, spatial experience is defined by its description, printed in verse form in the lavishly illustrated *Genre Don: China's First Book of Poetry-Architecture* (*Gediao: Zhongguo di yi bu shige lou shu*), a folio-sized book-cum-brochure distributed at the sales office to potential customers. Here, in one of a series of four "poems" comprising a section of the book entitled "Experience" (*tiyan*), we read:

> The spatial experience of Genre Don
> Arranges vision, discrimination, and exchange
> It awakens
> But a tiny minority of the same ilk
> In the spatial experience of Genre Don
> Space is subtly merged and split
> Infusion of the cultural element
> Brings space close. . . .
>
>   (*Gediao* n.d., 32)

By foregrounding the themes of cultural content, attention to aesthetic form, and appeal to an exclusive minority, this segment of advert-verse implies a homologous relation between highbrow, independent poetry and high-end real estate. Thus, whether one considers the physical construction of the sales office space or its discursive construction in accompanying print, the event space of the 2004 recital is inseparable from an attempt to mobilize the cultural cachet of poetry to enhance the economic value of property.

Conclusion

In their exploitation of the poetry-property connection, the Genre Don recitations certainly tend toward an extreme. Let me stress, however, that my analysis seeks, not to decry the "selling out" of the contemporary Chinese poetry scene, but to point to something larger: the multiple articulations among the performed poem, the concept of *huodong*, and the larger social and historical situation. What, then, are some of the implications of poetry and poetry recitation's involvement in the contemporary milieu of the cultural event? In one respect, let it be said that, due to their endlessly amorphous nature, *huodong* preclude generalization. Like contemporary poetry recitals, they come in all shapes, sizes, forms, and styles, and without doubt represent a dynamic symbol of the diversification of culture in contemporary China. But at the same time, underlying and even enabling this diversity is a unitary and deliberately state-engineered policy—the exploitation of the culture-economy—designed to harness market forces. So, even as poets and recitation enthusiasts might celebrate this poetic "renaissance," they should also keep in mind that while much has been gained in the shift from socialism to postsocialism, from a restrictive era of *yundong* to the heterogeneous cultural sphere of *huodong*, poetry of the spoken word is never as independent as one might think.

Yet in closing it seems more important not to stress a lack of freedom regarding where, when, and how the poetic word is spoken in China today but to recognize instead the prolific array of historical determinations that have come to inform the recited modern poem, and how these determinations, in all their mutual resistances and intersections, create potential for new forms of participation and innovation. This, I would venture, is the main discovery to come from this book. On the one hand, unraveling the ideological strands that inform a hundred years of discourse on poetic voice and recitation has meant conversing in detached, analytic silence with the documentary record spanning nearly a century. That conversation reveals, not just ideas from antiquity retooled to serve grandiose modern hopes for the sounding poetic voice, but also modalities of voice adopting words, techniques, and concrete situations to engage the multiply entwined, real-world aesthetics of literary invention, national crisis, personal tragedy, social exchange, political protest, and revolutionary ideology. On the other hand, the bodily engagement of fieldwork intimates the processes by which today's sonorous sites of poetry recitation continuously relay and remix all these strands. The event of recitation, as I have reminded friends and colleagues in China who are involved in sometimes quite insular poetic circles, creates spaces for creative exchange among seemingly discrete traditions. Open to all, these spaces are animated by the fanciful interventions of the artistic avant-garde, the quietly contemplative utterances of poetic intellectuals, the high bombast of state-sponsored orthodoxy, and the populist wordplay of wedding emcees and public-park amateurs. In 1922, we recall from Chapter 1, the young poet Yu Pingbo called for a "republic of poetry" springing from a return to a popular poetic essence. More than eighty years later, this promise unfolds in these evolving sound spaces of poetry's public life.

Notes

Introduction

Epigraph. Lu Xun 1981, 4:15.

1. McDougall and Louie seem to misread Cherkassky (1989) when suggesting that the wartime recitation poet Gao Lan himself performed at the 1937 Lu Xun memorial in Hankou, which he did not (see Chapter 4). Cherkassky notes only that Gao Lan's poetry was recited at that event. Also following an error in the Cherkassky article, they locate Gao Lan's native place as northwest China, when in fact he was born and grew up near the Amur River in China's northeast, Manchuria (McDougall and Louie 1997, 271-272). McDougall and Louie, like Cherkassky, give 1937 as the date of Gao Lan's first poetry collection. However, the Chinese-language sources I have viewed date Gao's first volume of recitation poems to February 1938. Finally, McDougall and Louie assert that "declamatory verse" of the war period was "usually performed on street corners and in other open venues" (262). As Chapter 4 demonstrates, however, modern poetry recitation in fact established itself in the more exclusive venues of literary events.

2. Beijing was renamed Beiping between 1928 and 1949, when the national capital was located in Nanjing. I refer to the city as Beiping when discussing events occurring during this twenty-year span.

3. For intriguing though fragmentary reminiscences of campus recitals during the 1980s, see Xi Du 2004.

4. In his 1945 essay "On Reading Aloud" (Lun langdu), Zhu Ziqing recognizes the entry of *langsong* into common parlance during the war period (1937-1945), but avers that because *song* suggests the recitation of classical texts, *langdu* is the preferred term to use when describing the reading or recitation of works in the modern vernacular (Zhu Ziqing 1994a, 15-16). In an essay published the following year, however, Zhu was referring to current, wartime, and even prewar poetry recitation as *langsong* (Zhu Ziqing 1948a, 97-106).

Chapter 1: Poetic Interiorities

1. While precise dating of the "Preface" remains in dispute, it is believed to have been composed during the early Han in the mid-second century B.C.E. (Lewis 1999, 173; Van Zoeren 1991, 85-86).

2. For seminal statements on the idea of national genius in literature, see Etienne Bonnot de Condillac 2001, 185-195, Thomas Carlyle 1951, 6-7, and Johann Gottlieb

Fichte 1922, 52–90. See also Bauman's study of Johann Gottfried Herder (2003). Studies that corroborate the modular appropriation of nationalist thought in regard to language reform, literature, and poetry include Gregory Jusdanis 1991, Uriel Heyd 1950, and Katie Trumpener 1997.

3. The term "national interiority" is adapted from Dimitrios Tziovas' study of nationalist thought and the Greek demoticist movement of the late nineteenth and early twentieth centuries (1986). I have chosen to use the expression "national interiority" to emphasize the idea of an inner subjectivity while avoiding confusion with the Resistance War period's geographical reference to China's inland provinces as the Interior or *houfang*.

4. According to Charles Ferguson's definition, diglossia refers to "a relatively stable language situation in which, in addition to the primary dialects of the language (which may include a standard or regional standards), there is a very divergent, superposed variety, the vehicle of a large and respected body of written literature, either of an earlier period or in another speech community, which is learned largely by formal education and is used for most written and formal spoken purposes but is not used by any sector of the community for ordinary conversation" (Ferguson 1964, 435).

5. Michel Hockx offers a fine-grained analysis of this positional shift among the contributors to the 1922 new poetry anthology *Snowy Morning* (*Xuezhao*) (1994).

6. Attempts to invigorate new poetry through invocation of a popular or oral tradition by no means came to a close in the early 1920s. The interest in collective origins of poetry persisted through the Republican and on into the Communist period of Chinese modern history, most notably in the call for proletarian literature during the 1930s, the debates on "national form" during the War of Resistance against Japan, and the campaign for a New Folk Song Movement during the late 1950s. Similar tensions, though in sublimated form, also animated the disputes over "popular" and "intellectual" poetry between 1998 and 2000 among mainland poets. For a thorough review and analysis of this dispute, see van Crevel 2008, 399–458.

7. For a detailed survey of the Chinese folklore movement, its influences, publications, and major proponents, see Chang-tai Hung 1985. On May Fourth intellectuals' selective appropriation of folklore, see Haiyan Lee 2005.

8. Translation from Stephen Owen 1992, 41.

9. On Vitale's influence on early Chinese folklorists, see Hung 1985, 18–19, 60.

10. On the debates over "commoner literature" and "commoner poetry," as well as the reactions to Yu Pingbo's "Return," see Hockx 1994, 88–95.

11. Yu's and his cohort's opponents were contributors to the "Poetic Studies Issue" of the *National Southeast University Nanjing College Teachers Daily*. See *Wenxue Xunkan* (Literary thrice-monthly), nos. 18–25 (1 November 1921–11 January 1922) for Yu's and others' attacks on this group.

12. See Kang's 1921 essay "My Views on New Poetry" (Xinshi de wo jian), reprinted as "Xinshi duanlun" (Notes on new poetry), in *Complete Poems of Kang Baiqing* (*Kang Baiqing shi quanbian*), edited by Zhu Xiaozheng and Chen Zhuotuan (Guangzhou: Huacheng chubanshe, 1990), 215–234. For responses to the essay, see Zhong Mi (Zhou

Zuoren), "The Effect of Poetry" (Shi de xiaoyong), *Morning News, Supplement* (*Chenbao fukan*; 26 February 1922) and Liang Shiqiu, "On Reading 'Return to Origins and the Evolution of Poetry'" (Du "Shi de jinhua de huanyuan lun"), parts 1–3, *Morning News, Supplement* (27–29 May 1922).

13. Yu's knowledge of Tolstoy was based on Geng Jizhi's 1921 translation of *What Is Art?* (Tuoersitai [Tolstoy] 1921).

Chapter 2: Poetry Off the Page

1. On twentieth-century poetry readings in the United States and Great Britain, see Morrisson (1996), Sivier (1983a, 1983b), and Edwards (1983). Though he does not provide a time frame, Shen Congwen mentions that Hu Shi enjoyed reading aloud his new poetic creations to guests (2002, 243). As for setting new poetry to music, in the 1920s linguist Yuen Ren Chao (Zhao Yuanren) produced phonographic recordings of sung new poems and, according to Zhu Ziqing, performed several times. Adapting poetry to music was not unusual at the time, as can be seen in Hu Shi's poetry collection *Experiments* (*Changshi ji*), which includes original song lyrics with musical notation. Another intriguing phenomenon, and one never mentioned by the Chinese poets and their critics, is that English poetry recitation seems to have been practiced at foreign-run schools for Chinese early in the twentieth century. My evidence for this is a handwritten inscription in a copy of F. T. Palgrave' s *The Golden Treasury* noting that the book was "a prize for recitation" at the Tientsin Anglo-Chinese College in 1914.

2. Yuen Ren Chao describes such chanting as "improvised tunes based on, but not uniquely defined by tones" (Chao 1956, 56). Although evidence is scanty, traditional modes seemed to guide early oral performance of new poetry. For instance, Yuen Ren Chao writes that for his 1928 *Songs of Contemporary Poems* (*Xinshi geji*; Shanghai: Shangwu yinshugan), the melodies he set to new poems were influenced by the chanting of classical poetry as well as by the "tonal composition" used in traditional drama (Chao 1956, 58 and fn). Also, Zhu Ziqing in his 1927 article mentions hearing Zhu Guangqian performing his own poems with an intonation resembling the spoken parts (*daobai*) of traditional Chinese opera (1996a, 223).

3. A possible factor in Chang's categorical equation of hearing, vision, and emotion is what Jane Geaney identifies as the tendency in early Chinese thought to treat the "heartmind" (*xin*) as behaving like one among the other senses, as it integrates them all (2002, 13).

4. Y. C. Chang writes that he would include the famous Chinese poets Du Fu, Li Bai, Bai Juyi, and Han Yu, except that they did not use punctuation (1924, 12).

5. According to my own calculation, Chang's count of lines in the second through fourth sections of *The Goddesses* (he omits the verse drama "Reincarnation of the Goddesses") is accurate, but he significantly overcounts the number of exclamation marks by about 360. The adjusted calculation, however, still gives Guo's poetry the highest frequency, with about one exclamation mark every 2.7 lines.

6. "Chinese Bloomsbury" is the term used by British poet Julian Bell, who taught at Wuhan University in 1935–1936 and visited Beiping in early 1936 (Bell 1938, 59).

See Laurence 2003 for an extensive study of the literary exchanges and dialogues between British modernists in Bell's circle and the Crescent Moon group.

7. It is interesting to note that at the present-day descendent of these academically inclined poetry salons, the annual Weiminghu Poetry Recital at Peking University, audience members are provided with a booklet of the poems to be read, which they dutifully scan during the readings.

8. In addition to "Stagnation" and Zhu Xiang's "Lotus-picking Song," other poems Shen mentions in this context include Wen's "The Old Cherry Vendor" (Mai yingtao laotouzi), "Mr. Wen Yiduo's Desk" (Wen Yiduo xiansheng de shuzhuo), Liu Mengwei's "Railway Ballad" (Guidao xing), and a number of unspecified poems by Xu Zhimo.

9. See Monroe and Zabel 1938, 444, and Harriet Monroe, Personal Papers, China Diary, II, 29 October 1934 and 13 November 1934, University of Chicago Library (Monroe 1934).

10. Zhu Xiang's friend Luo Niansheng substantiates that Zhu did indeed perform an "experimental" reading of this poem, writing that "with clear pronunciation, he gave a reading quite pleasing to the ear" (Luo Niansheng 1985, 72). Zhu Ziqing, who was also present at the reading, offers a different appraisal. According to him, Zhu Xiang delivered the same poem in a light and quick sing-song intonation similar to Beijing opera-style pronunciation, or yunbai, for an effect that Zhu Ziqing describes as "comical," though "grating on the ear" (1994a, 18).

11. Shen's list of deceased poets includes Xu Zhimo (1896–1931), Liu Mengwei (1900–1926), Zhu Xiang (1904–1933), Liu Bannong (1891–1934), Zhu Da'nan (1907–1930), Yang Zihui (?–?), and Fang Weide (1909–1935). Wen Yiduo survived until his assassination in 1946, but gave up writing new poetry in 1931.

12. Such attacks were by no means limited to poetry. As Chang-tai Hung points out, the idea of "propaganda first, art second" dominated arts and literature, especially during the early years of the war (1994, 276–277).

13. National Defense Literature was Chinese leftist writers' response in 1936 to the call for a political (Guomindang–Communist) united front against Japan. It was a loosely defined and short-lived movement fraught with factional posturing, but under whose rubric the primary aesthetic conflicts of the period can be discerned. For a detailed discussion, see Tagore 1967, 167–211.

14. Along with his poetic refutation of Dai Wangshu's critique (see n. 15 below), Pu Feng boasted that the readership for his National Defense Poetry included "middle school students, grade school teachers and students, progressive farming youth, and even some soldier comrades" (Pu 1938a, 43).

15. Responses include articles, such as Ren Jun's "Upon Reading Dai Wangshu's 'On National Defense Poetry'" (Ren 1948) and Yi Zhong's "The Chinese Poetry Scene in 1937" (Yi 1938), as well as satirical poems like Pu Feng's "Brother, Are You Going to Shanghai?" (Pu 1938a, 43). Ren Jun rebuts Dai point by point, arguing primarily that National Defense Poetry seeks to break with the formulaic sentimentalism and elitist opacity found in Dai's literary "camp"; that National Defense Poetry has in fact spread among the masses in the form of song; that Dai's isolated experiment on the train

provides insufficient evidence for his claims; and that, as less than a year has elapsed since its invention, one should not burden National Defense Poetry with unrealistic expectations. Yi Zhong simply declares that work by Dai and poets like him is doomed to extinction by the "cannon's roar" (*paosheng*) of the war, while Pu Feng's poem portray's Dai as an effete devotee of Shanghai's decadent dance halls.

Chapter 3: Inventing Recitation

1. Wanping is the town next to the Marco Polo Bridge, where wartime hostilities began on 7 July 1937.

2. The feminine element of Chinese new literature had been under attack since at least 1925, when "[c]ritics and writers called for a new literature of social commitment that denied the validity and importance of individual experience and emotion, substituting for it social and class awareness, knowledge, and especially action" (Larson 1998, 180).

3. This recital is discussed in detail in Chapter 4.

4. On Marinetti's recitation, or "combat *parole*," see Kahn 1999, 59–62.

5. The citation's source in Chinese can be found in Huang Zhongsu, *Langsong fa* (Recitational method; 1936). Huang, in turn, is citing University of London professor William Henry Hudson's *An Introduction to the Study of Literature* (Boston, New York, and Chicago: D. C. Heath and Co. Publishers, 1921), 166–167. Hudson takes the citation from Harvard literature professor Samuel Henry Butcher's *Harvard Lectures on Greek Subjects* (New York: The MacMillan Company, 1904), 229. Huang's book, it should be noted, deals almost exclusively with the recitation of classical Chinese poetry and prose for classroom education. He in fact expresses disappointment at the sloppiness of most new poetry and prose, disparaging it as "for the most part unreadable" (7). This may explain why Gao, along with the other believers in new poetry recitation discussed here, neglect to name him or his work.

6. Xu remarks in the preface to the *Handbook* that while in Hong Kong he practiced group recitation (*hesong*) with the Poetry Group of the Hong Kong branch of ACRAWA (All-China Resistance Association of Writers and Artists). Xu's large-scale recital was performed for an intellectual audience in the Hong Kong Confucius Hall (Yuan 1940).

7. As far as I can determine without being able to locate the poem as originally published in Guang's 1944 *Thunder* (*Lei*), the version of "Thunder at Midnight" closest to the original is the one published in Wang Wenchen, ed., *Selected Chinese Poetry of the 1940s* (Chongqing: Chongqing chubanshe, 1985). The versions included in *Selected Songs and Poems of Guang Weiran* (*Guang Weiran geshi xuan*) (Guang 1990) and *Collected Works of Zhang Guangnian* (Guang 2002) are both edited. Evidence of alteration includes the use of punctuation (poems of the mid-war period were often unpunctuated) as well as politically motivated changes to the final stanza, most notably the replacement of "I shall lead you" with "you shall lead us," and "neighbors on all sides" with "flame-red crowds." As for Gao's "Sufei," the version I cite appears in *Recitation Poems of Gao Lan* (Gao 1949). Aside from several corrections in punctuation, it is virtually identical to

the poem as it first appeared in print in the Chongqing *L'Impartial* literary supplement *Battle Line* on 29 March 1942.

8. It is also worth noting that the poetry volume of the *Compendium of Modern Chinese Literature, 1937–1949* provides the lyrics to three parts of *Cantata*, effectively presenting them to the reader as poetry.

9. Founded in Hankou in March 1938, ACRAWA organized and supported the activities and livelihood of writers and artists attached to its headquarters and branches throughout the war. See Chen Anhu, ed. 1997, 546–558 and Laughlin 2008. For more on the Poetry Recitation Team, see Chapter 4.

Chapter 4: Wartime Recitals and the Consolidation of a Genre

1. The two available volumes of these diaries, from 1931 and 1937–1938, were reportedly discovered some time after 1949 in a wastepaper recycling shop and sent on to Pu's relatives before being published (Huang and Chen 1985, 2: 996).

2. Gao Lan and a young employee of the Hankou City Radio Station would broadcast, often to musical accompaniment, nearly every recitation poem that appeared in the literary supplements of the local newspapers. Radio readings of this sort, frequently performed by stage and film stars, became common in Chongqing in the following years (Chen Anhu 1997, 558–562). The primary journal advocating poetry recitation as a form of "massified" literature was *Tunes of the Times* (*Shidiao*), which published a total of five issues beginning on 1 November 1937.

3. Interestingly, Ke Zhongping wrote later that his recitation, impromptu and at least partially sung, was of a poem originally dedicated to his wife (2002, 86–87).

4. For additional descriptions of wartime cultural work in the Chinese countryside, see Alber 2002, Hung 1994, and Laughlin 2002; 2008.

5. According to Zang's account, in the audience during his recitation was the teenage He Jingzhi, later to become deputy cultural minister and author of many poems that entered the Mao-era recitation repertoire.

6. Arranged performances for soldiers were standard for frontline cultural work groups like the squad working in Guomindang-controlled areas, as these groups were sponsored and hosted by the government and military, and were charged with the task of reporting back on the situation at the front lines (Laughlin 2008, 404–408).

7. The journal used *Xanglie* as its romanized name. To avoid confusion, I refer to it as *Rank and File* or, with the standard pinyin romanization, "Hanglie."

8. Whether the funds supplied by *L'Impartial* were in fact used to fund the Poetry Recitation Team in late 1940 is not clear, but seems likely given the prominence of Chen Jiying at the inaugural meeting and the lack of other major recitation activities between the spring and autumn of that year in Chongqing. One reason the team's formation was delayed until the autumn of 1940 may have been to await the arrival of the seasonal fog that helped protect the city from Japanese bombing raids from October to April (Tong 1945, 134).

9. Organizations represented included the China Motion Picture Corporation (Zhongguo dianying zhipianchang), Central Motion Picture Studio (Zhongyang

dianying sheyingchang), and the Experimental Theater (Shiyan juyuan) (Zhanxian 1940).

10. According to Zang Yunyuan, the event that immediately triggered this suppression was a large recital and rally held at Chongqing's Central University (Zang Yunyuan 1979, 75). More influential, however, was the notorious Wannan Incident of January 1941 in which Guomindang forces surrounded and nearly wiped out the Communist New Fourth Army. The incident put an end to the tenuous wartime United Front and initiated a period of suppression against perceived Communist sympathizers in the Guomindang-controlled areas.

11. Lao She describes the first staging of this event in 1941 (1999, 303–305).

12. According to Zhu Ziqing, due to the small radio audience during wartime, poets did not make a great effort to exploit that medium (1948b, 34).

13. On Feng's imprisonment, see Wu Changhua 1995, 109–122.

Chapter 5: Zhu Ziqing and Situational Poetics

1. The term "situation" as I use it is not to be confused with the Situationist International's concept of a "constructed situation," defined in 1958 as "A moment of life concretely and deliberately constructed by the collective organization of a unitary ambiance and a game of events" (Knabb 1989, 45).

2. Zhu's source on verse drama is J. Donald Adams, "Speaking of Books," *New York Times*, 22 October 1944.

3. The relevant student protest movements of 1946–1947 were the Anti–U.S. Brutality Movement, Guarantee of Human Rights Movement, and the Anti-civil War, Anti-hunger Movement (Beijing Dang'anguan 1991, 51–244).

4. On He Da's activities as a poet in the 1940s, see his biographical essay "Forty-five years of learning poetry" (Xue shi sishiwu nian) (1976, 154–157).

5. Regarding the poem "Our Talk" and the metaphor of literature as a "'weapon," it is interesting to note that while undergoing military training during the War of Resistance, He Da was greatly disappointed to discover that, due to a vision defect, he literally could not shoot straight (He 1976, 151–152).

6. As Zhu indicates in the essay "On Recitation Poetry," his conception of the "private" and "public" worlds, and poetry's place in both, were inspired by the Archibald MacLeish essay, "Poetry and the Public World" (1948b).

Chapter 6: Calculated Passions

1. Deputy Minister of Propaganda Zhou Yang wrote at the time, "Great Leap Forward folk songs reflect the laboring masses' ever-surging revolutionary vigor and passion for production, while also greatly inciting this vigor and passion, thus promoting the development of the forces of production" ([1958] 1995, 458). The founding cultural policy statement on this link between cultural and economic production appeared in *Wenyi bao* (Wenyi bao 1958). See D. W. Fokkema for an overview of the period (1965, 192–222), and Chen Shih-hsiang for a perceptive study of the Great Leap poems themselves (S. H. Chen 1966).

2. The "Three Red Banners" refers to the General Line for Socialist Construction, the Great Leap Forward, and the People's Communes.

3. As noted in Chapter 4, Poet's Day was established in Chongqing in 1941 by members of the All-China Resistance Association of Writers and Artists (Lao 1999; Chen Mingshu 1994, 383).

4. Traditional oral arts were essential to these performances, as the rural population did not as a rule recognize poetry recitation as a performance form. Veteran actress Zhu Lin clearly remembers a farmer praising the poetry recitation segment of one of these recitals by saying, "It sounds very nice when you talk that way" (Zhu Lin 2007).

5. For example, many of the *Poetry Journal* reports on recitation activities were contributed by Yin Zhiguang, an actor specializing in poetry recitation. Yin, along with *Poetry Journal*, organized the first poetry recitals for which tickets were sold: the famously popular Sunday Recitations (Xingqi langsong hui) held in Beijing in early 1963 (Ge 1963, 15; Yuan 1963, 49; Jia 2003, 88; Cao Can 2004; Yin Chih-kuang 1963, 28). He has continued to work as an impresario of recitals since the early 1980s.

6. In addition to Owen (1992, 38–49), see also Susan Daruvala's discussion of *zhi* and *qing* as regards Zhou Zuoren's ideas on the aesthetic (2000, 115–118).

7. According to one definition, this process of confession "begins with a stain and blemish, the purging removal of which is essential for enlightenment, not only for the self but for the collectivity, lest others become contaminated and polluted" (Apter and Saich 1994, 293).

8. I saw segments of "Song of Lei Feng" recited a number of times by amateur reciters in Beijing in 2005–2006. Excerpts from the poem are also commonly included in contemporary anthologies of poetry for recitation (Ling 2003; Lan and Liu 2006).

9. Note that I have retained the end-rhyme markers (Δ) in the English without in all cases reproducing rhyme endings. In the Chinese, the marked endings echo the first line's "Feng", i.e., *xiong, zhong, bing, ceng, ming*, etc. For an insightful discussion of the political-aesthetic function at work in the *–ng* rhyme ending, see Chen Shih-hsiang's study of Great Leap Forward poetry (S. H. Chen 1966, 400).

10. The poem has likewise become a standard in the repertoire of amateur poetry recitation enthusiasts.

Chapter 7: From *Yundong* to *Huodong*

1. Reducing the powers of the most important administrative institution behind *yundong*, the Ministry of Propaganda, was in fact one of Deng's strategies for weakening his leftist opponents (Kraus 2004, 16).

2. As Morris Wills, an American caught up in many early campaigns while resident in China from 1954 to 1965, laconically put it: "All life in China divides into 'movements'; the whole thing sort of dates from one movement to another. The Chinese word is *yun-tung*" (Wills and Moskin 1968, 97).

3. The state, as Richard Kraus observes and countless Chinese media reports corroborate, has identified and begun promoting culture as a growth industry (2004, 230).

4. Here I refer specifically to the "2004 Poetry Biennial" held in E'erguna, Inner Mongolia, as part of that city's Year of Tourism Publicity (Tan 2005, 18–22); the Guangzhou Zhujiang Real Estate Development Center's Evening at Hanjingxuan Poetry Recital held in coordination with the sales opening of its Hanjingxuan Humanist Community condominium project (Li Huifei 2002); the April 2006 Spring and Poets (Chuntian song ni yi shou shi) recital held in Ningbo during the Fourth Home Expo trade show (Ningbo China 2006; Zhejiang On-line 2006); and a variety of poetry recitals, besides the 2005 Kashgar event already mentioned, sponsored by the Zhongkun Investment Group's tourism operations.

5. According to my research, it seems that in fact neither the poetry competition nor the proposed poetry volume based on the competition results came to fruition; at least there is no subsequent mention of either in the media. The Yilianxuan Real Estate Development Company did, however, produce a folio volume entitled *Genre Don: China's First Book of Poetry-Architecture*, discussed in this chapter.

6. According to a media report, over twenty "celebrities of the poetry world" attended the 2004 recital, including Tang Xiaodu, Xi Chuan, Wang Jiaxin, Qiao Damo, Mo Fei, Hai Xiao, and Li Qingsong herself. Members of the all-female poetry club Hay Tribe, the report adds, provided "glittering scenery" (Zhao 2004).

7. The 2004 Peking University Poetry Festival opened on 2 April. It bears mentioning that the Hay Tribe, including Liu Bo, participated in one of the festival recitals (Liu Xia et al. 2005).

Glossary

a 啊
Ai Qing 艾青
"Ai Zhongguo" 哀中国
aiyo 哎哟
An E 安娥
ba 罢
Bai Yang 白杨
baihua 白话
Baihua shi yanjiuxuan 白话诗研究选
baogao shi 报告诗
Bian Zhilin 卞之琳
bu huazhuang de xi 不化装的戏
"Bu pa si—pa taolun" 不怕死—怕讨论
"Bu shi shi" 不是诗
"Cailian qu" 采莲曲
cailiao 材料
Cao Baohua 曹葆华
Cao Borong 曹伯荣
cao ta mama de 操他妈妈的
Cao'er 草儿
Chang Renxia 常任侠
chang shi 长诗
Changshi ji 尝试集
Chen Duxiu 陈独秀
Chen Jiying 陈纪滢
Chen Kaige 陈凯歌
Chen Nanshi 陈南士
"Chu dong" 初冬
chuangzuo 创作
Chunshui 春水
Chuntian song ni yi shou shi 春天送你一首诗
ci 词
cizao 辞藻

Dagongbao 大公报
dao 道
daobai 道白
Daqing 大庆
"Daxu" 大序
dazhong 大众
dazhong de pujixing 大众的普及性
dazhonghua 大众化
Deng Xiaoping 邓小平
difangyan 地方言
dong hang yi hu, wen zhe xing qi 动吭一呼，闻者兴起
Dongye 冬夜
Du Dongyan 杜东彦
Du Fu 杜甫
Duanwu jie 端午节
dufu minzei 独夫民贼
duisong 对诵
Dushi hui 读诗会
dusong 独诵
E'erguna 额尔古纳
Fang Yin 方殷
fangfu 仿佛
Fangzi 方子
Fanxing 繁星
Fei Ming 废名
Feng Naichao 冯乃超
Feng Xuefeng 冯雪峰
Feng Zhi 冯至
fenwei 氛围
fu shi 赋诗
Gan Yuze 甘雨泽
Gancao buluo 干草部落
Gangtie de gechang 钢铁的歌唱

ganrenli　感人力
gantan hao　感叹号
Gao Lan　高兰
Gao Lan langsongshi ji　高兰朗诵诗集
"Gaoliang hong le"　高粱红了
Ge Yuan　戈原
Gediao　格调
Gediao: Zhongguo di yi bu shige lou shu　格调：中国第一部诗歌楼书
geming de jiqing　革命的激情
geyao　歌谣
gongtong jinghun　共通精魂
Guan Lu　关露
guangchang shige　广场诗歌
Guang Weiran　光未然
guanhua　官话
guci　鼓词
Gudao　孤岛
"Guidao xing"　轨道行
guizu　贵族
Guo Dehao　郭德浩
guo min zhi sheng　国民之声
Guo Moruo　郭沫若
Guo Shaoyu　郭绍虞
"Guoyu de jinhua"　国语的进化
guoyu de wenxue he wenxue de guoyu　国语的文学和文学的国语
guoyu shi　国语诗
"Guoyu yu guoyu wenfa"　国语与国语文法
gushi　古诗
guwenjia　古文家
Hai Xiao　海啸
Han Bai　寒白
Hanglie she　行列社
"Hanjiao"　喊叫
Hanjingxuan　翰景轩
he　呵
He Jingzhi　贺敬之
He Qifang　何其芳
hesong　合诵
houfang　后方
Hu Feng　胡风

Hu Shi　胡适
huaju　话句
huan chun fan pu　还淳反朴
Huang Ningying　黄宁婴
Huang Nubo　黄怒波
Huangchuan　潢川
Huanghe dahechang　黄河大合唱
"Huanghe song"　黄河颂
"Huanghe yin"　黄河吟
"Huanying ci"　欢迎词
"Huida"　回答
huo　活
huobao shi　活报诗
huodong　活动
huodongjia　活动家
jianduan er gancui　简短而干脆
Jiang Guangci　蒋光慈
Jiang Xijin　蒋锡金
Jiang Xiangchen　姜湘忱
jiankang　健康
jianli　建立
jie　节
jiefang qu　解放区
jietou shi　街头诗
"Jigei Dunheshang de xiangrikui"　寄给顿河上的向日葵
"Jinye, women duguo Zhanghe"　今夜，我们渡过漳河
jitihua　集体化
jituan de gudongxing　集团的鼓动性
jizao　急躁
jueju　绝句
juexing　觉醒
Junxian　均县
juxianghua　具象化
Kang Baiqing　康白情
kao　考
Ke Zhongping　柯仲平
kongjian tiyan　空间体验
"Ku wangnü Sufei"　哭亡女苏菲
kuangxiao　狂啸
langdu　朗读
Langhua　浪花

langsong 朗诵

langsong qiang 朗诵腔

langsong shi 朗诵诗

Langsong tongxun 朗诵通讯

Langsongshi ji 朗诵诗集

langsongshi pai 朗诵诗派

lao 老

Lao She 老舍

"Lao Wang de si" 老王的死

le 了

"Lei Feng zhi ge" 雷锋之歌

Lei Shiyu 雷石榆

Li Bai 李白

Li Huiying 李辉英

Li Ji 李季

Li Lei 李雷

Li Qingsong 李青松

Li Zongren 李宗仁

Liang Zongdai 梁宗岱

"Liangge saoxue de ren" 两个扫雪的人

"Liming de tongzhi" 黎明的通知

Lin Geng 林庚

Lin Huiyin 林徽因

Liu Bo 刘博

Liu Mengwei 刘梦苇

Lu Xun 鲁迅

lunsong 轮诵

Luo Niansheng 罗念生

Luo Ying 骆英

lüshi 律诗

"Mai yingtao laotouzi" 卖樱桃老头子

mama 妈妈

manman 慢慢

Mao Zedong 毛泽东

Meng Chao 孟超

menglong 蒙胧

minban kanwu 民办刊物

mingbai ru hua 明白如话

mingxinpian shi 明信片诗

mingyun 命运

minjian de shi 民间的诗

minyao 民谣

minzhong wenxue 民众文学

Mo Fei 莫非

"Moluo shi li shuo" 摩罗诗力说

Mu Mutian 穆木天

ne 呢

ni yi sheng jiezhe yi sheng 你一声接着一声

nimen 你们

nuhou 怒吼

Nüshen 女神

"Nüwu" 女巫

pai 派

paosheng 砲声

paoxiao 咆哮

"Pingfan de yehua" 平凡的夜话

"Pingjing de hai maicangzhe bolang" 平
    静的海埋藏着波浪

pingmin 平民

pingmin shi 平民诗

Pu Feng 蒲风

pubian de qinggan 普遍的情感

puluo putonghua 普罗普通话

Qian Xuantong 钱玄同

qiang 腔

Qiao Damo 谯达摩

qing dong yu zhong er fa yu yan 情动于中
    而发于言

qinggan 情感

qinggan zhi qifu 情感之起伏

Qingnian jun 青年军

qingxu de boliu 情绪的波流

qu 曲

"Qu da youji zhan" 去打游击战

Qu Qiubai 瞿秋白

Qu Yuan 屈原

Rao Mengkan 饶孟侃

Ren Jun 任钧

renmen de qinggan he yizhi 人们的情感
    和意志

renmin 人民

renwen 人文

renwen dichan de juexing 人文地产的
    觉醒

renwen jingshen 人文精神

saishi hui 赛诗会

Shangcheng 商城
shan'ge 山歌
Shanghai shige zuotanhui 上海诗歌座
  谈会
"Shangxin de hudie" 伤心的蝴蝶
Shao Quanlin 邵荃麟
Shen Congwen 沈从文
sheng 声
sheng 聖
shengdiao 声调
shengyin yishu 声音艺术
shequ 摄取
shi 师
shi 诗
Shi 诗
shi de 诗的
shi de gongheguo 诗底共和国
shi de wangguo 诗底王国
"Shi shihou le, wo de tongbao!" 是时
  候了，我的同胞！
shi yan zhi 诗言志
"Shi yu kouyu" 诗与口语
shi zhe, zhi zhi suo zhi ye 诗者，志之所
  之也
shidai jingshen 时代精神
Shidiao 时调
shifu 师傅
Shige chubanshe 诗歌出版社
shige langsong 诗歌朗诵
Shige langsong dahui 诗歌朗诵大会
Shige langsong dui 诗歌朗诵队
Shige langsong yehui 诗歌朗诵夜会
Shige min'ge yanchang wanhui 诗歌
  民歌演唱晚会
shijian 实践
shijie geming 诗界革命
Shijing 诗经
"Shinian" 十年
"Shiren de huanxi" 诗人的欢喜
Shiren jie 诗人节
shisheng 诗声
Shiyan juyuan 实验剧院

"Shiyou ge" 石油歌
Shu Xiuwen 舒绣文
shuo hua 说话
shuqing changshi 抒情长诗
shuqing yanzhi 抒情言志
si 寺
sihu dingxing 四呼定形
sijiao 嘶叫
"Sishui" 死水
"Songbie nantong" 送别难童
"Songbie qu" 送别曲
songdu 诵读
suhua shi 俗话诗
Sun Daolin 孙道临
Sun Dayu 孙大雨
Tang Xiaodu 唐晓渡
"Tengtong" 疼痛
Tian Han 田汉
Tian Jian 田间
Tian Zhaoying 天照应
tigao qingxu 提高情绪
tiyan 体验
Wang Jiaxin 王家新
Wang Jinxi 王进喜
Wang Ying 王莹
wanzheng 完整
wanzhuan 宛转
wen 文
Wen Liu 温流
"Wen Liu, zuguo huzhao ni!" 温流, 祖
  国呼召你！
"Wen Yiduo" 闻一多
"Wen Yiduo xiansheng de shuzhuo" 闻
  一多先生的书桌
wende xingshi 文的形式
wenhua cheng 文化城
wenyao 文妖
wenyi bing 文艺兵
"Wo de jia zai Heilongjiang" 我的家在
  黑龙江
"Wo de jiaxiang–Yixing" 我的家乡—
  宜兴

"Wo wei shaonan shaonümen gechang"
我为少男少女们歌唱

women 我们

"Women bu yao rennai" 我们不要忍耐

"Women de jili" 我们的祭礼

"Women zhe shisi ge" 我们这十四个

Wu jing 五经

Wu xin guilai ya! Cong minjian guilai! 吾
心归来呀！从民间归来！

"Wuye de leisheng" 午夜的雷声

wuyin chuzi 五音出字

Xi Chuan 西川

Xian Xinghai 冼星海

xiang shan 向善

xiangqi le di yi sheng junhao 响起了第一
声军号

"Xiangxiang jilong tan" 想想吉隆滩

"Xiangyin" 乡音

Xiao Hong 萧红

Xiao San 萧三

xiaodiao 小调

Xiaoxiao 潇潇

xin de qingxu 新的情绪

Xin Qingnian 新青年

xin yangge 新秧歌

Xin Zhongguo jushe 新中国剧社

xinbang 新邦

xingshi 形式

xingshi luowu 形式落伍

xingxianghua 形象化

Xinhua ribao 新华日报

Xinli 心理

xinsheng 心声

Xinshi nianxuan 新诗年选

Xinshijie 新诗界

Xinyue she 新月社

xiu 秀

Xu Chi 徐迟

Xu Zhimo 徐志摩

"Xue de ge" 雪的歌

"Xuehua de baolie" 血花的爆裂

xunchang baixing 寻常百姓

ya 呀

yan 言

Yan'an 延安

Yang Zihui 杨子惠

yanwen yizhi 言文一致

yanyu 言语

Yi Zhong 伊仲

yin 音

yin 吟

Yin Zhiguang 殷之光

yinhang gaoge 引吭高歌

yinjie 音节

yinlü 音律

yinshuapin shi 印刷品诗

"Yiqie" 一切

yiqun 意群

yishi luowu 意识落伍

yong 咏

Yu Pingbo 俞平伯

Yuan Shuipo 袁水拍

Yue Bin 岳斌

yunbai 韵白

yundong 运动

yunlü 韵律

yuyan 语言

zai guzi li 在骨子里

"Zaihui ba! Xiaojie!" 再会吧！小姐！

Zang Yunyuan 臧云远

Zang Kejia 臧克家

zhan youshi de fengge 占优势的风格

Zhandi 战地

zhandouxing 战斗性

Zhan'ge she 战歌社

Zhanxian 战线

zhaohun 招魂

Zhang Guangnian 张光年

Zhang Hongchi 张洪池

Zhang Jiluan 张季鸾

Zhang Ruifang 张瑞芳

Zhang Tianyi 张天翼

Zhang Yaoxiang 张耀翔

Zhao Yuanren 赵元任

"Zhe bu shi liulei de rizi"　这不是流泪
　的日子

Zheng Zhenduo　郑振铎

zhengzhi shuqing shi　政治抒情诗

zhenzhi yu chengxin　真挚与诚心

zhi　志

zhijie de gandongxing　直接的感动性

zhisu　质素

Zhongguo dianying zhipianchang　中
　国电影制片厂

Zhongguo shige hui　中国诗歌会

Zhongguo shitan　中国诗坛

Zhongguo shitan she　中国诗坛社

Zhonghua quanguo wenyijie kangdi
　xiehui　中华全国文艺界抗敌协会

Zhongyang dianying sheyingchang　中央
　电影摄影厂

Zhou Gangming　周钢鸣

Zhou Zuoren　周作人

Zhu Da'nan　朱大楠

Zhu Guangqian　朱光潜

Zhu Weiji　朱维基

Zhu Xiang　朱湘

Zhuang Yong　庄涌

"Ziliujing de tianran wasi huo"　自流
　井的天然瓦斯火

zimian　字面

ziran de qingzhong gaoxia　自然的轻重
　高下

ziran de yinjie　自然的音节

ziran de yongyun　自然的用韵

ziyou shi　自由诗

"Ziyou xiang women lai le"　自由向我
　们来了

Zou Difan　邹狄帆

"Zuguo de tiankong kai le hua"　祖国的
　天空开了花

zuihou de beixiao　最后的悲啸

zuojia de shi　作家的诗

Zuoyi zuojia lianmeng　左翼作家联盟

Works Cited

Chinese-Language Sources

Ai Ke'en, ed. 1987. *Yan'an wenyi yundong jisheng, 1937.1–1948.3* (Chronology of literary and arts movements at Yan'an, January 1937–March 1948). Beijing: Wenhua yishu chubanshe.

Ai Qing. 1939. "Shi de sanwen mei" (Prose-style beauty in poetry). *Dingdian* (Climax) 1, no. 1 (10 July): 48–49.

———. 1991. *Ai Qing quanji* (Complete works of Ai Qing). 5 vols. Shijiazhuang: Huashan wenyi chubanshe.

Beijing Dang'anguan (Beijing City Archives), ed. 1991. *Jiefang zhanzheng shiqi Beiping xuesheng yundong* (Beiping student movements of the War of Liberation period). Beijing: Guangming ribao chubanshe.

Beijing Yilianxuan Fangdichan Kaifa Youxian Gongsi (Beijing Yilianxuan Real Estate Development Company, Ltd.). N.d. *Gediao: Zhongguo di yi bu shige lou shu* (Genre Don: China's first book of poetry-architecture). Beijing: n.p.

Benkan jizhe. 1963. "Langsong yishu zuotan" (A discussion of recitation art). *Shikan* (Poetry journal), no. 69, 55–58.

Cai Dingguo. 1994. *Guilin kangzhan wenxue shi* (Literary history of Guilin during the War of Resistance). Nanning: Guangxi wenxue chubanshe.

[Cao] Borong. 1964a. "Shigang gongren ai langsong" (Workers at Shijingshan Steel Factory love to recite). *Shikan* (Poetry journal), no. 75, 27.

Cao Borong. 1964b. "Wo dui shi langsong de chubu renshi" (My initial understanding of poetry recitation). *Shikan* (Poetry journal), no. 80, 113–116.

Cao Can. 2004. Interview. Beijing, 7 June.

Chang Y. C. 1924. "Xin shiren zhi qingxu" (The emotion of new poets). *Xinli* (Psychology) 3, no. 2 (April): 1–14.

Chen Anhu, ed. 1997. *Xiandai wenxue shetuan liupai shi* (A history of literary societies and schools in modern Chinese literature). Wuhan: Huadong shifan daxue chubanshe.

Chen Jiying. 1940. "Zhu shige langsong dui chengli" (Congratulations on the founding of the Poetry Recitation Team). In *Zhanxian* (Battle line) literary supplement, Chongqing *Dagongbao* (L'Impartial), 7 December.

———. 1941. "Xinshi langsong yundong zai Zhongguo (xia)" (The new poetry recitation movement in China, part two). In *Zhanxian* (Battle line) literary supplement, Chongqing *Dagongbao* (L'Impartial), 6 August.

———. 1987. "'Xu' Gao Lan langsongshi ji" ("Preface" to *Gao Lan's Poems for Recitation*). In *Shi de langsong yu langsong de shi* (Poetry recitation and recitation poetry), ed. Gao Lan. Jinan: Shandong daxue chubanshe: 29-33.

Chen Mingshu, ed. 1994. *Ershi shiji Zhongguo wenxue dadian, 1930-1965* (Annals of twentieth-century Chinese literature). 3 vols. Vol. 2. Shanghai: Shanghai jiaoyu chubanshe.

Chen Nanshi. 1922. "Shiren de huanxi" (The poet's joy). *Shi* (Poetry monthly) 1, no. 1 (January): 23.

Dai Wangshu. 1937. "Tan guofang shige" (On National Defense Poetry). *Xin Zhonghua zazhi* (New China journal) 5, no. 7 (10 April): 84-86.

Feng Xuefeng. 1948. *Xuefeng wenji* (Collected writings of Xuefeng). Shanghai: Chunming shudian.

Gan Yuze. 1975. *Shige langsong* (Poetry recitation). Harbin: Heilongjiang renmin chubanshe.

Gao Lan. 1937. "Zhankai women de langsong shige" (Launch our recitation poetry). *Shidiao* (Tunes of the times), no. 3 (1 December).

———. 1940. *Langsongshi ji* (Poems for recitation). Changsha: Shangwu yinshuguan.

———. 1942. "Ji Luan xiansheng yu shige langsong" (Mr. Ji Luan and poetry recitation). In *Zhanxian* (Battle line) literary supplement, Chongqing *Dagongbao* (L'Impartial), 6 September.

———. 1949. *Gao Lan langsongshi* (Recitation poems of Gao Lan). Shanghai: Jianzhong chubanshe.

———. 1987a. *Gao Lan langsongshi xuan* (Selected recitation poems of Gao Lan). Jinan: Shandong wenyi chubanshe.

———. 1987b. "Guoqu langsong yidian tihui" (Some lessons learned in recitation). In *Shi de langsong yu langsong de shi* (Poetry recitation and recitation poetry), ed. Gao Lan. Jinan: Shandong daxue chubanshe. Original ed., *Qingdao ribao* (8 May 1957): 141-148.

———. 1987c. "Qianyan" (Foreword). In *Gao Lan langsongshi xuan* (Selected recitation poems of Gao Lan), 1-17. Jinan: Shandong wenyi chubanshe.

———. 1987d. "Shi de langsong yu langsong de shi" (Poetry recitation and recitation poetry). In *Shi de langsong yu langsong de shi* (Literary Gazette), ed. Gao Lan. Jinan: Shandong daxue chubanshe. Original ed., *Shi yu chao wenyi* (Time and tide literature and art) 4, no. 6 (15 February 1945): 1-26.

Ge Luo. 1963. "Guangda qunzhong huanying shi langsong" (The broad masses welcome poetry recitation). *Wenyi bao*, no. 303, 15-16.

Guang Weiran. 1985. "Wuye de leisheng" (Thunder at midnight). In *Zhongguo sishi niandai shixuan* (Selected Chinese poetry of the 1940s), ed. Zhongguo sishi niandai shixuan bianweihui, 2: 403-409. 2 vols. Chongqing: Chongqing chubanshe.

———. 1990. *Guang Weiran geshi xuan* (Selected songs and poems of Guang Weiran). Beijing: Renmin wenxue chubanshe.

———. 2002. *Zhang Guangnian wenji* (Collected works of Zhang Guangnian). 5 vols. Vol. 5. Beijing: Renmin wenxue chubanshe.

Guang Weiran and Xian Xinghai. 1956. *Huanghe dahechang* (Yellow River cantata). Beijing: Yinyue chubanshe.

Hai Yang. 1944. "Guilin tongxun: shige langsong yehui" (Guilin dispatch: Evening of poetry recitation). In *Xinhua fukan* literary supplement, Chongqing *Xinhua ribao* (New China daily), 15 May.

Han Bai. 1940. "Lao Wang de si" (The death of old Wang). *Hanglie* (Rank and file) 1, no. 2 (12 February): 14–15.

Hanglie. 1940. "Bian houji" (Editor's postscript). *Hanglie* (Rank and file) 1, no. 3 (28 February): 24.

He Da. 1949. *Women kai hui* (We're in session). Shanghai: Zhongxing chubanshe.

———. 1976. *He Da shixuan* (Selected poems of He Da). Ed. Yin Zhaochi, Hong Kong: Wenxue yu meishu chubanshe.

He Qifang. 1995. *He Qifang shi quanbian* (Complete poems of He Qifang). Ed. Lan Dizhi. Hangzhou: Zhejiang wenxue chubanshe.

Hong Shen. 1950. *Xi de nianci yu shi de langsong* (Dramatic speaking and poetic recitation). Shanghai: Zhonghua shuju. Original ed., Chongqing: Zhongguo wenhua fuwushe, 1943.

Hong Zicheng and Liu Denghan. 2005. *Zhongguo dangdai xinshi shi* (A history of Chinese contemporary new poetry). Rev. ed. Beijing: Beijing daxue chubanshe.

house.sohu.com. 2004. *Gediao juzi zheng shi, dazao Zhongguo di yi bu shige lou shu* (Genre Don invests heavily in soliciting poetry to create China's first book of poetry-architecture). World Wide Web (accessed 11 January 2005). http://house.sohu.com/newshtml/59692.html.

Hu Shi. 1935a. "Wenxue gailiang chuyi." (A tentative proposal for reforming literature). In *Zhongguo xinwenxue daxi, jianshe lilun ji* (Compendium of Chinese new literature: Construction and theory volume), ed. Zhao Jiabi, 1: 34–43. 10 vols. Shanghai: Liangyou tushu gongsi.

———. 1935b. "Tan xinshi: banian lai yi jian da shi" (On new poetry: A major event of the past eight years). In *Zhongguo xinwenxue daxi, jianshe lilun ji* (Compendium of Chinese new literature: Construction and theory volume), ed. Zhao Jiabi, 1: 294–311. 10 vols. Shanghai: Liangyou tushu gongsi.

———. 1935c. "Jianshe de wenxue geming lun" (On the constructive literary revolution). In *Zhongguo xinwenxue daxi, jianshe lilun ji* (Compendium of Chinese new literature: Construction and theory volume), ed. Zhao Jiabi, 1: 127–140. 10 vols. Shanghai: Liangyou tushu gongsi.

———. 1935d. "Guoyu yu guoyu wenfa" (National language and national language grammar). In *Zhongguo xinwenxue daxi, jianshe lilun ji* (Compendium of Chinese new literature: Construction and theory volume), ed. Zhao Jiabi, 1: 228–232. 10 vols. Shanghai: Liangyou tushu gongsi.

———. 1935e. "Guoyu de jinhua" (The evolution of the national language). In *Zhongguo xinwenxue daxi, jianshe lilun ji* (Compendium of Chinese new literature: Construction and theory volume), ed. Zhao Jiabi, 1: 233–246. 10 vols. Shanghai: Liangyou tushu gongsi.

——. 1977. *Hu Shi liuxue riji* (Hu Shi's American diary). 2nd ed. 4 vols. Taibei: Shangwu shuguan. Original ed. 1947.

Huang Anrong and Chen Songxi, eds. 1985. *Pu Feng xuanji* (Selected writings of Pu Feng). 2 vols. Fuzhou: Haixia wenyi chubanshe.

Huang Zhipeng, ed. 2007. *Ni yisheng ying songdu de 50 shou shige jingdian* (50 classic poems you should recite in your life). Beijing: Beijing tushuguan chubanshe.

Huang Zhongsu. 1936. *Langsong fa* (Recitational method). Shanghai: Kaiming shudian.

Hui Lu. 1964. "Diantai tingzhong dui shi langsong de fanying" (The radio audience response to poetry recitation). *Shikan* (Poetry journal), no. 77, 66–68.

Invest Beijing. 2005. *Beijing Yilianxuan fangdichan kaifa youxian gongsi* (Beijing Yilianxuan Real Estate Development Co., Ltd.). World Wide Web (accessed 8 January 2006). http://www.bjinvest.gov.cn/qytj/200512/t105405.htm.

Jia Tubi. 2003. "Qiannian shiguo de yunque" (Skylarks in an age-old poem world). *Zhongguancun* (November), 88–89.

Jiang Guangchi. 1983. *Xinmeng, Ai Zhongguo* (New dreams, sorrow for China). Beijing: Renmin wenxue chubanshe.

Jiang Guipu. 1940. "Shige langsong dui chengli dahui ji" (Notes from the inaugural meeting of the Poetry Recitation Team). In *Zhanxian* (Battle line) literary supplement, Chongqing *Dagongbao* (L'Impartial), 7 December.

Jiang Tao. 2005. *"Xinshi ji" yu Zhongguo xinshi de fasheng* (New poetry collections and the emergence of Chinese new poetry). Beijing: Beijing daxue chubanshe.

Jiang Tian. 1964. "Kelamayi youkuang zhigong juxing shige langsong wanhui" (Karamay oil-field workers hold evening of poetry recitation). *Shikan* (Poetry journal), no. 73, 39.

Jiang Xiangchen. 1964a. "Langsong yanyuan shujian" (Letter from a reciting actor). *Shikan* (Poetry journal), no. 77, 29.

——. 1964b. "Langsong yi de" (A lesson in recitation). *Shikan* (Poetry journal), no. 80, 117–118.

Ke Fei. 1937. "Dazhonghua yu fangyan jietou shige" (Massification and dialect street poetry). *Zhongguo shitan* (China poetry forum) 1, no. 5 (December): 2–3.

Ke Zhongping. 2002. "Qing bu yao wuxin wo" (Please don't have false confidence in me). In *Ke Zhongping wenji* (Collected works of Ke Zhongping), ed. Zhao Jin. 3 vols. Vol. 3. Kunming: Yunnan renmin chubanshe. Original ed. Yan'an *Xin Zhonghua bao* (New China news) (20 October 1938): 85–87.

Kong Mi. 1943. "Chengdu de wenyi langsong hui" (Literary recital in Chengdu). Chongqing *Xinhua ribao* (New China daily), 28 May.

Lan Bo and Liu Miao, eds. 2006. *Langsong 365* (Recitation 365). Beijing: Dazhong wenyi chubanshe.

Langsong tongxun. 1941. "Langsong tongxun: Shige langsong dui zai Yu chengli." (Recitation dispatch: Poetry Recitation Team established in Chongqing). In *Women de shi, Shanghai shige congkan zhi san* (Our poetry, Shanghai poetry series no. 3), ed. Shi Yi et al., 145–149. Shanghai: n.p.

Lao She. 1999. "Di yi jie shiren jie" (The first Poet's Day). In *Lao She quanji* (Complete works of Lao She), 14: 303–305. 19 vols. Beijing: Renmin wenxue chubanshe.

Li Hongjie. 2005. *Dahua dichan: Nüxing yishu zhan ji shige langsong hui–Fangzi* (Big talk on real estate: Women's art exhibition and poetry recital–Fangzi). World Wide Web (accessed 18 January 2006). http://news.soufun.com/2005-03-09/382359.htm.

Li Huifei. 2002. *Yousheng de shige youse de shiren* (Sounded poems and colorful poets). World Wide Web (accessed 28 April 2006). http://www.zjdc.cn/news/displaynews. asp?id=179.

Li Lei. 1987. "Lun shige langsong de jiqiao" (On the technique of poetry recitation). In *Shi de langsong yu langsong de shi* (Poetry recitation and recitation poetry), ed. Gao Lan. Jinan: Shandong daxue chubanshe. Original ed., *Kangzhan wenyi* (War of resistance literature and art) 4, nos. 5–6 (10 October 1939): 55–57.

Li Xiaoyu, ed. 2004. *Jieri langsong shixuan, xiaoyuan ban* (Selected poems for holiday recitation, campus edition). Changsha: Hunan wenyi chubanshe.

Liang Zongdai. 1936a. "Wentan wang nali qu–'yong shenme hua' wenti" (Whither the literary scene?–The question of 'how to say it'). In *Shi yu zhen* (Poetry and truth), 1: 63–73. 2 vols. Shanghai: Commercial Press.

———. 1936b. "Tan shi" (On poetry). In *Shi yu zhen* (Poetry and truth), 2: 1–24. 2 vols. Shanghai: Shangwu yinshuguan.

———. 1939. "Tan 'langsong shi'" (On 'recitation poetry'). In *Xuedeng* (Lamp of learning) literary supplement, Chongqing *Shishi xinbao* (New times), 15 January.

Ling Shufang, ed. 2003. *Langsong shige jingxuan* (Essential recitation poems). Beijing: Chaohua chubanshe.

Liu Jianqiang. 2004. *"Taoli" shangye: sange dichan shangren de yishu mengxiang* ("Fleeing" commerce: The artistic dreams of three real-estate entrepreneurs). World Wide Web (accessed 4 January 2006). http://www.readcf.com/Html/20049211642-1.html.

Liu Qing. 1938. "'Langsong shi' yu 'jiti chuangzuo'" ("Recitation poetry" and "collective authoring"). In *Pingming* (Daybreak) literary supplement, Chongqing *Zhongyang ribao* (Central daily news), 29 December.

Liu Xia et al. 2005. *Gancao buluo* (Hay tribe). Beijing: Guangming ribao chubanshe.

Lu Mang. 1964. "Rang shige langsong geng shenru qunzhong" (Let poetry recitation penetrate more deeply into the masses). *Shikan* (Poetry journal), no. 80, 112–113.

Lü Ning and Chen Ziping. 1964. "Shanghai gongren wenhuagong juban 'Qingzhu qi-yi' gongren shihui" (Shanghai worker's culture palace holds "Celebrate July 1" workers' poetry event). *Shikan* (Poetry journal), no. 77, 68.

Lu Xun. 1981. "Wusheng de Zhongguo" (Silent China). In *Lu Xun quanji* (Complete works of Lu Xun), 4: 11–17. 16 vols. Beijing: Renmin wenxue chubanshe.

———. 2005. "Moluo shi li shuo" (The power of Mara poetry). In *Lu Xun quanji* (The complete works of Lu Xun), 1: 65–120. 18 vols. Beijing: Renmin wenxue chubanshe.

Luo Chuan. 1963. "Haerbin chengli qingnian yeyu langsong dui" (Harbin establishes youth sparetime recitation team). *Shikan* (Poetry journal), no. 64, 74.

Luo Niansheng. 1985. "Ping *Caomang ji*" (A review of *Wilderness*). In *Er Luo yi Liu yi Zhu Xiang* (Two Luo's and a Liu remember Zhu Xiang), ed. Luo Niansheng, 67–74. Beijing: Sanlian shudian.

Ma Bingshan. 1937. "Laba chuishou" (The bugler). *Zhongguo shitan* (China poetry forum), no. 4 (November): 8.

Mei Fang. 1964. "Zhiyuan Feizhou, Lading Meizhou renmin douzheng, shoudu juxing shige langsong yanchang hui" (The capital holds poetry and song recital to aid the people's struggles in Africa and Latin America). *Shikan* (Poetry journal), no. 74, 44.

Mu Mutian. 1937. "Muqian xinshi yundong de zhankai wenti" (Current issues in developing the new poetry movement). In *Kaituozhe* (Pathbreaker), ed. Gao Han, 109–124. Shanghai: Liaoyuan shudian.

———. 1938. "Qu da youjizhan" (Go wage guerilla war). *Wenyi yuekan–zhanshi tekan* (Literature and art monthly–wartime edition) 1, no. 7 (2 February): 140–141.

———. 1987. "Shige langdu he Gao Lan xiansheng de liangshou changshi" (Poetry recitation and two of Mr. Gao Lan's experiments). In *Shi de langsong yu langsong de shi* (Poetry recitation and recitation poetry), ed. Gao Lan. Jinan: Shandong daxue chubanshe. Original ed., Hankou *Dagongbao* (L'Impartial), 23 October 1937, 34–37.

———. 2000. "Lun shige langdu yundong." (On the poetry recitation movement). In *Mu Mutian wenxue pinglun xuanji* (Selected literary criticism of Mu Mutian), ed. Chen Dun and Liu Xiangyu, 221–228. Beijing: Beijing shifan daxue chubanshe.

Ningbo China. 2006. *"Chuntian song ni yi shou shi" Ningbo zhuhuichang huodong juxing* (Main venue of "Spring and poets" event held in Ningbo). World Wide Web (accessed 23 May 2006). http://gtog.ningbo.gov.cn/art/2006/04/10/art_3984_459411.html.

Ningying [Huang Ningying]. 1938. "Wen Liu, zuguo huzhao ni!" (Wen Liu, the Motherland cries out for you!). *Zhongguo shitan* (China poetry forum) 1, no. 6 (January): 4.

Niu Yunqing. 1988. "Gao Lan zhuanlüe" (Biographical sketch of Gao Lan). *Xinwenxue shiliao* (Historical materials on new literature), no. 3, 154–159.

Pu Feng. 1938a. *Heilou de jiaoluo li–fengci shiji* (In a dismal corner–satirical poems). N.p.: Shige chubanshe.

———. 1938b. "Women zai zuijin liu ge yue" (Our past six months). *Zhongguo shitan* (China poetry forum) 1, no. 6 (15 January): 26–27.

Qian Xuantong. 1918. "Changshi ji xu" ("Preface" to *Experiments*). *Xin qingnian* (New youth) 4, no. 2 (February): 136–142.

Qu Qiubai. 1953. "Lun dazhong wenyi" (On mass literature and art). In *Qu Qiubai wenji* (Collected writings of Qu Qiubai), ed. Qu Qiubai wenji bianji weiyuanhui, 2: 853–916. 4 vols. Beijing: Renmin wenxue chubanshe.

Ren Jun. 1936. *Lengre ji* (Hot and cold). N.p.: Shiren julebu.

———. 1948. *Xinshi hua* (Talks on new poetry). Shanghai: Guoji wenhua fuwushe.

Ren Jun et al. 1933. "Guanyu xiezuo xin shige de yidian yijian" (Some thoughts on writing new poetry). *Xin shige* (New poetry) 1, no. 1 (11 February): 8.

Sen Bao [Ren Jun]. 1933. "Guanyu shi de langdu wenti" (On the issue of reciting poetry). *Xin shige* (New poetry) 1, no. 2 (21 February): 1.

Sha Kefu et al. 1987. "Guanyu shige min'ge yanchang wanhui" (On the evening of poetry and folk song). In *Shi de langsong yu langsong de shi* (Poetry recitation and recitation poetry), ed. Gao Lan. Jinan: Shandong daxue chubanshe. Original ed., *Zhandi* (Battleground) 1, no. 3 (20 April 1938): 65–69.

Shang Jinlin. 1995. *Zhu Guangqian yu Zhongguo xiandai wenxue* (Zhu Guangqian and modern Chinese literature). Hefei: Anhui jiaoyu chubanshe.

Shen Congwen. 2002. "Tan langsong shi" (On recitation poetry). In *Shen Congwen quanji* (Complete works of Shen Congwen), ed. Xie Zhongyi, 238–252. Taiyuan: Beiyue chubanshe.

Shi Gang. 1943. "*Gao Lan langsongshi* ping" (Review of *Gao Lan's Recitation Poetry*). Chongqing *Xinhua ribao* (New China daily), 5 April.

Shikan. 1962a. "Shoudu jiang juxing Chunjie shige langsong hui" (Capital to hold Spring Festival recital). *Shikan* (Poetry journal), no. 55, 74.

———. 1962b. "Beijing juban shiren jie langsong hui" (Poets' Day recital to be held in capital). *Shikan* (Poetry journal), no. 58, 64.

———. 1962c. "Shaonian ertongmen de langsong huodong" (Teens' and children's recitation activities). *Shikan* (Poetry journal), no. 58, 64.

———. 1962d. "Guangbo shihui huodong" (Broadcast poetry rally activities). *Shikan* (Poetry journal), no. 59, 74.

———. 1962e. "Shoudu juxing zhiyuan Banama shige langsong hui" (Capital holds poetry recital to support Panama). *Shikan* (Poetry journal), no. 60, 74.

———. 1963a. "Beijing shi huaju, dianying yanyuan yeyu langsong yanjiu xiaozu chengli" (Beijing city spoken drama and movie actor's sparetime recitation research team established). *Shikan* (Poetry journal), no. 62, 74.

———. 1963b. "Beijing juban qingnian xuesheng langsong xunlian ban" (Youth and student recitation training course held in Beijing). *Shikan* (Poetry journal), no. 63, 70.

———. 1963c. "Beijing renmin yishu juyuan juxing xingqi shige langsong hui" (Beijing People's Arts Theater holds Sunday poetry recitations). *Shikan* (Poetry journal), no. 64, 74.

———. 1963d. "Nanjing, Xi'an, Hefei deng di juxing 'Zhichi heiren douzheng shige langsong hui'" (Nanjing, Xi'an, and Hefei hold "support the black people's struggle" poetry recitations). *Shikan* (Poetry journal), no. 67, 56.

———. 1964. "Zhichi Banama renmin fan Mei aiguo douzheng shige langsong hui" (Poetry recital to support the people of Panama's patriotic struggle against the United States). *Shikan* (Poetry journal), no. 72, 39.

Shikan she, ed. 1965. *Langsong shixuan* (Selected recitation poetry). Beijing: Zuojia chubanshe.

Shu Xu [Jiang Xijin]. 1941. "1940 nian Shanghai shige de huigu" (A look back at poetry in Shanghai in 1940). In *Women de shi, Shanghai shige congkan zhi san* (Our poetry, Shanghai poetry series no. 3), ed. Shi Yi et al., 12–32. Shanghai: n.p.

SouFun.com 2005. *Dahua dichan zhi: Nüxing yishujia shuo yishu yu dichan* (Big talk on real estate: Female artists discuss art and real estate). World Wide Web (Accessed 4 January 2006). http://news.soufun.com/subject/poetess/.

Sun Dangbo. 1996. "Guo Moruo dui xiandai xueshu sixiang de gongxian" (Guo Moruo's contribution to modern scholarly thought). In *Zhongguo wenxue yanjiu xiandaihua jincheng* (The process of modernization in Chinese literary research), ed. Wang Yao, 260–308. Beijing: Beijing daxue chubanshe.

Tan Kexiu, ed. 2005. *Mingtian* (Tomorrow). 2 vols. Vol. 2. Changsha: Hunan wenyi chubanshe.

Tongren deng. 1933. "Guanyu xiezuo xinshige de yidian yijian" (Some opinions on writing new poetry). *Xin shige* (New poetry), no. 1 (11 February): 8.

Tuoersitai [Tolstoy, Leo]. 1921. *Yishulun* (What is art?). Trans. Geng Jizhi. Shanghai: Shangwu yinshuguan.

Wan Qing. 1960. "Huayuan shihua biandi kai" (Flowers of poetry bloom all over the garden). *Shikan* (Poetry journal), no. 46, 46–47.

Wang Bingyang. 1939. "Langsong shi lun" (On recitation poetry). In *Xuedeng* (Lamp of learning) literary supplement, Chongqing *Shishi xinbao* (New times), 15 January.

Wen Shan. 1963. "Shi langsong xiaxiang xiaoji" (Notes on bringing poetry recitation to the countryside). *Shikan* (Poetry journal), no. 63, 64–67.

Wenyi bao. 1958. "Yangfan gulang, lizheng shangyou—wenxue jie dayuejin zuotan hui zonghe baodao" (Hoist the sails and stir up the waves, strive to go upstream—a comprehensive report from the Symposium on Literary Circles' Great Leap Forward). *Wenyi bao* (Literary gazette), no. 214, 20–25.

Wu Changhua. 1995. *Feng Xuefeng pingzhuan* (A critical biography of Feng Xuefeng). Shanghai: Shanghai shudian.

Xi Du. 2004. "Yanyuan xue shi suoyi" (Learning poetry at Peking University: Minor reminiscences). In *Shige Beida* (Poetic Peking University), ed. Chen Jun, 285–307. Wuhan: Changjiang wenyi chubanshe.

Xi Jin [Jiang Xijin]. 1937. "Langsong qu!" (Go and recite!). *Shidiao* (Tunes of the times), no. 3 (1 December).

——. 1938a. "Houji" (Postscript). *Zhandou xunkan* (Battle thrice-monthly) 2, no. 4 (18 February): 61.

——. 1938b. "Shige he langsong" (Poetry and recitation). *Wenyi yuekan–zhanshi tekan* (Literature and art monthly–wartime edition) 1, no. 12 (1 June): 259–262.

——. 1939. "Chenmo de shige" (Poetry of silence). In *Wo gechang: Shiren congkan yi ji* (I sing: Poets' series 1), ed. Bai Shu, 55–58. N.p.: n.p.

Xiao San. 1963. "Shi langsong mantan" (Some words on poetry recitation). *Shikan* (Poetry journal), no. 63, 56–63.

Xinhua ribao. 1941. "Wenhua huixun" (Culture digest). Chongqing *Xinhua ribao* (New China daily), 27 November.

Xu Chi. 1942. *Shige langsong shouce* (Poetry recitation handbook). Guilin: Jimei shudian.

Xue Wei et al. 1938. "Guanyu shige langsong: Shiyan he pipan" (On poetry recitation: Experiment and criticism). *Qiyue* (July), no. 9 (16 February): 263–264.

Yan Renyi. 1958. *Langdu jichu zhishi* (Recitation basics). Nanjing: Jiangsu renmin chubanshe.

Yang Li'ang. 1992. *Zhongguo xinshi shihua* (Talks on the history of Chinese new poetry). Changsha: Hunan wenyi chubanshe.

Yi Zhong. 1938. "1937 nian de Zhongguo shitan" (The poetry scene in China, 1937). *Zhongguo shitan* (China poetry forum) 1, no. 6 (January): 14–17.

Yin Zhiguang. 1962. "Beijing shi kaiban yeyu langsong jiangxi ban" (Spare-time recitation study group started in Beijing). *Shikan* (Poetry journal), no. 55, 74.

——. 1963a. "Gedi zhankai shige langsong huodong" (Poetry recitation activities launched all over). *Shikan* (Poetry journal), no. 62, 74.

——. 1963b. "Gedi zhankai 'Xiang Lei Feng xuexi' shige langsong huodong" ("Learn from Lei Feng" poetry recitation activities launched all over). *Shikan* (Poetry journal), no. 63, 70.

——. 1963c. "Shanghai, Tianjin shige langsong huodong" (Poetry recitation activities in Shanghai and Tianjin). *Shikan* (Poetry journal), no. 65, 74.

——. 1964. "Gedi juxing fandui Meiguo qinlüe Yuenan shige langsong yanchang hui" (Poetry and song recitations held all over to oppose the United States' invasion of Vietnam). *Shikan* (Poetry journal), no. 78, 58.

Yu Huiluo. 1963. "Rang guangbo ba shi songdao nongcun" (Let radio bring recitation to the countryside). *Shikan* (Poetry journal), no. 64, 73-74.

Yu Pingbo. 1922. "Shi de jinhua de huanyuan lun" (Return to origins in the evolution of poetry). *Shi* (Poetry monthly) 1, no. 1 (15 January): 30-48.

Yuan Shuipo. 1940. "Shi langsong" (Poetry recitation). Shanghai *Huamei wanbao* (Sino-American evening news), 30 March.

——. 1963. "Shige langsong zhide gao" (Poetry recitation is worth doing). *Shikan* (Poetry journal), no. 62, 49-52.

Zang Kejia. 1938a. "Shige langsong yundong zhankai zai qianfang" (The poetry recitation movement unfolds at the front). Chongqing *Xinhua ribao* (New China daily), 30 August.

——. 1938b. "Women zhe shisi ge" (We fourteen). *Wenyi zhendi* (Literature and arts frontline) 2, no. 1 (16 October): 419-421.

——. 1963. "Ting shi ji gan" (Feelings written down upon hearing poetry). *Shikan* (Poetry journal), no. 62, 53-54.

——. 1982. *Shi yu shenghuo* (Poetry and life). Hong Kong: Sanlian shudian.

——. 1985. "Shi de yinhe" (The Milky Way of poetry). In *Zhongguo sishi niandai shixuan* (Selected Chinese poetry of the 1940s), ed. Wang Wenchen, 1: 1-3. 2 vols. Chongqing: Chongqing chubanshe.

——. 1989. "Wo zai minzu geming de zhanchang shang gechang" (I sing on the battleground of the national revolution). In *Shige yanjiu shiliao xuan* (Selected historical research materials for poetry), ed. Long Quanming, 332-340. Chengdu: Sichuan jiaoyu chubanshe. Original ed., Zang Kejia, *Wo de shi shenghuo* (My life of poetry). N.p.: Dushu chubanshe, 1945.

Zang Yunyuan. 1979. "Wu Chongqing shi langsong xiaoji" (Jottings on poetry recitation in foggy Chongqing). *Shikan* (Poetry journal), no. 11, 75-77.

Zeng Chuanju. 1963. "Zuoxie Jiangsu fenhui deng danwei lianhe juban 'Baihua shige langsong hui'" (Jiangsu branch of the Writers Association and other units jointly hold "Hundred Flowers Poetry Recital"). *Shikan* (Poetry journal), no. 65, 74.

Zhang Jie and Lu Wencai. 1989. *Gao Lan pingzhuan* (Critical biography of Gao Lan). Qingdao: Qingdao haiyang chubanshe.

Zhang Tongwu. 2005. *2005 Nanjiang guoji lüyou jie kaimushi ji "Menghuan nanjiang Kashi-*

geer zhi chun" daxing shige langsong yinyue hui (2005 Southern Xinjiang International Travel Festival opening ceremony and "Southern Xinjiang reverie: Kashgar Spring" large-scale poetry recitation and concert). World Wide Web (accessed 26 December 2005). http://www.zhongkun.com.cn/tour/njlyj/gkmore1.htm.

Zhang Zhezhi. 1937. "O! Wo shi zhadan" (Ha! I'm a bomb). Zhongguo shitan (China poetry forum) 1, no. 5 (December): 20.

Zhanxian. 1940. "Langsong xiao xiaoxi" (The recitation grapevine). In Zhanxian (Battle line) literary supplement, Chongqing Dagongbao (L'Impartial), 7 December.

Zhao Liping. 2004. Gediao zai guoji shige jie longzhong kaimu (Genre Don holds grand sales opening on International Poetry Day). World Wide Web (accessed 27 July 2006). http://www.bjbusiness.com.cn/20040326/dichan2730.htm.

Zhejiang On-line. 2006. "Chuntian song ni yi shou shi" quanguo zhuhuichang huodong jianwen (Sights and sounds at the national main venue of "Spring and Poets"). World Wide Web (accessed 23 May 2006). http://www.yhnews.com.cn/xwzx/zhejxw/t20060411_71863.htm.

Zhi An. 1963. "Taiyuan juxing gongren shi langsong hui" (Taiyuan holds workers' poetry recital). Shikan (Poetry journal), no. 67, 8.

Zhongguo shitan. 1938. "Wen Liu xiaozhuan" (Biographical sketch of Wen Liu, 1912–1937). Zhongguo shitan (China poetry forum) 1, no. 6 (January): 4.

Zhou Yang. [1958] 1995. "Xin min'ge kaituo le shige de xin daolu" (New folk songs open up a new road for poetry). In Zhongguo dangdai wenxue shiliao xuan (Selected historical materials on contemporary Chinese literature), ed. Xie Mian and Hong Zicheng, 457–467. Beijing: Beijing daxue chubanshe.

Zhou Zuoren. 1923. "Geyao" (Folk song). Geyao zhoukan (Folk song weekly), no. 16 (23 April 1923): 7–8.

——. 1935. "Pingmin wenxue" (Commoner literature). In Zhongguo xinwenxue daxi (Compendium of Chinese new literature), ed. Zhao Jiabi. 10 vols. Vol. 1. Shanghai: Liangyou tushu gongsi. Original ed., Meizhou pinglun (Weekly review), no. 5 (1 January 1919): 236–239.

Zhou Zuoren et al. 1927. Xuezhao (A snowy morning). 5th ed. Shanghai: Shangwu yinshuguan. Original ed. 1922.

Zhu Guangqian. 1962. "Tan shige langsong" (On poetry recitation). Shikan (Poetry journal), no. 60, 58–61.

——. 1987. "Shilun." In Zhu Guangqian quanji (Complete works of Zhu Guangqian), ed. Ye Zhishan et al., 3: 3–331. 20 vols. Hefei: Anhui jiaoyu chubanshe.

Zhu Lin. 1960. Langsong chubu (First steps toward recitation). Beijing: Beijing chubanshe.

——. 1964. "Langsong geming shi, xian zuo geming ren" (To recite revolutionary poetry, first become a revolutionary). Shikan (Poetry journal), no. 77, 55–57.

——. 2007. Interview. Beijing, 2 August.

Zhu Weiji. 1940. "Women bu yao rennai" (We will not endure this). Hanglie (Rank and file) 1, nos. 5/6 (28 March): 34–37.

Zhu Xiang. 1935. "Cailian qu" (Lotus-picking song). In Zhongguo xinwenxue daxi: Shi ji

(Compendium of Chinese new literature: Poetry volume), ed. Zhu Ziqing, 8: 296. 10 vols. Shanghai: Liangyou tushu gongsi.

———. 1983. *Zhu Xiang shuxin ji* (Collected letters of Zhu Xiang). Ed. Luo Niansheng. Tianjin: Tianjin rensheng yu wenxue she. Original ed., 1936.

Zhu Ziqing. 1935. "Daoyan" (Introduction). In *Zhongguo xinwenxue daxi: Shi ji* (Compendium of Chinese new literature: Poetry volume), ed. Zhu Ziqing, 8: 1–8. 10 vols. Shanghai: Liangyou tushu gongsi.

———. 1948a. "Lun songdu" (On reading aloud). In *Biaozhun yu chidu* (Standards and criteria), 97–106. Shanghai: Wenguang shudian.

———. 1948b. "Lun langsong shi" (On recitation poetry). In *Lun yasu gongshang* (On appreciating the elegant and the common), 33–43. Shanghai: Guanchashe.

———. 1948c. "Meiguo de langson shi" (American recitation poetry). In *Lun yasu gongshang* (On appreciating the elegant and the common), 44–56. Shunghai: Guanchashe.

———. 1994a. "Lun langdu" (On reading aloud). In *Zhu Ziqing sanwen, xia ji* (Prose writings of Zhu Ziqing, vol. 3), ed. Yan Jingli and Xu Xing, 3: 15–24. 3 vols. Beijing: Zhongguo guangbo dianshi chubanshe.

———. 1994b. "Yibang zhi xing riji" (Diary of travels abroad). In *Zhu Ziqing sanwen, xia ji* (Prose writings of Zhu Ziqing, vol. 3), ed. Yan Jingli and Xu Xing, 3: 213–342. 3 vols. Beijing: Zhongguo guangbo dianshi chubanshe.

———. 1996a. "Chang xinshi dengdeng" (Singing new poetry, etc). In *Zhu Ziqing quanji* (Complete works of Zhu Ziqing), ed. Zhu Qiaosen, 4: 220–225. 12 vols. Nanjing: Jiangsu jiaoyu chubanshe.

———. 1996b. "Jintian de shi–jieshao He Da de shi ji *Women kai hui*" (Today's poetry—introducing He Da's poetry collection *We're in Session*). In *Zhu Ziqing quanji* (Complete works of Zhu Ziqing), ed. Zhu Qiaosen, 4: 501–509. 12 vols. Nanjing: Jiangsu jiaoyu chubanshe.

Non-Chinese-Language Sources

Alber, Charles J. 2002. *Enduring the Revolution: Ding Ling and the Politics of Literature in Guomindang China*. Westport, CT, and London: Praeger.

Allen, Joseph R. 1992. *In the Voice of Others: Chinese Music Bureau Poetry*. Minneapolis: University of Minnesota Press.

Anderson, Benedict. 1991. *Imagined Communities: Reflections on the Origin and Spread of Nationalism*. Rev. ed. London: Verso.

Anderson, Marston. 1990. *The Limits of Realism: Chinese Fiction in the Revolutionary Period*. Berkeley, Los Angeles, Oxford: University of California Press.

Apter, David E., and Tony Saich. 1994. *Revolutionary Discourse in Mao's Republic*. Cambridge, MA: Harvard University Press.

Arbuckle, Gary. 1994. *Literacy and Orality in Early China* (World Wide Web). David C. Lam Institute for East-West Studies (text of a lecture given in 1994; cited 22 December 2006). Available from http://www.cic.sfu.ca/nacc/articles/litoral/loraltext.html.

Barthes, Roland. 1977. *Image, Music, Text*. Trans. Stephen Heath. New York: Hill and Wang.

——. 1985. "Listening," trans. Richard Howard. In *The Responsibility of Forms: Critical Essays on Music, Art, and Representation*, 245–260. New York: Hill and Wang.

Bauman, Richard. 1992. "Performance." In *Folklore, Cultural Performances, and Popular Entertainments*, ed. R. Bauman, 41–49. New York and Oxford: Oxford University Press.

——. 2003. *Voices of Modernity: Language Ideologies and the Politics of Inequality*. Cambridge: Cambridge University Press.

Bauman, Richard, and Charles L. Briggs. 1990. "Poetics and Performance as Critical Perspectives on Language and Social Life." *Annual Review of Anthropology* 19: 59–88.

Bei, Dao. 1990. *The August Sleepwalker*. Trans. Bonnie S. McDougall. New York: New Directions.

——. 2000. "Reciting." In *Blue House*. Trans. Theodore Huters and Feng-ying Ming, 249–262. Brookline, MA: Zephyr Press.

Bell, Julian. 1938. *Julian Bell: Essays, Poems, Letters*. Ed. Quentin Bell. London: The Hogarth Press.

Bennett, Gordon. 1976. *Yundong: Mass Campaigns in Chinese Communist Leadership*. Berkeley: Center for Chinese Studies, University of California, Berkeley.

Berlin, Isaiah. 1976. *Vico and Herder: Two Studies in the History of Ideas*. New York: Viking Press.

Bernheimer, Charles. 1995. "Introduction." In *Comparative Literature in the Age of Multiculturalism*, ed. C. Bernheimer, 1–20. Baltimore: John Hopkins University Press.

Bernstein, Charles. 1998. "Introduction." In *Close Listening: Poetry and the Performed Word*, ed. Charles Bernstein, 3–26. New York and Oxford: Oxford University Press.

Braester, Yomi. 2005. "Chinese Cinema in the Age of Advertisement: The Filmmaker as a Cultural Broker." *China Quarterly* 183: 549–564.

Bruns, Gerald L. 1974. *Modern Poetry and the Idea of Language: A Critical and Historical Study*. New Haven and London: Yale University Press.

Carlyle, Thomas. 1951. *Carlyle's Unfinished History of German Literature*. Ed. Hill Shine. Lexington: University of Kentucky Press.

Chao, Yuan Ren. 1956. "Tone, Intonation, Singsong, Chanting, Recitative, Tonal Composition, and Atonal Composition in Chinese." In *For Roman Jakobson: Essay on the Occasion of His Sixtieth Birthday*, ed. Morris Halle et al., 52–59. The Hague: Mouton.

Chen, Duxiu. 1996. "On Literary Revolution," trans. Timothy Wong. In *Modern Chinese Literary Thought: Writings on Literature, 1893–1945*, 140–145. Stanford, CA: Stanford University Press.

Chen, S. H. 1966. "Multiplicity in Uniformity: Poetry and the Great Leap Forward." In *China Under Mao: Politics Takes Command*, ed. Roderick MacFarquhar, 392–406. Cambridge, MA, and London: MIT Press.

Cherkasskii, L. E. 1980. *Kitaiskaia poeziia voennykh let, 1937–1949* (Chinese poetry of the war years, 1937–1949). Moscow: Nauk.

Cherkassky, Leonid. 1989. "Gao Lan." In *A Selective Guide to Chinese Literature 1900–1949*. 5 vols. Vol. 3: *The Poem*, ed. Lloyd Haft, 106–108. Leiden and New York: E. J. Brill.

China Reconstructs. 1959. Poets in Competition. *China Reconstructs* (March), 29.

Chow, Rey. 1995. *Primitive Passions: Visuality, Sexuality, Ethnography, and Contemporary Chinese Cinema.* New York: Columbia University Press.

———. 1998. *Ethics after Idealism: Theory-Culture-Ethnicity-Reading.* Bloomington: Indiana University Press.

Chow, Tse-tsung. 1968. "The Early History of the Chinese Word *Shih* (Poetry)." In *Wen-lin: Studies in the Chinese Humanities,* ed. Tse-tung Chow, 151–209. Madison: University of Wisconsin Press.

Condillac, Etienne Bonnot de. 2001. *Essay on the Origin of Human Knowledge.* Trans. and ed. Hans Aarsleff. Cambridge: Cambridge University Press.

Connor, Steven. 1997. "The Modern Auditory I." In *Rewriting the Self: Histories from the Renaissance to the Present,* ed. Roy Porter, 203–223. London and New York: Routledge.

Daruvala, Susan. 2000. *Zhou Zuoren and an Alternative Chinese Response to Modernity.* Cambridge, MA, and London: Harvard East Asia Center.

Davenport, Russell W. 1944. *My Country.* New York: Simon and Schuster.

Debord, Guy. 1994. *The Society of the Spectacle.* Trans. Donald Nicholson-Smith. New York: Zone Books.

de Certeau, Michel. 1984. *The Practice of Everyday Life.* Trans. Steven Rendall. Berkeley: University of California Press.

Denton, Kirk, ed. 1996. *Modern Chinese Literary Thought: Writings on Literature, 1893–1945.* Stanford, CA: Stanford University Press.

Dolar, Mladen. 1996. "The Object Voice." In *Gaze and Voice as Love Objects,* ed. Renata Salecl and Slavoj Zizek, 7–31. Durham and London: Duke University Press.

Doleželová-Velingerová, Milena. 1977. "The Origins of Modern Chinese Literature." In *Modern Chinese Literature in the May Fourth Era,* ed. Merle Goldman, 17–36. Cambridge, MA, and London: Harvard University Press.

Dutton, Michael. 2004. "Mango Mao: Infections of the Sacred." *Public Culture* 16(2): 161–187.

Edwards, Paul C. 1983. "The Rise of 'Expression.'" In *Performance of Literature in Historical Perspectives,* ed. David W. Thompson, 529–548. Lanham [MD], New York, and London: University Press of America.

Feld, Steven. 1996. "Waterfalls of Song: An Acoustemology of Place Resounding in Bosavi, Papua New Guinea." In *Senses of Place,* ed. Steven Feld and Keith H. Basso, 91–135. Santa Fe: School of American Research Press.

Ferguson, Charles A. 1964. "Diglossia." In *Language in Culture and Society: A Reader in Linguistics and Anthropology,* ed. Dell Hymes, 429–439. New York: Harper and Row.

Fichte, Johann Gottlieb. 1922. *Addresses to the German Nation.* Trans. R. F. Jones and G. H. Turnbull. Chicago and London: The Open Court Publishing Company.

Finnegan, Ruth. 1992. *Oral Poetry: Its Nature, Significance and Social Context.* 1st Midland Book ed. Bloomington and Indianapolis: Indiana University Press. Original ed. Cambridge: Cambridge University Press, 1977.

Fitzgerald, John. 1996. *Awakening China: Politics, Culture, and Class in the Nationalist Revolution.* Stanford, CA: Stanford University Press.

Fliegelman, Jay. 1993. *Declaring Independence: Jefferson, Natural Language, and the Culture of Performance.* Stanford, CA: Stanford University Press.

Fokkema, D. W. 1965. *Literary Doctrine in China and the Soviet Influence, 1956–1960.* The Hague: Mouton.

Foucault, Michel. 1970. *The Order of Things: An Archaeology of the Human Sciences.* New York: Vintage Books.

Fussell, Paul. 1979. *Poetic Meter and Poetic Form.* Rev. ed. New York: Random House.

Geaney, Jane. 2002. *On the Epistemology of the Senses in Early Chinese Thought.* Honolulu: University of Hawai'i Press.

Goldman, Merle. 2002. "A New Relationship between the Intellectuals and the State in the Post-Mao Period." In *An Intellectual History of Modern China*, ed. Merle Goldman and Leo Ou-fan Lee, 499–538. Cambridge: Cambridge University Press.

Goodman, David S. G. 1981. *Beijing Street Voices: The Poetry and Politics of China's Democracy Movement.* London and Boston: Marion Boyars.

Gourgouris, Stathis. 1996. *Dream Nation: Enlightenment, Colonization, and the Institution of Modern Greece.* Stanford, CA: Stanford University Press.

Gummere, Francis B. 1908. *The Beginnings of Poetry.* New York: The MacMillan Company.

Gunn, Edward. 1991. *Rewriting Chinese: Style and Innovation in Twentieth-Century Chinese Prose.* Stanford, CA: Stanford University Press.

——. 1993. "Literature and Art of the War Period." In *China's Bitter Victory: The War with Japan, 1937–1945*, ed. James C. Hsiung and Steven I. Levine, 235–274. Armonk, NY: M. E. Sharpe.

Heyd, Uriel. 1950. *Foundations of Turkish Nationalism: The Life and Teachings of Ziya Gökalp.* Westport, CT: Hyperion Press.

Hobsbawm, E. J. 1990. *Nations and Nationalism since 1780: Programme, Myth, Reality.* Cambridge: Cambridge University Press.

Hockx, Michel. 1994. *A Snowy Morning: Eight Chinese Poets on the Road to Modernity.* Leiden: Centre for Non-Western Studies, Leiden University.

Holm, David. 1991. *Art and Ideology in Revolutionary China.* Oxford: Clarendon Press.

Hsia, T. A. 1968. *The Gate of Darkness: Studies on the Leftist Literary Movement in China.* Seattle and London: University of Washington Press.

Hung, Chang-tai. 1985. *Going to the People: Chinese Intellectuals and Folk Literature, 1918–1937.* Cambridge, MA: Council on East Asian Studies.

——. 1994. *War and Popular Culture: Resistance in Modern China, 1937–1945.* Berkeley: University of California Press.

Ihde, Don. 1976. *Listening and Voice: A Phenomenology of Sound.* Athens: Ohio University Press.

Jakobson, Roman. 1987. *Language in Literature.* Ed. Krystyna Pomorska and Stephen Rudy. Cambridge, MA: Belknap Press.

Jay, Martin. 1993. *Downcast Eyes: The Denigration of Vision in Twentieth-Century French Thought*. Berkeley and Los Angeles: University of California Press.

Jeffreys, Mark. 1995. "Ideologies of Lyric: A Problem of Genre in Contemporary Anglophone Poetics." *PMLA* 110 (2): 196–205.

Jusdanis, Gregory. 1991. *Belated Modernity and National Culture: Inventing National Literature*. Minneapolis: University of Minnesota Press.

Kahn, Douglas. 1992. "Introduction: Histories of Sound Once Removed." In *Wireless Imagination: Sound, Radio, and the Avant-Garde*, ed. Douglas Kahn and Gregory Whitehead, 1–28. Cambridge, MA, and London: MIT Press.

———. 1999. *Noise, Water, Meat: A History of Sound in the Arts*. Cambridge, MA, and London: MIT Press.

Kedourie, Elie. 1993. *Nationalism*. Oxford and Cambridge, MA: Blackwell. Original ed. 1960.

Kidson, Frank, and Mary Neal. 1972. *English Folk Song and Dance*. Totowa, NJ: Rowman and Littlefield. Original ed. 1915.

King, Vincent V. S. 1966. *Propaganda Campaigns in Communist China*. Cambridge, MA: Center for International Studies, MIT.

Knabb, Ken, ed. 1989. *Situationist International Anthology*. Berkeley: Bureau of Public Secrets.

Knechtges, David R. 1976. *The Han Rhapsody: A Study of the Fu of Yang Hsiung (53 B.C.–A.D. 18)*. Cambridge: Cambridge University Press.

Kraus, Richard Curt. 2004. *The Party and the Arty in China: The New Politics of Culture*. Lanham, MD: Rowman and Littlefield Publishers.

Larson, Wendy. 1998. *Women and Writing in Modern China*. Stanford, CA: Stanford University Press.

Lastra, James. 2000. *Sound Technology and the Modern Cinema: Perception, Representation, Modernity*. New York: Columbia University Press.

Laughlin, Charles A. 2002. *Chinese Reportage: The Aesthetics of Historical Experience*. Durham and London: Duke University Press.

———. 2008. "The All-China Resistance Association of Writers and Artists." In *Literary Societies of Republican China*, ed. Kirk A. Denton and Michel Hockx, 379–411. Lanham, MD, and Boulder, CO: Lexington Books.

Laurence, Patricia. 2003. *Lily Briscoe's Chinese Eyes: Bloomsbury, Modernism, and China*. Columbia: University of South Carolina Press.

Lee, Gregory B. 1996. *Troubadours, Trumpeters, and Troubled Makers: Lyricism, Nationalism, and Hybridity in China and Its Others*. Durham, NC: Duke University Press.

Lee, Haiyan. 2004. "Sympathy, Hypocrisy, and the Trauma of Chineseness." *Modern Chinese Literature and Culture* 16 (2): 76–122.

———. 2005. "Tears That Crumbled the Great Wall: The Archaeology of Feeling in the May Fourth Folklore Movement." *Journal of Asian Studies* 64 (1): 35–65.

———. 2007. *Revolution of the Heart: A Genealogy of Love in China, 1900–1950*. Stanford, CA: Stanford University Press.

Levin, David Michael, ed. 1993. *Modernity and the Hegemony of Vision*. Berkeley: University of California Press.

Lewis, Mark Edward. 1999. *Writing and Authority in Early China*. Albany: State University of New York Press.

Li, Fukang, and Eva Hung. 1992. "Post-Misty Poetry." *Renditions* 37: 93–98.

Link, Perry. 2000. *The Uses of Literature: Life in the Socialist Chinese Literary System*. Princeton, NJ: Princeton University Press.

Liu, Alan P. L. 1971. *Communications and National Integration in Communist China*. Berkeley, Los Angeles, London: University of California Press.

Lotman, Yuri M. 1990. *Universe of the Mind: A Semiotic Theory of Culture*. Trans. Ann Shukman. Bloomington and Indianapolis: Indiana University Press.

Lu, Hsün [Lu Xun]. 1977. *Selected Stories of Lu Hsün*. Trans. Yang Hsien-yi and Gladys Yang. New York: W. W. Norton.

Lu, Xun. 1996. "On the Power of Mara Poetry," trans. Shu-ying Tsau and Donald Holoch. In *Modern Chinese Literary Thought: Writings on Literature, 1893–1945*, ed. Kirk Denton, 96–109. Stanford: Stanford University Press.

Mackinnon, Stephen R. 2008. *Wuhan, 1938: War, Refugees, and the Making of Modern China*. Berkeley: University of California Press.

MacLeish, Archibald. 1940. "Poetry and the Public World." In *A Time to Speak, Selected Prose of Archibald MacLeish*, 81–96. Cambridge, MA: The Riverside Press.

McDougall, Bonnie S. 1979. "Dissent Literature: Official and Nonofficial Literature in and about China in the Seventies." *Contemporary China* 3 (4): 49–79.

McDougall, Bonnie S., and Kam Louie. 1997. *The Literature of China in the Twentieth Century*. New York: Columbia University Press.

McLuhan, Marshall. 1962. *The Gutenberg Galaxy: The Making of Typographic Man*. Toronto: University of Toronto Press.

Middleton, Peter. 1998. "The Contemporary Poetry Reading." In *Close Listening: Poetry and the Performed Word*, ed. Charles Bernstein, 262–299. New York and Oxford: Oxford University Press.

Monroe, Harriet. 1934. China Diary, II. Harriet Monroe Papers. The University of Chicago Library.

———. 1935. "In Peking." *Poetry* (46): 30–39.

Monroe, Harriet, with Morton Dauwen Zabel. 1938. *A Poet's Life: Seventy Years in a Changing World*. New York: MacMillan Company.

Morris, Adalaide. 1997a. "Introduction." In *Sound States: Innovative Poetics and Acoustical Technologies*, ed. Adalaide Morris, 1–14. Chapel Hill and London: University of Carolina Press.

———, ed. 1997b. *Sound States: Innovative Poetics and Acoustical Technologies*. Chapel Hill and London: University of North Carolina Press.

Morrisson, Mark. 1996. "Performing the Pure Voice: Elocution, Verse Recitation, and Modernist Poetry in Prewar London." *MODERNISM/modernity* 3 (3): 25–50.

Mukarovsky, Jan. 1976. *On Poetic Language*. Trans. and ed. John Burbank and Peter Steiner. Lisse: The Peter de Ridder Press.

Ong, Walter J. 1990. "Foreword." In *Oral Poetry: An Introduction*, i–xii. Minneapolis: University of Minneapolis Press.

Owen, Stephen. 1992. *Readings in Chinese Literary Thought*. Cambridge, MA, and London: Council on East Asian Studies, Harvard University.

Parkes, M. B. 1993. *Pause and Effect: An Introduction to the History of Punctuation in the West*. Berkeley and Los Angeles: University of California Press.

Perkins, David. 1976. *A History of Modern Poetry: From the 1890s to the High Modernist Mode*. Cambridge, MA: The Belknap Press.

Perry, Elizabeth J. 2002. "Moving the Masses: Emotion Work in the Chinese Revolution." *Mobilization: An International Journal* 7 (2): 111–128.

Schmidt, Leigh Eric. 2000. *Hearing Things. Religion, Illusion, and the American Enlightenment*. Cambridge, MA: Harvard University Press.

Sivier, Evelyn M. 1983a. "Penny Readings: Popular Elocution in Late Nineteenth-Century England." In *Performance of Literature in Historical Perspectives*, ed. David W. Thompson, 223–230. Lanham, New York, and London: University Press of America.

———. 1983b. "English Poets, Teachers, and Festivals in a 'Golden Age' of Poetry Speaking, 1920–1950." In *Performance of Literature in Historical Perspectives*, ed. David W. Thompson, 283–300. Lanham, New York, and London: University Press of America.

Smith, Bruce R. 2003. "Tuning into London c. 1600." In *The Auditory Culture Reader*, ed. Michael Bull and Les Back, 127–135. Oxford and New York: Berg.

Smith, Mark M. 2000. "Listening to the Heard Worlds of Antebellum America." *Journal of the Historical Society* 1(1): 65–99.

———. 2001. *Listening to Nineteenth-Century America*. Chapel Hill: University of North Carolina Press.

Tagore, Amitendranath. 1967. *Literary Debates in Modern China: 1918–1937*. Tokyo: The Centre for East Asian Cultural Studies.

Tam, Koo-yin. 1975. "The Use of Poetry in the Tso Chuan: An Analysis of the 'Fu-shih' Practice." PhD diss. University of Washington.

Tang, Tao. 1993. *History of Modern Chinese Literature*. Beijing: Foreign Languages Press.

Tang, Xiaobing. 2000. *Chinese Modern: The Heroic and the Quotidian*. Durham, NC, and London: Duke University Press.

Tong, Hollington K. 1945. *China after Seven Years of War*. New York: The MacMillan Company.

Trumpener, Katie. 1997. *Bardic Nationalism: The Romantic Novel and the British Empire*. Princeton, NJ: Princeton University Press.

Tziovas, Dimitrios. 1986. *The Nationism of the Demoticists and Its Impact on Their Literary Theory (1888–1930)*. Amsterdam: Adolf M. Hakkert.

Valéry, Paul. 1972. "Concerning *A Throw of the Dice*." Trans. Malcolm Cowley and James R. Lawler. In *Collected Works of Paul Valéry*, ed. Jackson Mathews, 307–316. Princeton, NJ: Princeton University Press.

van Crevel, Maghiel. 2008. *Chinese Poetry in Times of Mind, Mayhem and Money*. Leiden and Boston: Brill.

Van Zoeren, Steven. 1991. *Poetry and Personality: Reading, Exegesis, and Hermeneutics in Traditional China*. Stanford, CA: Stanford University Press.

Vitale, Guido Amedeo. 1896. *Pekinese Rhymes*. Peking: Pei-t'ang Press.

Wang, Ban. 1997. *The Sublime Figure of History: Aesthetics and Politics in Twentieth-Century China*. Stanford, CA: Stanford University Press.

Wang, Jing. 2001. "Culture as Leisure and Culture as Capital [in post-1992 China]." *positions: East Asia Cultures Critique* 9(1): 69–104.

Wank, David L. 1995. "Bureaucratic Patronage and Private Business: Changing Networks of Power in Urban China." In *The Waning of the Communist State: Economic Origins of Political Decline in Hungary and China*, ed. Andrew G. Walder, 153–183. Berkeley, Los Angeles, and London: University of California Press.

Wasserstrom, Jeffrey. 1991. *Student Protest in Twentieth Century China: The View from Shanghai*. Stanford, CA: Stanford University Press.

Wei, Su, and Wendy Larson. 1995. "The Disintegration of the Poetic 'Berlin Wall.'" In *Urban Space in Contemporary China: The Potential for Autonomy and Community in Post-Mao China*, ed. Deborah S. Davis et al., 279–293. Cambridge: Woodrow Wilson Center Press and Cambridge University Press.

Wills, Morris, and J. Robert Moskin. 1968. *Turncoat: An American's 12 Years in Communist China*. Englewood Cliffs, NJ: Prentice-Hall.

Xia, Ming. 1999. "From Camaraderie to Cash Nexus: Economic Reforms, Social Stratification and Their Political Consequences in China." *Journal of Contemporary China* 8 (21): 345–358.

Yeh, Michelle. 1998. "The Cult of Poetry in Contemporary China." In *China in a Polycentric World: Essays in Chinese Comparative Literature*, ed. Yingjin Zhang, 188–217. Stanford, CA: Stanford University Press.

Yin, Chih-kuang. 1963. "Poetry Heard by Millions." *China Reconstructs* (August), 27–29.

Zumthor, Paul. 1990. *Oral Poetry: An Introduction*. Trans. Kathryn Murphy-Judy. Minneapolis: University of Minnesota Press.

——. 1994. "Body and Performance," trans. William Whobrey. In *Materialities of Communication*, ed. Ludwig Pfeiffer and Hans Ulrich Gumbrecht, 217–226. Stanford, CA: Stanford University Press.

Index

Page numbers followed by the letter *f* refer to figures and tables.

About the Author

John A. Crespi received his doctoral degree in East Asian Languages and Civilizations from the University of Chicago. He has taught at Valparaiso University and Swarthmore College and is currently Henry R. Luce Associate Professor of Chinese at Colgate University.

Production Notes for *Crespi* | VOICES IN REVOLUTION

Design and Composition by the University of Hawai'i Press Production Department

Text in Goudy Old Style and display type in Warnock Pro

Printing and binding by The Maple-Vail Book Manufacturing Group on 50 lb. Glatfelter Offset D37, 400 ppi